In Her Defence

Philippa Malicka

HODDER &
STOUGHTON

First published in Great Britain in 2026 by Hodder & Stoughton Limited
An Hachette UK company

The authorised representative in the EEA is Hachette Ireland, 8 Castlecourt Centre, Dublin 15, D15 XTP3, Ireland (email: info@hbgi.ie)

2

Copyright © Philippa Malicka 2026

The right of Philippa Malicka to be identified as the Author of the Work has been asserted by her in accordance with the Copyright, Designs and Patents Act 1988.

All rights reserved. No part of this publication may be reproduced, stored in a retrieval system, or transmitted, in any form or by any means without the prior written permission of the publisher, nor be otherwise circulated in any form of binding or cover other than that in which it is published and without a similar condition being imposed on the subsequent purchaser.

All characters in this publication are fictitious and any resemblance to real persons, living or dead, is purely coincidental.

A CIP catalogue record for this title is available from the British Library

Hardback ISBN 978 1 399 72172 1
Trade Paperback ISBN 978 1 399 72173 8
ebook ISBN 978 1 399 72174 5

Typeset in Sabon MT by Manipal Technologies Limited

Printed and bound in Great Britain by Clays Ltd, Elcograf S.p.A.

Hodder & Stoughton policy is to use papers that are natural, renewable and recyclable products and made from wood grown in sustainable forests. The logging and manufacturing processes are expected to conform to the environmental regulations of the country of origin.

Hodder & Stoughton Limited
Carmelite House
50 Victoria Embankment
London EC4Y 0DZ

www.hodder.co.uk

In Her Defence

Philippa Malicka grew up in Essex and now lives in London. Her journalism has appeared in the *Sunday Telegraph* and *Sunday Times* and she is a graduate of the Fiction MA at the University of East Anglia. *In Her Defence* is her first novel. It was longlisted for the Bridport First Novel Award.

You remember too much,
My mother said to me recently.

Why hold onto all that? And I said,
Where can I put it down?

>   Anne Carson, 'The Glass Essay'

A cage went in search of a bird

>   Franz Kafka, Aphorism no.16

People can be removed from the world
They don't tell you that, but it's true
I mean, they do tell you, but they don't tell you
People you love can be removed from the world
(They can remove themselves)
They will be removed from the world
Didn't anybody ever tell you that

>   Emily Berry, Ghost Dance

For Hilary and Nick

PART ONE

GUEST V FINBOW: DAY ONE

Watch her, Anna Finbow, as she approaches the Royal Courts of Justice in a glossy Land Cruiser. The windows are dark, so it's not immediately clear who is inside yet, but the photographers sense that, finally, this must be her. Abruptly, they break out of their conversations, turn and point their lenses, jostling for the right position to take her picture. The car door opens to the sound of cheers and some heckling. A woman in her fifties gazes out.

Pivoting on the leather seat, she raises her chin and slips carefully out of the car, pausing only when an assistant, someone new, passes her phone and a box-shaped handbag. She's wearing her favourite square sunglasses, and her dark hair is blow-dried firmly in place like a helmet. When her lawyer approaches, Anna greets her with a kiss on each cheek. Together, they link arms.

You must know my old boss, Anna Finbow. Her smile will be familiar from *Anna's Advent*, the festive cookery show – now in its tenth season – that runs throughout December. She will have smirked at you in print from the masthead of the lifestyle column that she pens in the weekend newspaper. Chances are, you'll own one of Anna's collectible ceramics somewhere, too. An eggcup, or perhaps even a cereal bowl, in one of her famous designs. *Finbow Flora* – a cottage-kitsch, filigree pattern of intersecting willow leaves and little daisies – which she glazed onto almost everything she made. Nauseatingly chintz, I always thought, but that's what Anna's brand represented. Her name was synonymous with a lost vision of Britain: rosebuds over the door, cricket on the village green, a huge kitchen filled with happy children. A myth, basically. A fiction that Anna's bitter courtroom feud will soon expose.

There was a time when Anna wasn't so sweet. She had hell-cat years, back in the early nineties, when she was still with Albion.

That was her band, which she joined as a singer when she was twenty-four years old and completely off her head. I would feel uneasy as a little girl when I saw her on my parents' television – an impish, punky muse in flamboyant outfits and pencilled-on beauty spots. Witty and outrageous; our nation's cause for concern.

As I watch her approach the courthouse, I realise that has never changed. There never was a moment, during my brief employment, where I *didn't* feel uneasy around Anna. That's the effect of famous people on those like us. You're not meant to feel at ease. In their enlightened view, there is always a 'them' and always an 'us'. Anna's universe was binary: those who were with her and those who were against. It made her paranoid and suspicious of those who she surrounded herself with.

Almost everyone. For a short while, she was willing – far too willing – to trust me.

Anna stops to interact with the well-wishers who have gathered along the Strand in the late-September sunlight. I am still awed to see her squeezing hands and signing old photographs, her smile dazzling and mendacious. In the months we worked together, Anna often complained about how this whole legal nightmare had aged her. During the long conference calls with her legal team, she'd drag a jade roller over her face in a panic, as if trying to seal some essence of youthful vitality back into herself. She needn't have worried. Her beauty is resilient, baked into her heart-shaped face and the perfectly symmetrical features, which often made me want to sculpt her.

Before long, Anna is bustled away from her fans. Leaving them without a backwards glance, she ascends the small flight of steps leading up to the entrance of the courthouse. There, by the great doorway, Anna is joined by her husband, Bonamy. As he bounds up to her, my body stiffens with shame. He's dressed smartly in a grey linen suit and yet there's always something elegantly scrappy about Bon's appearance, like he's been sketched with a pencil. He and his wife turn back around for one last photo. For a moment, it's big waves and cautious, toothless smiles. Everything about their bearing suggests gratitude, then, beneath that: grim defiance. Above the sound of camera lenses closing, their fans call out, pledging love and wishing them luck. It is a surprise to catch myself saying it, too.

The couple turn, now encircled by police officers. Behind the railings, the crowd loosens; mobile phones are lowered, but I manage to keep sight of them. This is when I notice their hands. Bonamy and Anna are holding each other in the secret way I know they sometimes do. Not the usual palm to palm clasp; instead, they are linked by their fingertips which curl around each other.

Abruptly, the scene ahead of me blurs with tears. I cling tightly on to the railing in order to stay upright. This was the special way that Mary used to hold their hands, Anna once confessed, referring to their only daughter. When she was very little, it was the way Mary grasped them; how they all led each other through her early years. It was the family's secret handshake. When Mary first disappeared, Bonamy and Anna regressed into this childish handholding all over again. Just one of many strangely comforting habits the couple fell into almost two years ago, when their dark ordeal first began.

When I first got a job in Anna's household, she'd talk about Mary as if she was still just an infant asleep in the next room. She went on about how adorable her little girl was. How loved. She spoke of the embroidered Bonpoint dresses Mary wore, and the croquembouche they had delivered from Stohrer each year for her birthday. How Mary had delivered their wedding rings on rollerskates, gliding down the church aisle to 'Love Me Do,' before reciting a Yeats poem from memory. '"Tread softly",' Mary had lisped, aged seven. '"Because you tread on my dreams."' Every year at Anna's and Bonamy's wedding anniversary party, Mary would recite it again and bring the house down. I would smile patiently, as Anna made me watch the old grainy videos on her phone, and say how much I wish I'd seen the real thing. I'd pretend I hadn't noticed the strange language that my celebrity-boss lapsed into – that instinctive way she talked about her daughter's childhood, in the present tense.

I'm ashamed, now, of how I indulged those nostalgic fantasies. When in reality, Mary is an adult and bitterly estranged from her mother. Their last interaction was almost two years ago and coincided with the same time Mary began seeing Jean Guest, a maverick new therapist. Welsh, mid-fifties and unlicensed, this is the same woman who dares to sue Anna Finbow in court this week.

When Mary first vanished at the age of twenty-two, devastating letters were penned to those who loved her most. She explained how she would be cutting herself off, dedicating her life to Jean and that the girl they once knew should be forgotten. But Anna would not forget. She went straight to the internet to tell the world what had happened, warning everyone about the wicked witch who carried her daughter away. Jean Guest quickly retaliated with a lawsuit, claiming defamation. Anna countered that she was simply telling the truth. Mary has abandoned her mother and instead taken up her therapist's cause.

I am dedicating my life to my healing now, Mary had written to her parents in the brutally cold email she'd sent as she cut herself off. *Do not try to find me.*

The worst bit of that message, Anna later reflected, wasn't their daughter's tone – haunted and angry though it was. Nor was it the way Mary accused her parents of destroying her life and every chance of happiness. It was the fact that she addressed her parents by their Christian names. Anna claimed she was never *Anna* to Mary. She insisted on *Mummy*.

By the way, I no longer think of, or refer to, you as my mother and father, Mary wrote in her bitter postscript to the email. *Because those are names you earn.*

With the couple now inside, the crowds disperse. I pause for a sensible amount of time, then head for the law-court steps, passing a group of protestors wielding placards and signs.

A thin man with bright blue eyes pushes a petition towards me, calling for regulation in the therapy industry. Another pamphlet calls out the reckless use of psychedelic drugs by unlicensed practitioners posing as healers. The Finbows have paid these attendants, but still, I take a leaflet, burying it deep into my rucksack, which is then taken from me and scanned for chemicals or explosives.

The atrium of the Royal Courts of Justice is vast and splendidly gothic, like some great hall of a fairy-tale castle. My voice shakes as I give my name at the reception, and then I receive directions to Courtroom Six. When I reach the upper gallery, it is chaos: court reporters are vying for the best seats and ushers patrol about, reminding us to sit down so that spaces can be filled. I manage to find one at the back, so that my presence won't be too obvious, but close enough to get a clear view over the dark wooden benches below.

There are only fifteen minutes to go before proceedings will begin, and the atmosphere is turning nervy and airless. An older woman next to me sighs and asks if I think the air conditioning is malfunctioning. I shrug, but as our arms touch, I notice how cold and damp her skin is. Fanning the air, she admits she's feeling faint. I rummage in my rucksack for my water bottle and offer it to her. I find it touching when she accepts.

'What's your connection to all this?' I ask, quietly tucking the bottle away. I glance downwards at the woman's loafers and her expensive handbag, then back up at her lined face. Her brown eyes brim with pain.

'My daughter got involved with this woman, too. Five sessions a week at one point. She ruined her life.'

My voice catches in my throat. 'I'm so sorry—'

She thanks me solemnly. 'I used to fantasise so often about her facing justice. But the police never got enough evidence to criminalise her.'

My pulse rises. 'What is your daughter's name?'

The woman's lips tighten. 'Oriel.'

For a moment, we fall quiet, watching the remaining spectators take their seats.

'And you?' The woman's gaze returns and flits over my cropped hair and the antique man's watch I like to wear. I can feel her trying to get the measure of me. 'What brings you to the show?'

There is a pause. I glance around me. 'My name's Augusta,' I say, quietly, using my full name, in case any journalists overhear.

'Lucy Ayres.' She extends a small hand. 'I take it you know the Finbows?'

'Just a friend of the family,' I say.

Somewhere in the court papers, I am referred to as Anna's 'aide' but the truth is that I am much closer to her than that. For now, though, I don't go there.

The woman smiles a faint approval, then straightens in her seat. In the courtroom beneath us, two groups of lawyers bustle in, wheeling suitcases of paperwork. The clock hands skip towards ten. The clerks ready their bundles of evidence. Any moment now, Justice Larkin will appear. Our sensational trial will soon unfold.

STOKE-ON-TRENT, APRIL

Six months ago

Whatever they will accuse me of later, I never sought to be Anna's *aide*, and I'm not the kind of person who makes a habit of messaging celebrities out of the blue, either. But the thing about Anna Finbow is that you felt as if you knew her. It was – and still is – her greatest skill. Her fortune was carved out of that knowing familiarity she fostered. I resisted it at first, but I turned out to be no different from everyone else. Before long, I fell for it, too.

I could argue in court that, as a ceramicist myself, I had no choice but to apply for work with Anna's business; that the forces acting on me were purely economic. We certainly weren't a creative match – Anna was famous for her bone-thin, floral uniformity, whereas my style is more like me: earthy-toned and slightly misshapen. I never make dainty teacups, but mugs the size of tankards, with their surfaces roughly hewn. *The texture of cauldrons,* as a teacher once put it.

In my defence, I could claim that I needed a part-time job to support my own fledgling pottery business; that there wasn't much other work around. So, when I happened to see her out walking her dog one evening near her factory in Stoke, of course I seized the moment and got in touch.

But that would only be one version of the story. Told differently, another version would say that I was obsessed with Anna, seeking her out and exploiting my privileged access to her, once I had gained it.

The truth sits somewhere between the two.

It was her coat that had caught my attention first. Chocolate-coloured, suede and long, there was no mistaking the expensive drape of it. Then it was the way Anna stood. Her shoulders were hunched up close to her ears and her hands were buried in her pockets. As my bus stalled, I noticed she was staring into the window of a toy shop. That was probably the first moment that disrupted my original image of Anna Finbow as a steely, untouchable edifice. Standing there in front of those brightly lit toys, she looked cowed, like a woman – or even a little girl – who had lost something. Human posture tells us so much more about a person than we ever realise. It has its own alphabet.

Was it grief that brought her here? I had wondered as I studied her. Or embarrassment? I'd read everything I could find about the public spat with her daughter, Mary, and the massive legal case – now a defamation claim – that was mounting between her and Mary's therapist. The news was so full of gossipy updates, it made sense that Anna might want to escape her home in London for Stoke-on-Trent. To get her head down and work, just for a while. Until things quietened down.

My bus pulled away and I gained another sight of that famous profile. My heart pattered with the thrill of coincidence.

Here it comes, I thought. *A chance.*

A year ago, I'd done the same thing as her and escaped London, too. The Potteries, once the fiery heartland of British ceramics, holds a certain appeal to broken people. For one, there's no town centre: we're instead made up of six small towns, which compete for primacy and wrestle for council funds like a nest of underfed chicks. To live somewhere so geographically fragmented makes you feel a bit more whole, and I wondered if Anna knew that, too. On her website, she called Bellinter, her factory, the 'cradle' of her brand, but the city itself was curative. I had moved here after a series of break-ups. Gradually, as the months passed, the Potteries fused me back together.

Later that night, on the mezzanine of my studio where I slept, I'd opened an application on my phone. Anna's profile was never far from the top of my recent searches. I clicked on the envelope sign and introduced myself, telling her that I'd literally just gone past her in the street and that her brown coat was amazing. Then I gave a little background. I made a great deal of the art foundation course that I'd actually never finished, as well as the calibre of my references, which, I assured, could be provided on request. I pasted across the sales pitch from a previous application I had submitted.

26 years old. Ceramicist. Born and bred in Stoke. Worships your brand: songbook of English interiors.

Trained in Rome. Team player, self-starter. Loves to be challenged. Ambitious. Determined.

Needing experience, so happy to muck in and do (just about) anything.

If your team is already full, no problem at all!! I'd still love to take you for a coffee and hear about your career?

I pressed send. A minute later, I opened the app and typed another message.

Not sure if you remember, but we actually met once before! At a party.

Then I hesitated, remembering that brutal occasion when she had ignored me. In the end, I thought the better of it. It was a night I wanted to forget, anyway. I highlighted that bit of text and pressed delete.

Those messages were the first of many untruths I told Anna.

I'm not a native Stokie, by any stretch. I moved up here the February before last. Before that, it had been the cheapest fringes of London; before that, school in the southwest. Kingsfold had been one of the last remaining Evangelical Christian schools in the country. By the time I arrived, it had changed to a secular status, but many of the fanatical teachers remained. My parents worked there, too, and though they weren't organised enough to be truly religious, our house was still imbued with their employer's stiff morality. I got out as soon as I could.

After a few wrong turns along the way, I ended up in London. But really, in its suburbs. In Wanstead, I rented a room within a large house owned by an older American lady who lived on cruise ships for six months of the year, and who raised the rent slightly before each passage. Her saving gesture was the job in the café she found for me. Any money I had left over, I spent booking time in the pottery studio nearby. Back then, I suppose I was only playing about, shaping things, copying the skills and techniques of the more talented ceramicists I observed around me. But, as I sat at that wheel on those alternate Saturday afternoons, I felt grounded for the first time in my life. There is a primeval, essential quality to working with clay. Humans have always done it. And in my studio, as I cut and weighed those cool blocks of material, I reconnected to an imagined lineage of past potters; a kinship I'd never found in romantic or even platonic relationships. Looking back, you could say I rediscovered a spirituality that had been stamped on in school. It never once occurred to me that I could make money from it.

The fact that the whole practice felt so essential to my being meant I was frightened to pursue any formal training. How many art foundation courses did I get onto, only to drop out on day one? Art school was too expensive, I told myself; it only dampened raw talent or was otherwise simply too indulgent. So I opted, instead, to contain my deepest-felt desire in a hobby, rather than gamble my life on it. For a few years, the café work rolled on and I didn't improve. Then I moved away to a different part of London and got a job in the local cinema. My trips to the studio became less frequent. I tricked myself into pretending this didn't make me dreadfully sad.

Occasionally, I read online about residencies. Back then, it seemed the most outrageous privilege to me, to receive a stipend and accommodation for weeks at a time, just to improve your craft. That was why, I reasoned, my applications were never successful. I didn't believe, deep down, that I really deserved it. Then, one morning, a couple of years ago, during a painful creative dry spell, a surreal email arrived. My eyes scanned for the usual letting-down phrases: 'unfortunately', 'we're sorry', or 'not this time'. But nothing appeared. I had won a place on a residency in Rome. My world was about to change. Which, of course, it did, but so differently from how I would have wanted.

After Italy, I couldn't face London again. It felt too much like going backwards. What I needed, desperately, was a place to live, and a studio with north light – the flat, grey kind of light that would reflect my heartbroken mood. I decided on Stoke. Beautiful studios were being created from its iconic old pottery factories, the rare kind of workspaces where you could also live. But when I first moved up here, nothing inside shifted. For months, I wandered the streets and supermarkets, bewildered with heartbreak. I realised how that dragging longing for someone didn't miraculously lift from your chest just because you'd changed cities. When I saw Anna Finbow from the bus that day, I wondered if she was reaching the same conclusions. How the loneliness remains. Their absence carries day and night. It takes up residence inside you, wherever you live.

A week after I saw Anna, my phone flashed with a message.

Hi Gus. Good to hear from you. Just confirming you are based in SOT?

My heart dropped. I had been cleaning tools in my studio but now things were different; I had received a direct message from Anna Finbow. Quickly, I wiped my hands, then hoisted myself onto my workbench, letting my legs dangle free as I read it over and over. The green glow around her name suggested she was still online.

My hands shook as I typed my reply.

Yes! Not far from your HQ.

Anna was typing. The dots shimmered and rippled. I gripped the handset, muttering an inward prayer of thanks to the miracle of the internet. Then waited.

Would you be available to discuss a role at Anna's this evening?
I lowered the phone, feeling stupid for thinking Anna would handle her own communications.

What time?

7 ok?

Of course.

At home, not Bellinter.

My correspondent gave me the address of Anna's home in Hanley. I thanked her, amazed to learn how close it was.
Will Anna be there in person? I texted, fear swimming in my stomach. *Just so I'm prepared!*
No response came, but throughout the rest of the afternoon, I started to feel the old heaviness in my chest begin to lift. I sketched a plan in my mind of how I might position myself if I actually came to meet Anna; the ways I might win her over. For the first time in months, a feeling of clear-headed purpose came over me. I switched apps and texted a friend.
So I might have good news.

GUEST V FINBOW: DAY ONE

Gazing around Courtroom Six, I am astonished at the sheer circus of it all, at how the Finbow family estrangement has resulted in this very public trial. The absurdity of the situation strikes me again: how can a rift between a mother and daughter end up in the highest court in the country? Don't we all have the right to disappear? Not according to Anna, who refuses to accept that Mary simply wanted out of her old life. No: it is her therapist who has poisoned her, to the point that Mary no longer knows her own mind at all.

All stories have a source tale that precedes them, an origin myth.

Talk to me about your childhood, asks the probing therapist, in the recurring stereotype, when we are invited to make sense of our lives. In this case, the seed of Anna's legal battle was planted online via her newsletter, *The Peony*, which was circulated to millions of inboxes on Friday afternoons. Anna often uploaded posts about the agony of her family estrangement. Usually, there were no consequences to this public outpouring of emotion; her fans had come to expect it. But the legal mistake she made, and which landed Anna in court on charges of libel, was to name Jean Guest outright. The defamatory text was sandwiched between a recipe for Earl Grey granita and a feature on summer garden games for kids:

Many of you will have read about the plight of our family in recent months… To all of you who have got in contact to offer me your sympathy and support, thank you from the bottom of my heart.

Before Mary began working with her so-called therapist, **Jean Guest**, she was the happiest, brightest girl. Everyone who met her was touched by her joy. But after receiving hours of "healing" our daughter has been turned against us. False memories have been inserted in her mind to isolate her and make demons out of those who love her most. Stay ALERT to unqualified therapists, new-age healers, life coaches, etc. They are modern-day cult leaders, twisted, dangerous and sick people who recruit talented young women like my daughter for their own financial gain. Bonamy and I shall fight this. We will not rest until this industry is properly regulated in the United Kingdom and psychological manipulation has been made a criminal offence. So please do support our cause by signing this **petition**.

In the meantime, keep me in your thoughts. Hold your loved ones close for me.

x Anna

I often imagine Anna writing the newsletter. It makes me want to shake her by the shoulders. What kind of mental fog must have descended upon her to pen something so irresponsibly provocative and hit send? When it was first published, almost eighteen months ago now, the press described it as a 'blind' and 'broken-hearted' post. But I'm not sure I believe that. I picture Anna crafting it with purpose, sitting in that cathedral-sized kitchen in Notting Hill, typing, as she always did, with her index finger, a frosted glass of white wine within reaching distance. I see her posting the piece, then taking a deep, vitriolic swig. This is the way she views the world, of course. 'Them' and 'us'.

A letter from Jean Guest's solicitor arrived before lunchtime the following day. Mary's therapist was seeking seven-figure damages from Anna Finbow, for reputational harm. But even as the legal case against her mounted, Anna always dismissed the newsletter as her 'little rant'. She refused to make any out-of-court settlements to Jean Guest, because she believed that what she had written was true.

Since then, Anna has not wavered from that defence. Yet, discerning the truth behind her 'truth defence' is what brings us to the High Court today. Jean Guest will insist she is a dedicated healer who only wants the best for the troubled people she works with. Anna will counter that she is a cultic abuser, ripping families apart. At the centre of it all, there is the poor young woman, Mary, who has repeatedly stated that she only wants to be left alone.

Still, the two women will go on with this battle about her life choices, fighting over her like a torn doll.

For all the horror of the circumstances, I know that Anna is actually looking forward to seeing Mary in court. She's had only one brief sighting of her daughter in the twenty months that have passed since Mary began her sessions. The first day of trial will be, at least Anna is hoping, a family reunion. So, now, when a door in the upper gallery opens, I watch as Anna swivels round, her gaze scanning desperately along the row of spectators. Bonamy catches her eye from the front row and shakes his head. They can only bitterly conclude that Mary has not come.

At five minutes to ten, another commotion catches their attention. Bonamy looks down and the tips of his ears redden. Jean Guest is arriving with her legal team.

It is a remarkable thing, to feel the presence of another human travel up and down your spine. There is a tingling feeling in the base of my skull – my hackles rising – then a slow heat which seeps down to my seat bones. Jean lingers by the wooden desk she will sit behind, conferring with polite ushers. Her modest handbag and navy crepe skirt suit give her a soft appearance: the bearing of a harmless academic, as if she poses no threat other than beady intelligence. She greets her team with terse smiles, thanking them graciously. All the while, she avoids Anna's furious stare.

'That *fucking* witch!' mutters the woman next to me, Lucy, in an accent unused to swearing. Together, we watch Jean take her seat to the left of the raised judge's bench, sitting parallel with Anna, whose defiant gaze is now trained forward. Shaking her head, Lucy whispers, 'She took my little girl. My only little girl.'

I consider reaching over and squeezing her hand or making some other kind of gesture that would comfort us both, but soon the usher is calling us to rise for the judge's arrival. We clatter to our feet as Justice Larkin settles himself down, reading out information on fire exits and issuing a long apology for the heat in the room.

'But moving on from our air conditioning: a word of warning about your own circulation. No doubt you will have encountered the cameras outside.'

He glances upwards and addresses the gallery. Do I invent the harsh way his stare fixes mine?

'Please refrain from speaking to any members of the press during the course of this trial. We are fortunate enough to have invited a number of journalists up here in the gallery, so we may trust that the fourth estate will report on our proceedings accurately and adequately without our input. These proceedings already deal with the complex nature of public discourse. Please do not add any more noise to it.'

And with that, Justice Larkin invites opening submissions. Jean Guest's barrister rises and a momentary calm descends. I wonder if it is relief that the moment has finally arrived; that we have risen from the tabloid gutter into the more upright realm of reason and procedure.

Still, I can't help praying that I will somehow be spared all of this. The desperate hope that, before my part, a key legal precedent will be unearthed at the last minute and unravel the case entirely. I summon the scene: after a day or two of debate, a loophole is discovered. *Bang*, the judge brings his hammer down. The trial is over. I remain merely a spectator, not an actor.

Fantasies. I'm good at those. I was once told that it stemmed from all the shame I carried around. I had developed a capacity that made me inventive – deviant, even – to avoid exposure. I was encouraged to see how this emerged from an impulse to protect myself, a survivalist instinct to secure my part in an alternative world, a better life than my own.

Others will say that I was grasping upwards. An ambitious social climber. The lawyers will soon hurl the same insult that Anna once spat in my face, too. Perhaps without her sneer. Perhaps without her hand snatching my arm.

The sting of it, all the same.

'*Leech*.'

STOKE-ON-TRENT, APRIL

It was dark by the time of my interview at Anna's home. Gusts of rain blew about, falling into the top of my shoulder bag and threatening to spoil the portfolio of my recent work I'd hurriedly printed out. As I turned onto Glass Street, a quiet road filled with beautiful old Victorian factories, my footsteps slowed. I took slow, steady breaths, but my stomach – all my organs – felt knotted together. Anna's entrance was marked by stylish cylindrical lights on either side of her front door, and a camera crouched above them like a tiny gargoyle. I checked up and down the street in case anyone had seen me. The door opened almost as soon as I pressed the bell. Someone had been watching.

Anna's assistant, Clover, must have been in her mid-forties. She was dressed in the comforting way of artsy women her age: a turquoise boxy jacket; wide-legged, ankle-skimming trousers; a striped Breton top tucked into them. She blinked at me through her tortoiseshell glasses for a few moments. Her tired expression melted into relief.

'Thanks for making it,' she said, extending a warm hand to mine and leading me inside.

The hallway had a seagrass matted carpet and smelt overpoweringly floral, like one of Anna's shops. We climbed up a narrow, curved staircase into a vast open-plan living space which ran long and narrow beneath a vaulted ceiling. There were framed photographs of Anna's family everywhere, aligned meticulously in rows on every surface like chess pieces. I was desperate to stop and look, but Clover led me towards its very end where the kitchen was separated off by sliding glass doors. A light sprang on as we entered: a huge Murano-glass chandelier which hung down over a moon-coloured marble countertop. I made an involuntary sound of recognition; this was where Anna's festive cookery shows were filmed. For the last three series, she had baked and broiled, her tattoo peeking out of her sleeve as she whisked egg whites in her own range of glazed bowls.

'Anna will be with you soon,' she said, fetching me a glass of water and bringing me into the living area. 'She's finishing a call.'

I nodded. Then I noticed Clover's coat in her hands. 'You've already provided references, haven't you?' she asked, looking distractedly for her bag. 'We need emails and phone numbers.'

'Sent them earlier,' I lied.

Clover made a murmuring sound, which made it unclear whether she'd actually heard me. Glancing down again at her phone, she swore. Her husband was going to be late. She needed to get home and put dinner on for the kids. As she began to make excuses, she kept looking nervously towards a doorway at the end of the living space. Anna's office, I guessed.

'I can wait,' I said, in a voice that was too high-pitched to be casual. The prospect of sitting alone in Anna Finbow's loft apartment could never be casual. Clover wavered as she looked me over, her eyes agitated and uncertain. 'But do you have any advice for me?'

She sighed wearily. 'The magic word is yes. Always agree with her. Whatever it takes. And don't mention the legal nuisance. Not unless she brings it up.'

'Of course I won't,' I reassured gently. 'That's private.'

Clover departed and I sat on the sofa for several minutes, stunned. With its cathedral proportions, the living space looked more like a museum than a home. I loved the wide openness of the space. How the kitchen evolved effortlessly into the lounge, and the gorgeous way it was all knocked through. For several moments, I took it in: the Francis Bacon on my left, the Lucian Freud to my right. With my fingertips, I pressed down onto the tightly sprung plushness of all her upholstery, thinking of how cold it was in my own studio. Inside my head, there was a voice announcing and re-announcing itself: *I'm here. I'm actually inside her home.*

And then, the study door opened and Anna strode in.

'So wonderful of you to come so late!'

I rose quickly from the sofa, goosebumps flooding my skin. She was wearing slim black trousers and a long, sleeveless cardigan that billowed as she approached. By the hearth, we faced each other, and she held my gaze. I wondered then if there was a flicker of remembrance; whether she recognised me, too. For a moment, my legs, my knees – my entire lower half – turned to air. Then her stare melted into a wide but vacant smile. Of course, she had no idea who I was. People like her never do.

'Clover's an angel to have let you in,' Anna said, letting the small dog who followed her run over and lick my hand.

I cast my eyes over her face. There was an old-fashioned aspect to her beauty. It was in the soft waves of her dark hair and the way her features aligned so evenly, like a five on a dice. But, up close, Anna also looked pale and under-slept; you could tell from the red rims of the lower lids and the slightly swollen bags under her eyes. I didn't pity it. Part of me enjoyed the signs of suffering and fatigue that were legible in her face.

'You weren't waiting long, were you?' she asked.

'Hardly five minutes.'

'Well, that's a good start,' she said, grinning sappily as her dog jumped up against my legs. 'He likes you. Pick him up, will you?'

I did as I was told. Quill was the dog's name. Anna constantly posted pictures of him. He was a stout and beady-eyed little dachshund, with russet-coloured rings of fat that collected in rolls along his front legs like Indian bangles.

Anna turned and went into the kitchen, expecting me to follow. I carried the dog through to where she lingered by the wooden dresser, absently flipping through some paperwork.

'Clover assured me she vetted you, but I always like to meet people first, just to check they're not a loony.' She laughed heartily; somewhere beneath the sound was the smoking habit I knew she hadn't kicked. 'And vice versa, I expect. Did she get the agreement across to you?'

'Yup,' I said tightly, feeling a coldness settle in my chest. Botching references to Clover was one thing, but did Anna mean an employment contract or an NDA?

'Good. Because we need absolute discretion. Okay?' She discarded an envelope and fixed her attention back onto me. 'Now, a couple of questions I always like to ask my team. What's your single biggest passion? Clover told me you're a potter?'

I thought back to one of the phrases I'd once used in a cover letter to her.

'I make pots to live. Ceramic sculptures to breathe,' I said, smiling warily as it came back to me. 'I've actually printed a few photos of my—'

Anna interrupted me with a hand. 'And what would you say is your best attribute?'

Ignoring a flare of irritation, I answered her. 'My loyalty. Not only to the projects I work on, but also to people.' There was a terrible thinness to my voice.

'And now your worst?' Anna barked, quickfire style.

I hesitated.

'Go on,' she goaded. 'I actually love this question and I'll tell you why. We humans, we don't reflect on our faults enough.'

I stared for a moment at Anna's pointed finger, before the perfect answer appeared.

'I always speak my mind. If you were to ask my opinion on something, I'd easily give it. I actually find it very difficult to lie.'

Anna softened. 'That's good. I'm surrounded by too many people who only tell me what they think I want to hear. It's imprisoning.' She got up from her stool then, and offered to show me round. 'It might be a little premature, but we may as well go over it now. Come on. Over here.'

To my surprise, she led me further into the kitchen, to a cupboard beside the fuchsia-coloured Aga. 'Here's where we keep Quill's lead,' she said while I nodded, feeling totally lost.

Then she showed me the glass jar containing all his Bonios, his cod-liver oil supplements and the plastic bags I was to use to pick up his shit. Slowly, the reality dawned. Anna wasn't looking to resource her design team; she needed a dog walker.

His bed was there, by the Aga, she said, and over in the main living space, was a cage I could shut him into if he was getting chewy. The instructions went on for so long, I couldn't bring myself to interrupt her. When she had finally finished, I opened my mouth to explain that there had been a mistake. I didn't walk dogs. I was a ceramicist. Once again, Anna silenced me with a hand.

'Hold on, we'll get to your questions in a moment. I'll just show you how the alarm works while it's fresh in my mind. We've had to get it changed because of all the photographers,' she said grimly, tapping her fingernails against the alarm keys. 'And the fact I keep breaking it.' She leaned in and whispered theatrically, 'I'm actually number dyslexic.'

'How often should I come?' I asked carefully, half-frightened by how fast things had spiralled away from my original intention. I couldn't conceive of a job that was further from what I wanted to do. Briefly I reflected: *but could this access actually help me?*

'Will Quill be staying up here a lot?' I went on to ask, tactfully. I knew, like the rest of the country, that Anna's trial was expected to take place later this year. The fact that I was already worrying about her return to London told me then what I needed to know: this was a good opportunity. As her domestic help, I could boast of a far more intimate relationship with Anna than I might have gained at work. I would become part of her home, which might lead to something better.

Anna glanced downwards. A strand of dark hair fell in front of her face and she brushed it aside modestly, with the heel of her palm. 'I plan to be here rather a lot. So, assume I'll be needing you, rather than not.'

My heart skipped at that word, *needed*. There was a vulnerability to it that I couldn't help responding to. I found myself smiling at her. Briefly, she returned it, then looked pointedly at her phone: a subtle gesture of dismissal. I gathered my things. But then, when I was halfway out of the door, she called out, sternly.

'Hang on. Just a moment.'

My chest froze. Had she remembered something? I turned and looked upwards. Anna was standing at the top of the stairs, holding the dog and pouting.

'You haven't said goodnight to Quill.'

My footsteps were light, both from the rush of our meeting and embarrassment at her ridiculous charade. I ran my fingers over the cold, black button of Quill's nose, telling him that I looked forward to working together. Anna nodded her approval. There was a hierarchy in her household and, evidently, I would sit on the lowest rung of it. Now that this had been established, I was free to go.

Once I reached the end of Glass Street, I collapsed against a wall and shut my eyes. I was taken aback by Anna's instant trust, by that daffy sentimentality, and the strange force of our whole interaction. But, at the same time, when I thought of the background checks, and the legalities I had pretended to have signed, a sense of panic closed in.

Not long, I soothed myself, counting six seconds for the in-breaths, six for the out. *And if you do it right and give her what she wants, it'll be worth it.* 'Grip the earth,' I muttered aloud, flexing my toes in my boots. 'Name the sounds.' A siren nearby, the slick crawl of car tyres across wet tarmac. But, louder than the outside world, was the recent echo of Anna's frantic instruction.

'Do not let Quill off the lead,' she had warned, her tone suddenly shifting. 'Whatever you do. Do not undo him, okay?' I understood then, that behind that fear, was the loss of her daughter. Knots of pain loosened in my chest as I grew aware of it. 'He'll just run away,' Anna continued, wide-eyed with worry. 'Either that, or someone will take him. Promise me?'

We had locked eyes, there in her magnificent kitchen, and I had promised her. She had made me promise as if he were the last thing she had left.

'You won't let anyone carry him off?'

'I swear, Anna,' I had said, remembering Clover's words: *the magic word is yes*. 'Don't worry. You have my word. He'll be safe with me.'

GUEST V FINBOW: DAY ONE

Ms Ibrahim, acting on behalf of Jean Guest, stands first.

'My Lord, here's the unfortunate situation,' she begins carefully. 'Your adult child decides they no longer wish to maintain a relationship with you. How should you respond? Those circumstances may indeed be sad, and they may be very painful, but they are not grounds for causing wilful damage to the reputation of those individuals who happen to retain contact with the estranged.'

There is a pause as she waits for that to sink in. Her fingertips rest on the desk, flexing and unflexing.

'That is why this particular case, however costly it has already proven, is not at all complex. There can be no disputing the defamatory language used by the defendant, Mrs Finbow, in her published newsletter, *The Peony*, nor the wide extent of its readership. And, since this is a question of libel, it is not my client's responsibility to *disprove* the defamatory accusations levelled against her. We are merely bringing the claim. The burden of evidence,' she says, gesturing elegantly towards Anna, 'sits with the defence, whose evidence we look forward to examining later this morning.'

Ms Ibrahim pauses briefly for water, then spends several minutes running over the failed attempts to get the case settled outside of court. 'It is with deep regret that we are even here, My Lord. We decry the defendant's resistance to mediation, despite mounting costs and emotional harm caused to those involved. Because, above all, it is Ms Guest's own clients whom she cares for most. She cherishes their wellbeing *far above* her own reputation. For years, she has dedicated herself to the psychological regeneration of her clients, many of whom present with extremely challenging mental disorders. She is not interested in engaging in this proxy custody battle with her client's mother. She simply wants to do her job.'

Ms Ibrahim turns and addresses the wider courtroom.

'This has been her vocation since she left the family home in North Wales as an eighteen-year-old, to undertake her role as a mental health nurse in London, first at the Maudsley Hospital in Camberwell, then at HMP Feltham. Eventually, and at great personal cost, my client embarked on her own training in psychotherapy at Regent's University. Unfortunately, she was unable to complete that training, due to her dedication to her day-job, but that struggle informed her pioneering practice. Today, she runs a successful coaching business out of her house in Primrose Hill, blending psychodynamic techniques with holistic treatments such as reiki, hypnosis and nutritional guidance. Many of her clients, from whom we will hear during the trial, credit her with altering the course of their lives for the better and in doing so, giving them the strength to launch careers, and achieve deeper self-acceptance.' She pauses and glances towards Anna. 'Or to leave certain relationships which no longer serve them.'

Ms Ibrahim's manner softens as she concludes. 'We extend sympathy towards Mrs Finbow for her anguish surrounding her daughter's life choices. But we also posit that my client's professional reputation must be respectfully upheld and cleared of these wholly destructive allegations.'

Ms Ibrahim thanks the judge and sits back down. In the gallery, there is the hum of thoughtful conferring.

'It's not a coaching business,' Lucy hisses aloud as those nearby acknowledge her uneasily. 'It's a *cult*.'

I place a hand briefly on her arm. An act of support, though I am not yet sure if I agree. Not when my body remembers old loyalties. Not when the softest part of me witnesses the deceit. Calls me *traitor*.

'Are you a therapist, My Lord?'

It is now Ms Carr's turn to stand. An older, twig-thin woman, her heels clipping noisily on the ground, approaches the judge's bench.

The question elicits weak laughter from the gallery. Judge and barrister exchange a brief smirk; there is a twinkle of recognition between the two of them that alludes to a relationship beyond the courtroom. Perhaps they are college buddies, distant cousins, or family friends.

'No, you are not a therapist, My Lord, though you may very easily claim to be. Throughout the United Kingdom, this industry is dangerously unregulated. The terms "therapist", "counsellor" and "life coach", are not protected. I could go online this evening and purchase credentials that would allow me to set up practice as any, or all three, of those occupations tomorrow morning.' She pauses and looks at her colleagues. 'Frightening, isn't it? My Lord, the petition that my client circulated in her newsletter sought to raise awareness about the harm caused by unlicensed therapists. It gained millions of signatures and will shortly be debated in Parliament. There is no doubting the truth of the problem that extremely vulnerable people, such as is the case with my client's daughter, are exposed every day to dangerously misguided individuals like the claimant, Ms Guest. There can also be no doubting the truth of my client's words: that her daughter sought relief from her therapist, and has instead been subjected to coercion, manipulation and exploitation. In short, she is one of many young women who have been caught up in Ms Guest's brutal and calculating network, which we will prove *is*, in practice, a therapy cult.'

The gallery falls silent. The heat of the room is beginning to seep into my skin now and my armpits prickle damply with it. Lucy has withdrawn a tissue from her handbag, which she presses against her lips. Ms Carr turns her page and continues.

'Coercive relationships happen very easily in therapy. We meet a practitioner. We trust them. We transfer all sorts of complex feelings onto them. We might even fall in love. It's very common, My Lord. Freud called it "Transference". An awareness of this tendency within such an intimate relationship is a key matter of professional ethics. Professionals are trained to create a boundary between themselves and their clients. This is not the case with Jean Guest because her professional credentials are, in fact, only superficial; she has twisted what little training she has undertaken to sound more credible than she really is.'

Justice Larkin's gaze moves to the table where Jean is sitting. I wonder what he is making of her now, whether his mind is struggling to reconcile these assertions with the bookish woman in front of him. Ms Carr follows his gaze, then gestures in the same direction.

'My esteemed colleague may believe that this case is, what was her phrase? "Not at all complex," she said, but we argue quite the opposite. It is an astoundingly complicated case, since it centres on our understanding of what our memories are capable of. As my client wrote in her newsletter, Ms Guest embeds false memories in the minds of her patients as a means of wielding control over their lives. She exploits the fallibility of human memory for her own gain. This is the part *that is not at all complex*: our personal memories, indeed, our entire sense of self, can be led astray in an astonishing number of ways. The memories we hold about those we love are not stable. They are not insects suspended in resin, perfectly preserved. Our memories are suggestible, prone to contamination, slippery as eels. Easily warped in the wrong hands. And, My Lord, Mary Finbow is in the *most wrong* hands. Before she met Jean Guest, Mary was a dedicated and loving daughter. Today, Mary is ostracised from her entire social milieu. In her newsletter, my client only wanted to speak this truth.'

There is a pause as Ms Carr smiles grimly, waiting for the rumble of voices to die down. 'Over the coming days, we will learn how the claimant never fosters the psychic liberation that her followers are seeking. Instead, she annexes their social freedoms and creates dangerously co-dependent devotees who are isolated from everyone except Ms Guest, their cunningly charismatic, self-appointed leader. Through coercion, she severs her followers not only from their families but from their once-bright futures. It is from this position that we defend the statements and sentiments of *The Peony* as accurate and genuine. Put simply: my client was delivering the facts. And a fact cannot be libellous.'

The judge thanks both barristers for their opening statements and announces the beginning of witness evidence. First, he calls Mrs Anna Finbow to the stand, and as she rises, she glances towards the gallery one more time, just to check. Mary has not come, but Anna won't be defeated. Her eye briefly falls on me and she gives a curt nod. Perhaps it is a threat, or it could be something else, a kinder signal. Not a warning but a *watch this*.

STOKE-ON-TRENT, APRIL

During the course of my first week, Anna's dog and I established a routine. I left my studio at eight o'clock and arrived shortly afterwards to take Quill outside, so he could relieve himself. Then I made his breakfast: a strange porridge-like milk and rice mixture that Anna insisted on because it disguised all the oily supplements she had him take. By nine, we were ready to walk. I would dress the dog in his little clip-on wax jacket and take him to a park about twenty minutes away. Circling the muddy field three times, we'd get to ten o'clock, when we would start our journey homewards, stopping off at the butcher for a pig's ear. Then, when we were back, I'd dry his paws with a muslin cloth, fill a large bowl of water, and put the radio on so that he had voices to keep him company after I left. By then, it would be almost lunchtime – a horribly long time to wait until my arrival the following day. As I rubbed my thumb and index fingers against his silky ears to bid him goodbye, I felt an almost unbearable affinity. I also knew how it felt to count down the hours until my next chance of human contact. The greasy aloneness of an empty weekend, with no plans, no one to see.

So, throughout that week, knowing Anna was away, I sent her pictures and little updates, trying to keep my tone light and irreverent. Quill was being such a good dog, I assured her.

He loved his lunch today. Barked bravely at a Doberman.

I signed off with a 'G' from me, and an emoji of a paw print from him. By the end of the week, I had even dared to add an 'X'. Sometimes, Anna responded with a heart, or an emoji of hands in prayer, or a *superstar, thanks*. Other times, she flatly ignored me.

It was also because Anna was away that I was able to gain an intimate understanding of her home. Or at least, of the rooms I could get into. I could have explored every inch of the loft, but my access was restricted to the main living space and the kitchen, which I nevertheless crept lightly through, avoiding Quill's eye as he observed me from his basket.

The kitchen was a beautiful room and clearly Anna's chief domain, yet the longer I spent there, the more I sensed its profound isolation; really, it was a film set, not a home. With a twinge of unease, I realised that Anna's existence up here was pretty solitary: there was just one bowl on the drying rack, and only a single washed-up wine glass, along with the stale tang of tobacco that hung low in the air.

Inside the kitchen dresser, things were more intriguing. Each drawer contained a chaos of unopened post, cosmetic paraphernalia, half-finished pill packets, unlidded lipsticks, and a wadge of parking tickets from the Borough of Kensington and Chelsea, all bunched up in their yellow plastic wrappers like the heads of daffodils. At the bottom of one drawer, I noticed a round tin, sweetly decorated with roses. I opened the lid and inhaled the scent of a perfumed balm. It was amazingly familiar, an old perfume I'd loved years ago but struggled to find again. The fruity notes had warped with age and blended into each other, but its peppery base remained the same. As I rubbed it onto my wrists and neck, I imagined for a moment that Anna had appeared and was standing before me. A frightening thought. I turned then, and closed the drawer, slipping the perfume tin into my coat pocket.

The living space was even better. I loved to linger there, inspecting the books on the shelves or the artworks on the wall. But far better than the paintings were the Finbow family photographs, which I spent hours poring over, partly nauseated, partly enthralled. Over in the corner, on a semi-circular table near the fireplace, were all the photographs of Mary. Some of the photos I had seen before in the press, but there were private images from her childhood, too. My favourite was a silver frame, showing a fair-haired girl of about six, jumping up and down on a beautiful sleigh bed. Somewhere in France it looked like, or maybe Italy, but it was somewhere warm and European. The sheets were strewn everywhere and the ornate purple headboard was shaped like a bishop's hat. The girl wore a navy corduroy dress with a lace collar and was grinning widely. You could see all her missing teeth, and her clenched little fists, as she jumped into the air. I came back to this one over and over, pushing deeper upon the shard of pain it lodged in my chest. This photo had been captured by someone who evidently adored her, and who had revelled in her glorious girlhood. It felt pitiful to compare myself to her, but Mary and I were not too different in age, and nothing like this existed of me. My family photos captured me in my Kingsfold uniform. After I reached my teenage years, they had abruptly stopped. Around the same time, I had first cut my hair short.

In other frames, Mary was older, glossier. In these images, she looked beautiful and excessively well-connected; someone who modelled clothes elegantly and enjoyed going to parties. There she was, captured at an event, perhaps a birthday, wearing biker boots and a stringy black dress, double fisting glasses of champagne. In another, she was surrounded by men, many of them older. They slung arms around her, knuckles grazing her collar or breasts. Instantly, I resented their social ease. How they squared their groins towards the camera, opening up their mouths slightly, so that the shape of them resembled little crescent moons. But, as I studied this picture closely, I noticed how sad Mary looked behind the wide smile. There was a vacancy in her eyes; a jelly layer of sadness that I couldn't bring myself to look at.

A bitterness rose up in my chest as I reflected on how publicly Anna was pursuing her daughter in court and in the press: a woman who perhaps *needed* to disappear, and who was well within her rights to do so. I had done it myself, several times before – when

I first left home, and then again when I fled London after my break-up. What if someone had stopped me closing one chapter of my life and opening another?

When I dropped Quill home each day, carefully checking the drawers and the photo frames so that my rifling left nothing disturbed, I imagined talking to Anna about her court case, and helping her see the error in her approach. She needed to understand that sometimes you have to give people up, and just hope it's not forever.

That had been the hardest lesson of my break-up: to wait and see if they come back to you. That the true art of loving is in the letting go.

Towards the end of the second week of my employment, I approached Anna's loft on Glass Street to find two men going through her bins. My first assumption was that they were homeless. The fact that they were journalists took longer to register. One man was young and tubby with a shaved head, the other rake-thin and markedly older, but they were dressed in similarly cheap, green coats. Their hands moved fast as they hunted through Anna's rubbish bags. The younger guy held up a camera. The other ripped apart the black bin liner with two hands, like a doctor tearing open a shirt to get at the heart. I hung back for several moments on the other side of the street, watching as they lifted out wine bottles, paperwork, packets of medication. Some they photographed, the rest they discarded carelessly over their shoulders.

Suddenly, a large, black-framed Crittall window was tipped open overhead, and boiling water poured down onto the pavements. As it hit the ground, the hot water hissed into steam like a witch's potion.

'Cunts!' Anna roared at them from above. 'Fucking cunts!'

She was back.

A ceramic planter smashed by the journalists' feet; lumps of soil and dried out geraniums spread across the ground as they danced backwards, raising camera lenses to their faces in self-defence. Next, the Aga kettle was thrown, bouncing as it fell.

One of the men gestured over his shoulder to leave, but the other cocked his head towards the blue front door. It swung open. Anna stepped out in her bare feet and a long white nightie, her hair hastily knotted on the top of her head.

'This is harassment,' she shrieked, not noticing me. Her face was free of make-up and her eyes looked puffy and red. She picked up an almond-milk carton and threw it. 'You brutes! I'll call the police!'

The men retreated up the street, still photographing Anna as she tossed whatever she found: a glass jar, then a wine bottle. When they were almost parallel to where I was standing, I stepped into the road and put my hand in the way of their lenses.

'Leave her alone!' I yelled, pointing to the rubbish on the ground. 'You're making a disgusting mess. Get out of here.' The two men looked at me with confusion. I pointed towards the end of the street. 'Go on. Leave her alone. Get out,' I called, as they turned back up the street. 'Scumbags.'

The sun was dazzlingly low in the sky and we both shielded our eyes as the men jogged away. When they were gone, Anna glanced across at me.

'Oh, it's you,' she said breathlessly, relief washing over her face. 'Thank you.'

I guided her back towards the door.

'We'll blame it on the foxes,' I said, gesturing to all the trash.

'Not foxes, *vultures*.'

I surveyed the rest of the strewn litter. There, dented in the gutter, was the kettle she had thrown. I bent down and held it up. 'Tea?'

Back upstairs, Anna paced the kitchen, incensed.

'How the hell did they find out where I live?' she railed. Then she turned on herself. 'I shouldn't have yelled at them like that,' she said, pulling at her cheeks in horror. 'Those photos – I'll look *ancient*.'

I persuaded her to sit down while I made drinks and fed us all: a Bonio for Quill, a couple of ginger biscuits for us, for the shock. It felt good to bustle around the kitchen, making things; even better to be granted the intimacy of her rant.

'You don't look old,' I soothed, eventually settling down next to her on a kitchen stool. It was true; she was still in her nightie, a sleeveless cotton thing which made her look like a child.

Anna sighed gratefully and stared into her mug of tea. On the island between us lay her iPad and a pouch of rolling tobacco. It was mid-morning now, and the radio murmured quietly on the dresser shelf. Above, the Murano-glass chandelier reflected a soft, milky light.

'Distract me, Gussie,' she said eventually, rising from her thoughts. 'Tell me about you. What is it you do? As in, what *else* do you do?'

'You're asking me if there's other dogs?' I asked jokingly. It made her laugh, which again made me feel good. 'Don't worry, Quill and I are exclusive.' I held out my hands and showed how dry they were; the clay beneath my fingernails. 'The rest of my time, I'm in the studio.'

'Oh yes, you're an artist!' Anna bloomed. 'Same as my daughter. I remember now actually. Clover sent me the link. Your stuff is *amazing*.'

My spirits soared at the compliment, but I found myself underplaying things. I told her about the monastic way I lived in my frosty studio: the mattress on pallets atop the chipboard mezzanine; the electric shower that zapped you when you stood on its metal drain. Anna gushed over it. She told me how romantic that work sounded, compared to her own.

'Should we swap lives?' I joked.

Anna flinched. 'I'm not sure you'd want that. And besides,' she pursed her lips and looked under the table, 'you look better in those dungarees than I ever did.'

'Really?'

'It's strange. I used to have that exact pair.' Anna's eyes glinted. 'I'm sure no girl, no *woman*, could resist you in those.'

There was a pause. Anna looked at me knowingly. Her blunt reference to who I was raised first a defensiveness, then a surge of affection; a thawing of my emotions that I couldn't control. We laughed awkwardly; coy laughter, which was also an admission. I reached over and made a point of drinking a large mouthful of tea. Eye contact was impossible.

So, it was a relief when Quill interrupted us, skidding into the kitchen and running in nutty circles. I got up to clear our mugs and fussed over him.

'Here's our little guard dog!'

'You're taking such good care of him,' Anna commented, watching me fill his water bowl.

'I enjoy it.' I set down the bowl, then stood to face her on the other side of the counter. 'To tell you the truth, I've been pretty animal-starved.'

'You live alone?' Anna's gaze flitted to my wedding finger.

'Not even a cat.'

'Your parents?'

'We're not close.'

'Oh,' said Anna, sensing animosity in my tone. She studied me with new interest. 'Do you speak?'

'Not regularly.'

'How often? Monthly?' I shuddered as if that was impossible. 'Quarterly?'

'Christmas-ly.'

Anna acted like it was fate. 'But this is uncanny,' she said, knocking her knuckles against the counter, half-triumphant. 'Another estrangement. It's an epidemic!'

'I wouldn't like to put a label on it,' I shrugged. 'We're different animals. They find me strange, I find them strange. Does that count as estrangement?'

'Gussie, you really must call them,' she said in a maternal tone.

'Why?' I said, feeling myself bristle. Another part of me was touched by her interest.

'Because they're your parents. You can't carry resentment, Gussie. For one, it *wrecks* the skin. But also, what people don't understand is, no one gives you a manual for motherhood. No one tells you how on earth to do any of it. Then, just at the moment you work it out – *bam*! Your children are grown up. They've got this *scorecard* on you, but it's too late. They're gone.'

I couldn't look Anna in the eye, for the sadness in what she had admitted.

'I mean, it's not really a conscious decision. We just don't have that much to say to each other.'

Anna's voice wavered. 'Well, I suppose you're in your right mind. And my daughter very much is not. She's struggled off and on for years. How else can she face standing up and giving evidence against me in the highest court of the land? *Me*, her own mother. Isn't that the most unnatural thing you ever heard?'

There was a heavy pause.

'It's probably not my place to say,' I ventured gently, 'but I'm really sorry about what's been happening. Especially with everything before – the photographers.'

'Nonsense. It's hardly your fault, is it?'

'I know I've only worked here a few weeks, but you seem like a really good person.'

Anna blinked at me for several moments. The cold outside had made her eyes stream, melting dark blotches of yesterday's mascara into her lower eyelids. 'Thank you,' she whispered. 'That actually means a lot.' She smiled gratefully, then her phone sounded a message. Anna read it over and began moving brusquely around the kitchen, apparently in search of something. Her manner had hardened, and I wondered if the intimacy of our exchange had unsettled her. We'd gone too deep, perhaps. Or she'd revealed more of herself to me than she wanted to.

'Didn't the post come yesterday?' She frowned and walked over to the dresser.

'I don't think so,' I said, feeling my chest kick at the lie. There was silence as she rifled on. I began to search for Quill's lead.

'My lawyers sent some documents,' she said, and sighed. 'You didn't sign for anything?'

'I wasn't really here for long,' I said brightly, clipping the leash to Quill and announcing his walk. 'It was always pretty early.'

Anna made a low sound of frustration. 'They've sent it to the office instead,' she muttered, slamming a drawer closed and marching out of the room. 'Bunch of total *fucking* amateurs.'

When I was out of the house, I checked my phone. Hardly two hours had passed and yet those photographs of Anna were already online. As I scrolled them, I couldn't help smiling. Anna was right to have panicked; without her make-up on, she looked deranged and raw.

Yet as I walked home, I kept revisiting the intimacy of our conversation with queasy pleasure. The connection I had built with Anna felt strangely effortless and her company had nourished me in unexpected ways. She was far more accepting that I had imagined, and my mind kept rounding back on the familiar warmth of her expressions; the comfortingly ripe musk of sleep on her skin.

Maybe Anna didn't need a dog walker at all, but a surrogate. An understudy for the girl she had lost. It was unnerving, how ready I was to play that part. But perhaps that shouldn't have come as a surprise. A long time had passed since I'd had anyone to lean on.

GUEST V FINBOW: DAY ONE

After repeating the oath, Anna smooths down her starchy black dress and rotates her shoulders. The atmosphere in the gallery stiffens; we are all making mental adjustments to the sight of Anna off-screen, comparing it to the more flattering soft-focus of her television image. Still, a lightly sycophantic laugh ripples around the gallery when, after thanking her for attending, the judge asks if she is comfortable. Anna quips, 'Rather warm, Your Lordship.'

Then Ms Carr, Anna's barrister, begins, her black onyx earrings swinging as she talks. 'I'll first take you through the statements that you have provided for this case, Mrs Finbow. You should find to your right an impressive array of documents and files. We'll need the second file, the yellow one.' Anna primly wets her finger against her lip, then turns the pages. 'You have it there, Mrs Finbow? Very good.'

Ms Carr warms her up by asking a few questions about her career. First the band, then the yoga videos she made in the mid-nineties as she tried to soften her image. Anna's face lights up as she talks. She has always been her own favourite subject.

'That's right,' Anna preens. 'I am credited with bringing the concept of downward-facing dog to every British housewife.'

And when she is quizzed on the company, she says, 'I launched it when I was pregnant with Mary and was rather bored. The band had imploded, the DVDs were out and selling. I suppose I was feeling a little rudderless. In the back garden of our London house, I made a few cereal bowls and some egg cups. Just as a hobby. But then, as luck would have it, they were featured rather prominently in a dear friend's film. It ended up doing very well, here and in the States. After that, demand went *berserk*. We moved our production from our poky garden shed to Bellinter.'

'That's your factory in Stoke-on-Trent?'

'Correct. We're British-made and very proud of it.'

From there, Ms Carr asks Anna about her broadcasting work.

'Would you say that you understand the great responsibility of a public platform, Mrs Finbow?'

'Very much so.'

They run through presenting stints she has had. Her newspaper column. The time she guest-edited *Woman's Hour*.

'Did you fully understand,' Ms Carr asks, 'the legal limitations on discussing real people on these platforms?'

'Yes. As I wrote in my statement, I'd received media training on an annual basis.'

Ms Carr tilts her head in enquiry. 'Have you ever experienced any complaints from the media outlets you worked for throughout your career?'

Anna thinks for a moment. 'Once, yes. I was referred to the Broadcasting Standards Commission. It was live, a Children in Need thing, or Red Nose Day, I can't remember which.'

'Are you referring to the broadcast on the thirtieth of October 2005?'

'Yes.'

'Would you care to explain what happened?'

Anna smiles. 'I put on my jumper during an ad break and when we went live again, there was a wasp trapped inside it. I'd plucked it straight from our washing line at home, you see. The insect stung me three times.'

Ms Carr winces. 'And that was the only time you have been reprimanded for any statement made in public?'

'Yes, it was. It is.'

'To confirm, they found fault with you for—'

'—swearing, yes. I said "fuck". Repeatedly.'

A laugh goes around the gallery. Even the corners of the judge's mouth are twitching.

Ms Carr allows the laughter for a moment, then she asks calmly, 'Did you fear any reprimand over your newsletter, *The Peony*? The email that mentions Ms Guest?'

Anna's nostrils flare. 'No, I did not.'

'And why was that, Mrs Finbow?'

'Because I was telling the truth.'

Ms Carr leaves a pause to allow the simplicity of that defence to land. Then she enquires about the dynamics within the Finbow family.

'I'm referring to the time *before* the fracture,' she says. 'Your relationship... how would you describe your bond with Ms Mary Finbow?'

For the first time today, Anna's voice falters. 'It was the strongest of bonds. We were a perfect trinity, the three of us: Mary, my husband and I.' Her chin quivers. 'We loved her, still love her, to death.'

Ms Carr takes her through a number of affectionate text messages that have been submitted as supportive evidence. Then a handmade Mother's Day card is projected onto a television screen nearby. The judge pivots on his chair; Ms Ibrahim's team manoeuvres itself to see.

On the front of the card is a cut-out of a glossy photograph showing the Finbows at a dinner table beneath a palm tree. Anna and Bonamy are in matching linen clothes, wearing identical suntans. Mary is between them, breast buds visible beneath her vest top, hair in holiday cornrows. She has stuck stars and furry animal stickers around the photograph.

'"To Mummy and Papa",' Ms Carr reads, as she flicks the screen to reveal the message Mary had written inside the card. '"Never forget how much I love you."'

Anna fails to stifle a cry with the back of her hand. While someone brings her a tissue and she collects herself, the journalists in the gallery scribble furiously. My chest aches as I imagine them publishing these details later this evening. Mary's intimate correspondence. The intrusion of it. The transgression of boundaries: exactly what a therapist would seize on.

'This note was written when Mary was twelve years old. How did your relationship change as your daughter grew up?'

'We remained close. Mary was always a confident, active, happy and curious teenager. There were a few bumps along the way, of course. But what teenager doesn't face the odd setback as they navigate life?'

'Could you be specific?' Ms Carr asks, head tilted.

'Well,' Anna ponders. 'Schooling was sometimes a bit contentious. Mary wasn't hugely academic, but then, neither was I.'

I study Anna closely to see if her face betrays the far more complex truth she is concealing. She hardly blinks, because she is desperate to convince the court that her daughter's upbringing was perfect. The two women labour this point for some time, with Anna producing more and more evidence of her daughter's devotion: holidays in Kenya she had organised for her parents' wedding anniversaries; the fact that she dutifully followed their advice and attended the art school of their choosing.

'An art school in Rome, is that correct?'

My breathing turns shallow. I concentrate my gaze onto the palms of my hands; the grey sweat beads in their shallow creases. The abrupt ending of my lifeline.

'Yes. She was very happy there. Her view on the place only changed when she met Ms Guest.'

'You claim that, shortly after your daughter began sessions with Ms Guest, she left school and severed all contact with you. Is it your evidence that Ms Finbow is being coerced by Ms Guest? Encouraged by the claimant to ostracise herself from those she loves?'

'Yes. We were told as such in the first email we received from her.'

There is a pause as the email is located within a folder of evidence, and Ms Carr reads out loud, '"The longer I spend in session, the clearer it becomes that I must enforce a healing separation from you both."'

Mrs Ayres makes a small cry of recognition. '*Healing separation*,' she whispers, shaking her head. 'We got the same line.'

Ms Carr lowers her file. 'How could you tell these were not the words of your daughter?'

Anna scoffs like it's obvious. 'The very fact that it was spelled correctly. My daughter has many talents,' she says drily. 'Spelling is not one of them.'

In the row behind me, someone laughs, but Anna's criticism feels jarring. Ms Carr senses this and recovers it.

'My Lord, this advocation for isolating the individual from their social milieu closely aligns to Temerlin and Temerlin's 1982 definition of cultic organisations that we have relied on in pre-hearing. Typically, charismatic cult leaders identify, or else invent, faults with their target's network of social relations, in order to gain control over their lives.'

'—In this case it is *sheer invention*,' Anna interrupts.

Ms Carr nods. 'Let's return once again to the email, shall we?' Ms Carr reads. '"As I journey backward into my past, I am rediscovering many frightening moments from my childhood that I have tried to bury. These cannot be reintegrated into my consciousness nor healed while I maintain our poisonous relationship."'

There is a creeping feeling in my scalp at the assumed privacy of her words. A feeling of relief that Anna's daughter is not around to hear this.

'Do you have any knowledge of what these "frightening moments" are, Mrs Finbow?'

'None whatsoever. They are being invented by Ms Guest. She's persuaded our daughter that we have done deplorable things. And the worst thing about it is, we cannot defend ourselves. It is impossible, when we have no idea what Mary has been made to believe.'

'Your newsletter asserted that Ms Guest has, for want of a better phrase, a *modus operandi*. That she inserts false memories into her clients with deliberate intent. Do you still stand by this statement? That Ms Guest has *purposefully* ruptured this bond with your daughter?'

'I will stand by it forever. That's why I wrote the newsletter. It was a warning, published in good faith. A decent practitioner should seek to unite families.' Anna's face darkens as she points towards Jean's table. 'That woman over there only seeks to break us apart.'

Ms Carr nods gravely, then places her folder of notes on her desk. She cocks her head at her client and asks, 'Before we close, Mrs Finbow, I'd like to ask the simple question, *why?* Why would the claimant deliberately pursue your daughter in such a calculating way that you felt it was your duty to call it out in public, as you did in *The Peony?*'

'She goes after wealthy women, girls of independent income. We certainly wouldn't be here if that woman wasn't obsessed with material gain.' Anna's jaw tightens. 'But it's also my belief that there are other sinister reasons at play.' She pauses and haughtily shakes her hair. 'This is also about me. I have something of a public profile. Ms Guest wants that for herself.'

A journalist sitting close to me smirks and makes a note of what has been said.

'So your view is that Ms Guest is motivated by envy?'

Anna scowls over to where Jean sits, her hands primly clasped on the table. 'Perhaps it's fruitless to hypothesise about someone so evil. But, at the deepest level, this has always been about me. About who I am. That woman *wrongly* sees me as someone who has everything. And so, she takes my only daughter. In doing so, she has shattered our lives.'

Ms Carr nods silently, allowing the courtroom to digest her words. Then she places her palms together. 'My final question then, Mrs Finbow. If it's not too painful to reflect upon, please, tell the court: how does it feel to live without Mary?'

Anna considers the question for a moment. She looks down at her hands, then back at her lawyer. Her eyes brim with the tears I know they have rehearsed. 'I'm lost,' she admits quietly. 'When your child is born, it's like you get these strange new coordinates. One is your life and the other is theirs. They might grow up, but their life is still inside you. They remain always inside you. Nested, just like a Russian doll. Without her, it's like there's something missing inside me. I feel – not just lost – but utterly hollowed out.'

A subdued silence descends over the courtroom. Up in the gallery, Lucy Ayres covers her face with her hands. Ms Carr returns to her desk and sits back down. The curtain falls on Anna's first performance.

There will be no further questions, My Lord.

STOKE-ON-TRENT, MAY

About a month after I first started working for Anna, I began to be trusted with other jobs in her household. They began as small favours, really: a request to print something out on the computer in her study. To wait around and let a builder in, or to receive and then put away the luxurious groceries someone delivered every couple of days to the house, even when she was in London. The menial tasks were not coordinated by Anna, but rather Clover, her PA, who was grounded at home with an ill child. Clover thanked me profusely for helping her out.

Anna really likes you, she assured me over text. *In a design meeting the other day, she described a customer profile as edgy and cool. 'Sort of like Gus.'*

I replied with a single exclamation mark. The beat in my heart was running all over.

Speaking of customers, Clover continued, *where are your invoices? Send them over, or you won't get paid!*

When I ran into her, Anna seemed content with the quieter days she was spending at Bellinter, buried in her design work. Bonamy was staying in London, but Anna said she was calmer away from the family home in London; there were fewer photographers and no social obligations to fake her way through. As I worked out the rhythms of her working day, I adjusted my own schedule accordingly, sometimes walking Quill a little later in the hope of running into her as she returned home. Depending on her mood, we might have a glass of wine together while she perched at the kitchen island, scrolling her iPad and monologuing about Mary or her lawyers, whom she was very critical of. During those conversations, we slowly became closer. Although, even when we chatted intimately,

Anna's tone could shift like quicksilver and she'd suddenly task me with something: *bin out; broccoli on. Would you be an angel and shut off my machine?* Anna was paying for my obedience, so I had to bite my lip. Like everyone else around her, I was obliged to agree with her on all matters. Though it was exhausting, she always praised my candour. Right up until the end, Anna used to say, *you're the only one who is honest with me*.

The fact of it was, she hated to be told the truth about anything. I learnt my lesson one crisp morning in May when we were out walking together.

'Can I ask you a question?' Anna asked. There was a bright sun overhead and a low mist lying upon the canal. Quill was trotting between us, his tail curled up like an aerial. I had run into Anna on my way out with him. At the last minute, she'd decided to join me. 'A private question?'

My stomach always lurched when I heard that word, *private*. Still, I smiled cautiously, offering myself up to Anna's needs.

'Always.'

'Have you ever done therapy?' She was breathing heavily.

'Couldn't afford it,' I quickly answered, feeling my cheeks colour. 'Plus, it's not really my thing.'

'What, speaking your feelings?'

'Having feelings.' I laughed.

'It's bollocks, though, isn't it?' Anna interrupted. 'It's not even a science. All this blaming other people for your problems; it's just cowardice. I mean, my mother could be a *perfect hag* to me, but I recognise she was only ever doing her best.'

'It probably helps to talk about things openly—'

'—things you already know about, though,' said Anna, interrupting. Little red flecks of bumpy skin had appeared on her neck above her Lycra sports vest: defensive colours, like a threatened lizard. 'You don't go to therapy to uncover more bad crap. You actively remember the bad things that have happened to you, right?'

'Too readily,' I said, swallowing hard.

It was over a decade ago, yet the episode that got me kicked out of my school always hovered in my awareness. The look of disgust on my parents' faces. I had risked their jobs. I had let them all down. The sneer on Mr Greening's face as he described what I had done, and who I was, as *unnatural*. The scene returned, often at night, in haunting detail, running through my mind like a black ribbon.

'I wish I could forget them,' I admitted.

'Precisely!' said Anna triumphantly. She gestured towards herself. 'I was a female musician in the nineties. Some fucked-up things happened to me and I recall *plenty*. If something that terrible happened to Mary – something *dark* – then we'd have known about it. She would have told me.'

Now, she claimed, they were going to try something different. A new strategy, to convince the courtroom that Mary was mad. Her legal team was seeking to organise a psychiatrist in the hope that Mary might allow herself to be assessed.

'A brilliant guy, ex-Home Office,' she gushed. 'An independent expert in coercive control and ideological radicalisation.' She saw it as key evidence for her case. 'We've got to show the judge exactly what a *fucked-up* young woman Mary now is.'

'How is it independent if you arranged it?' I was irritated by her elated tone, how she couldn't see the irony in what she was trying to prove. Anna ignored me. 'And what if they conclude that she's flourishing? Living happily, or making good art?'

There was a pause. Anna turned and fixed me in a flinty stare. I immediately saw my error in challenging her, but I couldn't back down, not when the point I was making felt so important. 'That won't happen.'

'Why not?' I countered.

'Because it's not true.'

'But what's this psychiatrist going to ask her?'

'It's more that he *observes*.'

I felt a squeezing in my chest. 'Don't you see how traumatising the way you're proceeding will be for Mary? Spying on her with private detectives, making out that she's *mad*?

'—I'm not *implying* she's mad,' Anna retorted, 'I'm proving it.'

'You're pushing her further away!'

Anna made a frustrated noise and pointed. 'Don't *you* start this, too. Do you know how impossible it is to love someone and let them go?'

'Of course, I do,' I muttered through gritted teeth.

'With respect, Gussie,' she sneered, 'you don't have the first idea. You've never had a child of your own. No. My daughter needs to know that I'll fight for her.'

'But who knows? The sessions she's undertaking, the search for self-improvement. Maybe it's all just a phase?'

'—You don't know my daughter!' Anna cried. 'This isn't improvement and it's not a phase. We're not talking about her painting her bedroom black or getting one of her *silly crushes* on girls. She has a dangerous dependency on this woman.'

That phrase, *silly crushes,* irked me. My mind was still thinking of Mr Greening. The frightening prospect of my own childless future. Quill pulled on the lead and I wrenched him harshly backwards.

'But this is so public, Anna. You'll humiliate her. You'll humiliate yourself. Just think, those lawyers will throw anything they like at you. Accuse you of any number of things. I don't understand why you won't just settle it, like we discussed before. There's still time. It would be much smarter, especially if—' I paused. This was delicate. Anna sat down on a nearby bench and leaned heavily on her elbows, knitting and unknitting her fingertips as I talked.

'If what?' She stared up at me. Her breathing had deepened, as if she was spoiling for a fight. 'We have nothing to hide,' she thundered. 'Not me, not her father.'

I sat next to her, daring to rest a hand on her arm. 'But every family has secrets. This whole ordeal will be so public. Aren't you scared?'

'Of course, I'm terrified, Gussie!' Anna yelled, colour blooming into her face as she got up and started walking. 'Of course, we're afraid of everything that will come out! The witch records all sorts of collateral so she can blackmail people. So, yes, I'm *fucking* terrified. And my whole career is probably on the line. But you also know what? No secret is more important than bringing her home. It's worth it,' she said breathlessly. 'My only daughter is worth it.'

A furious quiet hung between us. It stung to be shouted at, but it wasn't Anna's defensiveness that disturbed me most. It was her utter self-certainty. I had never met anyone more obsessed with the maintenance of her public image, and yet she was willing to risk all of it. Although we disagreed over her approach, I couldn't help but admire her commitment, her maternal defiance.

We walked in silence for a while, then I apologised, holding Anna lightly by the elbow.

'I wanted your advice, Gussie,' Anna responded, her mouth twitching with pain. 'Your support. Not your *judgement*.'

'I know,' I said, soothingly. 'And you know Mary better than anyone else.'

'Exactly.'

It was at that point that Anna abruptly stopped walking. Quill had made a mess. Anna stared pointedly towards the ground, then back at me. I squatted down as she looked away, her arms folded.

Weeks would pass before I dared to advise Anna again.

GUEST V FINBOW: DAY ONE

Anna has mastered the art of the subtle gesture. It's all those years in front of the camera. When she returns to the witness stand in the early afternoon and removes her jacket, revealing her yoga-toned arms, she's conveying her strength. Moving slowly and purposefully, her very thinness reflects her self-discipline, which sits at the heart of her legal defence. Anna needs the judge to conclude that she is a restrained woman in all her dealings. Her piece in *The Peony* wasn't carelessly published, but thoughtfully contrived. Factually accurate. Steadfastly true.

But under the pressure of cross-examination, Anna soon buckles. Her oral evidence proves far harder to control.

'I'd like to ask some questions,' Ms Ibrahim says, 'about the events of the seventh of March this year. Could you talk me through the events of that day?'

Anna's chin dips as if she is anticipating a blow in the face. 'That was Mary's twenty-fourth birthday. It will have been quiet.' Her voice trembles. 'Since she left, that day is a source of great pain for us.'

'Specifically, if you can tell me, what did you get up to?'

'I did some yoga, as I generally do in the mornings. We might have had a few friends for lunch.'

'And after that?' Ms Ibrahim presses her. 'In the early evening, just before seven o clock?'

Anna looks straight ahead. 'I was visited at home by two members of the Metropolitan Police,' she says with strained dignity. 'They arrested me.'

Up in the gallery, the journalists fidget and whisper. Those press photographs were notorious: the domestic goddess, tripping down the steps of her frothy-pink villa in Notting Hill, flanked by two policemen. The scandal that this caused, I knew, was partly what drew her up to Stoke the following month. She couldn't face the humiliation of it.

'Would you inform the court of the reason behind your arrest?' Ms Ibrahim enquires.

'I believe my crime was delivering a birthday card to my daughter.'

Ms Ibrahim wipes the skin beneath the seam of her wig. 'You were arrested for breaching an injunction to stay away from your daughter, Mary. According to the police report, you even resisted arrest. You kicked a police car.'

Anna colours. 'It wasn't my intention for things to turn physical—'

'—You didn't mean them to, but they did.'

'I have since apologised to everyone involved,' she snaps. 'I wasn't myself. I was deranged with grief. And nothing came out of it. They brought me in for questioning, and I was eventually released without charge, only a warning.'

'Let's return to the birthday card,' Ms Ibrahim says. 'Do you confirm that you entirely disregarded your daughter's clear wish not to be contacted by you?'

'It was not her real wish.'

'But, more importantly, you entirely disregarded an Order of the Court, didn't you? An Order that was made for Mary Finbow's protection?'

The muscles in Anna's neck stiffen.

'Do you believe that you are above the law, Mrs Finbow?' Ms Ibrahim continues.

'Of course not.'

'Then why did you disregard the law?'

'I was desperate,' Anna cries. 'I didn't think that—'

'Did you think you could get around it, just as you thought you could defame my client's reputation and face no repercussions?'

'No.' Anna's voice cracks. 'That is not the case at all. I was simply telling the truth.'

There is a grim pause. A smile passes across Ms Ibrahim's face. She has wound Anna up in precisely the way she wanted to.

'Let's move on. Could you tell me a little about the book you are writing now? According to your publishers, this is your *third* memoir?' She clasps her slim hands in front of her in a posture which no longer belies rapt attention, but sarcasm.

Anna straightens. 'Well, this one's rather different. It's about our current situation; it's full of practical advice for families who are going through the same thing as us.' She turns to address the judge. 'Your Honour, there are hundreds of families facing this exact nightmare.'

'May I ask if your daughter is named in the book?'

Anna's expression hardens. 'It's a work in progress. I can't give too much away. Not without my publisher's permission.'

'What about Ms Finbow's permission?'

Anna snaps back defensively. 'It's been pretty bloody hard to get a message to Ms Finbow.'

Ms Ibrahim gives a withering smile. 'But you don't think she'll mind? Is it much the same as when you published your piece in *The Peony*, Mrs Finbow? That you haven't considered the risk?'

'She won't read it,' Anna scoffs. 'My daughter doesn't read books. And never has.'

I flinch at this blunt admission. Meanwhile, the force of Ms Ibrahim's argument is building. It is undeniable: Anna Finbow plays out all her family dramas in public, utterly ignorant of the impact her public statements will have on the lives of others.

'Your daughter has faced this level of media intrusion from the moment she was born,' the barrister continues. 'For instance – and this is just one example out of many – photographs of Mary's childhood birthdays were published each year in *Hello!* magazine.' Ms Ibrahim sighs heavily. 'Could it be possible that your daughter simply wants a break from all this?'

Anna shakes her head. 'She may say that she does, but I know it is not her real wish.'

Ms Ibrahim pauses, allowing the court to reflect on the insubstantiality of Anna's claim.

'In her witness statement, Ms Finbow talks of how unhappy she was, growing up in your home. Is this also your understanding?'

'No. That is not my *understanding* nor the reality,' Anna quips. 'My daughter's notion of her childhood has been poisoned by your client. Her present selfhood, too. Just look at that independent report we commissioned. He concluded that my daughter was suffering with depression.'

Ms Ibrahim's eyes widen. 'But, Mrs Finbow, it also concluded that your daughter displayed no obvious indicators of psychological entrapment during the meeting.' She reads aloud. '"No impulsivity, no signs of cultic indoctrination or aggression. Mary also referred proudly to her growth as a professional artist, which has helped her to overcome a previous dependency on recreational drugs. She pointed to the fact that she no longer engages in substance abuse as evidence of her life satisfaction." Is it not your view that this sounds healthy and well-adjusted?'

'There was never any real substance abuse going on,' Anna scoffs, off script now and avoiding her lawyer's furious glare. 'Nothing excessive. More a case of having fun.'

Ms Ibrahim looks purposely grave. 'Most people,' she says slowly, 'would see any drug misuse as a reason to seek the professional help of a counsellor or therapist.'

'Your client is not a professional.'

Ms Ibrahim sighs. 'But nor can your witness statement be relied on as factual. For instance, you describe Ms Finbow's home life as a happy one. Whereas she has made allegations of drug-taking in your family home.'

My pulse quickens. Ms Carr rises with an objection, which Ms Ibrahim calmly rebuts. 'My Lord, my questions are relevant to refute the defence's preposterous idea that my client harbours some fanatical demand for separatism. To the contrary, Mrs Finbow's daughter chooses to live apart from her family milieu for incredibly logical and sensible reasons. She alleges that her home life, for example, was not a safe nor healthy environment to grow up in. Here, we have a typical text exchange – there are many, but in the interests of time, let's just study this example at page 311. The defendant writes to her daughter, Mary, "Darling, have you seen Daddy's weed?" Ms Ibrahim turns to Anna. 'Do you have it there, Mrs Finbow?'

Anna is thin-lipped. 'I do.'

'And have you located your daughter's reply? I'll read it for you. She says: "it's with me upstairs". She sends an emoji of a devil. You reply: "save some for us". Can you confirm the dates of this exchange for the courtroom?'

Ms Carr rises again. 'My Lord, I think we are now in an area where my client cannot be compelled to answer, and ought to be fairly and properly given the usual warning.'

Anna quickly cuts across Ms Carr. 'No, I want to answer. I have nothing to hide.' She glances towards her barrister, who shoots her a warning stare. 'I expect it was our Carnival party.'

'August of which year, Mrs Finbow?'

Anna's voice grows quieter. '2009.'

'When your daughter was how old?'

Anna pauses as she calculates. 'Fourteen.' There is the stirring of voices in the gallery. Jean smiles down at her notebook, her cheeks pink with excitement. 'We've always had a permissive household.'

'In the eyes of the law, that isn't permissive, Mrs Finbow, it is criminal. But, as we have already seen, you prefer to pick and choose when the law applies to you, don't you?'

'That's not right.'

'In her statement, Mary talks of how badly this – what was your term? – *permissiveness* affected her mental health. But, then again, you were already aware of that, weren't you?'

'There had been some issues,' Anna says softly. 'But when she was a lot younger.'

'And did you and your husband support your daughter during those previous bouts of poor mental health?'

Anna's posture stoops. She bites her lip as she looks helplessly over to Ms Carr. Finally, in a defeated voice, she admits, 'We hired a therapist.'

Ms Ibrahim smirks. 'What is the difference between Mary Finbow's choice to work with my client now, and the care you provided for her in her adolescence?'

Anna stumbles over her words. 'Yes. We engaged experts. People with real accreditations.'

'Is it possible that you are simply not satisfied with the outcome?'

'No!'

'Is that why you are seeking revenge against my client?'

Anna brings one hand to her forehead and uses the other to steady her at the witness box. 'You're wrong...' she stutters.

Ms Ibrahim smiles beatifically and nods at the judge to signal she has reached the end of her cross-examination. Her manner softens. 'We understand how unhappy you are with your daughter's life choices, Mrs Finbow. Your desire to place blame on my client is understandable in these contexts, given your great personal sadness. But that does not mean it is right.'

STOKE-ON-TRENT, JUNE

Just before Anna left for her summer holiday in Greece, I arrived back from walking Quill one rainy afternoon, to find a small group of people perched on stools in her kitchen. They were corporately dressed, with notebooks and large files spread across the marble counter. Anna stood in front of them all, wearing the kind of luxuriously comfortable clothes she did at home: a fawn-coloured cashmere poncho and a pair of large gold hoop earrings. She had weights attached to her ankles and was performing leg raises while briefing the team. I hesitated outside by the glass kitchen doors, unsure whether to enter.

'Everyone, this is Gussie,' Anna announced, beckoning me through. 'Quill's carer. *My* carer. And guess what: she's also a ceramicist, just like me! *Mega* talented. Sells it all from a little branded storefront online. No overheads. Just *genius*.'

I waved uneasily at the group who blinked at me with tired faces. Then, with a jolt of panic, I realised their stationery bore the name of a legal firm. I had overheard Anna many times on the phone to these people, but never encountered them in person. I thought anxiously of the NDA, unsigned, in my inbox; the background checks Clover had neglected to run. It wasn't sensible to stay. But my curiosity overruled it.

'It's pouring outside,' I murmured quietly to Anna. 'Can I wait here until it stops?' There was a nervous edge to my voice that I regretted.

'I'll have to park you in the lounge,' she whispered with exaggerated secrecy. She was now making slight pulsing squats from the knee. There was a manic energy to her today, which I found even more alarming than the presence of her legal team. I left the dog lead on the table and the kitchen door slightly ajar. That way, Quill could come and go with ease, and their conversation would also be audible.

After some minutes of subdued exchange, their meeting grew more animated.

'We have to get hold of that other girl, Oriel,' Anna ordered, her folded arms barricading her chest. 'What's her surname?'

'Ayres?' one lawyer suggested. 'Oriel Ayres.'

'Yes, well done,' Anna said, irritably. 'Where are we with her?'

'I'm afraid she's just been hospitalised again. She's fine, but it's unlikely she'll talk. Overdose.'

'Again?' Anna said. '*Fuck*. And her mother?'

'Her mother won't speak without Oriel's consent. We'll have to wait.'

'Well, actually,' Anna snapped, 'I'm done waiting.' There was a deferential silence. 'She must know that it's *me* seeking help?' She made a low, frustrated sound. 'What have we offered her? Whatever it is, raise it. Double it.'

Someone delivered vague assurances, then the group fell quiet again. When I looked through the ajar doorway, the lawyers were squinting towards laptops or studying their notebooks. Anna had her back to me, was busy scrolling her phone.

After a while, she sighed. 'Dare I ask, then, where we got to with Lawrence?'

'You mean Lawrence Melrose?'

'Who else?'

My chest skipped at the name of that renowned artist. I held tightly on to Quill's body to quieten his breathing. Together, we listened.

'We need to have him there. Just his name, you know. It adds gravitas.'

One of the more senior lawyers cleared his throat. 'We've actually got a development. He seems to have got into a spot of trouble. A rather ugly accusation. From an ex-student.'

My chest pounded with interest.

'I know about that,' said Anna, flatly. 'It's nothing—'
'Well,' he insisted, 'it's becoming something. We're not sure how good it would look if we summoned him for our side.'
'He told me it had blown over.'
'There's an update for you here,' one of the lawyers said. 'We could summarise now, or…?'
'Later,' Anna blustered impatiently. 'I'll read it later. Please let's move on.'

It was seven o'clock by the time the lawyers packed up and filed down the stairs. When the front door slammed and I was certain they were gone, I crept into the kitchen.
'Christ,' said Anna, clutching her chest with one hand. With her other hand, she held a glass of white wine. 'I'd forgotten you were still here.'
'I'm sorry,' I said, and hesitated. 'It's still too wet to go out.'
'Oh, forget it,' Anna said, and passed me the wine bottle and a glass.
There was a pause as she crossly scrolled through something on her phone, then she sighed, tossing it to one side.
'Cheers, then,' I said, watching her carefully and settling at the counter.
Anna's eyelids flickered as she leant back against the Aga and swallowed. '*Jesus,* Gussie, I don't think I can manage *cheers*. Not after today.'
My gaze floated to a black notebook one of Anna's lawyers had left behind, on the counter by the fridge. I wondered if they'd return for it, or even miss it at all. 'Was it a difficult meeting?' I asked gently, wanting to fill in the gaps of what I'd overheard.
Anna dipped her chin. 'It's always difficult,' she said. 'But today, yes, today was bad.' There was a brief silence as she concentrated on rolling a cigarette. 'We've had some strange news. A sighting. Bonamy bumped into her. Mary.'

The air in the room began to feel very thin, as if there were no oxygen left in it. 'Where?'

Anna grimaced as she exhaled smoke. 'Maida Vale Tube station, of all places. Mary wouldn't even speak to him. And my husband – the *idiot*. The class A *cunty* coward – he just let her go. He just walked off.'

'It must have been an awful shock,' I began, trying to keep my face even. 'Maybe it was the wiser choice, to approach things gently—'

'—No, Gussie.' Anna said, flicking her lighter. 'It was absolutely *spineless* of him.'

I proceeded carefully. 'Did Bonamy say where she was going?'

'She wasn't going anywhere. Apparently, she looked like a tramp, standing alone in the cold, handing out flyers. Recruiting more victims for that witch. Can you imagine it? *My* daughter. Practically begging in public?'

My skin chilled as I pictured the scene. The harrowing coincidence of it. A family reunion in such a painfully public place.

Anna stubbed out her cigarette and I gestured for her to join me at the counter. She slumped forward on the stool, her chin in her hands.

'When did this happen?' I said, wondering if I dared touch her.

She replied in a low, unguarded tone. 'Three days ago. Bonamy didn't even come to me with the news. That *bastard*. He told our private investigator first. Before telling me.' She reached for her wine glass. 'They think that if I found out where Mary was, I'd just turn up and start looking for her. They're frightened about another arrest. They all see me as a liability.'

'That doesn't make you a liability,' I said soothingly, placing a hand, not yet on her body, but on the back of her seat. Her long hair tickled the inside of my wrist, where my pulse was beating rapidly. 'That makes you a mother.'

Anna considered this for a moment, then slowly shook her head. Her manner had quietened now. As I noticed the wilted movements of her eyes and the irregular clenching of her jaw, I wondered if she was on something stronger than the wine in her hand. In the bathroom cupboards, there were stacks of painkillers and anti-anxiety pills. Had she taken something to deal with the pain of her husband's encounter? It would be understandable, I decided, with a flutter of nerves. And it could be useful. If Anna was high, or stoned, I might be afforded a different kind of intimacy. Tentatively, I filled her glass. She soon began to repeat herself.

'I promise I'm not normally like this, Gussie,' Anna slurred, making a light sound of exasperation. 'So *weepy*. I just can't bear the thought of my daughter, standing out there, advertising the services of a crook who steals her money. I refuse to let it happen.' She pointed to herself. 'And I won't let that witch get a penny of my money, either.'

'But she's not interested in your money, right?' I hesitated, unsure whether I should use Anna's term. 'The *witch*, isn't she giving anything she wins through the case to charity?'

Anna looked mystified. 'What do you mean?'

An indignant lump rose to my throat. 'Aside from legal costs; those damages she's seeking—?'

'—Where did you read that?' Anna interrupted. 'This woman wants money. She's always wanted our money.' She briefly reflected, then raised her voice. 'Is that what they're saying now? Is that what they're writing?'

'No, I'm sorry,' I said and shook my head. 'Forget it. I must have it wrong. Really, I have no idea.'

'—No one does!' Anna stared at me, though she could no longer focus. 'You know, Gussie, I never stop dreaming of her coming back. I have this fantasy where she remembers that she loves us again. And that we were good parents to her. When I wake up, I think that she's still in her bedroom, fast asleep in her tartan pyjamas.'

Tears streaked from the corner of her eyes. I reached over to wipe them. 'Some mornings, after I dream, I even go into her room.

I can't tell you how disappointed I am when I see her bed's empty. Do you think that's strange?

'A little—'

'—And I hear her voice *all the time*. And I think that I see her, too. Walking around, I get these glimpses. It's like I have a thousand missing daughters, all just out of reach.' Anna's reddened eyes roamed over my face. 'Every young woman reminds me of her.' She frowned. 'Even you. I mean, obviously, you're so different, but you seem somehow similar, too.'

I smiled warily, desperate now for Anna to stop talking. An unbearable pain was building in my chest. I kept picturing the flickering lights of the Tube station, the sluicing sound, like sharpening knives, as trains passed through it. Bonamy meeting his daughter like she was a stranger.

When Anna began massaging her temples, complaining of a headache, I seized my chance to get away.

'I've had it since this morning,' she whispered weakly. 'Can't shake it. This terrible tearing sound. From behind my eyes.'

I pointed towards her bedroom. 'Have a rest. I'll clear up.'

'Isn't it too early for bed?' She looked at me with an expression of such childlike trust, I had to look away.

'I'll wake you before I leave,' I said, getting up from the counter. 'Once I've done the kitchen.'

I guided Anna unsteadily towards her bed, drawing a blanket over her small body. Framed on her bedroom walls were giant posters of her most famous designs: illustrated ducks and dancing soldiers, all entwined with her signature witticisms. They were hung up high, but meaningless now, like old flags in a baronial hall.

'You know,' Anna said, still tearful as she settled into the pillows. 'If that had been me, *me* in that fucking Tube station, I never would have left. *Ever*.'

I sat on the edge of the bed and looked kindly into her face. 'I know.'

'I'd have just grabbed hold of her. Like that—'

Limply, I let her seize my wrist as she made her point.

'And got her *straight* back home,' she gasped, finally letting me embrace her. 'Where she was *happy*.'

'Of course you would,' I hushed, taking in her comforting smells: the moth-repellent beneath her cashmere, the liquorice sweetness of the wine we had been drinking.

'I wouldn't have let Mary go, Gussie.'

'I know,' I whispered, feeling my own throat narrowing. I held Anna close towards me, just as my lips made the words. 'Neither would I.'

I waited for a while in the kitchen, just in case Anna re-emerged. Her words haunted me as I shifted anxiously around the room: *you remind me of her.* They made me want more for myself. They made me want out of the whole situation. But it was also true that, over the course of this evening, and even over the weeks before, my feelings towards Anna had shifted. Perhaps it was the nearness to her suffering, or the fact I had started to share her conviction: she had done nothing wrong.

So I told myself the task was simple: clean up and ignore the notebook. Things were straightforward: wash the glasses, feed Quill, then go. *It doesn't exist.* As my thoughts circled, I even cut myself a tragic little bargain: if I left the lawyer's book alone, I would buy myself something. Some new clay, the gorgeous, mineral-rich stuff that made my studio smell like a dairy. Or perhaps a trip somewhere, far away from the tormenting situation I'd waded into.

The bribery was delusional. My will was too weak. Just before I left, I persuaded myself that I needed a piece of paper to write Anna a quick note. She'd be disturbed, I reasoned, if she woke up to see I'd gone, after I promised to wake her. It was important to thank her for the wine and tell her when I'd be back again. As I opened the cover to the first page, my gaze fell on Quill as he lay dreaming in his basket. It felt absurd to envy him, but I did. I wanted a spotless conscience, too. But it was much too late for that.

Tucked inside the notebook was the briefing document that the male lawyer had referenced, the one about the artist. With my heart in my mouth, and pausing every so often to check Anna hadn't woken up, I scanned it quickly, jaw locked stiff as I repressed the urge to scream with outrage. Retrieving my phone from my bag, I squared the document in front of me so I could get a good angle. Then there was an unexpected sound. I had just started to capture each page, when it came again, the sound of the rain at the window, but also of a key tickling the lock of the front door. I froze. The squeal of door hinges as it swung open; then a slamming as it shut.

'Anna?' a male voice called breathlessly. Footsteps darted up the stairs. Frantic, I shut the book and moved it to the side. 'Anna?'

A man appeared: a tall, slim-hipped figure, dressed in loose-fitting chinos and a long navy coat. Bonamy Finbow. I grabbed a tea towel to wipe my trembling hands.

'Hullo there,' he said, entering the kitchen and shaking off his overcoat. He had thick, sandy-coloured hair, far more than was usual for a man over sixty. It rose up from his chest, too, protruding through the undone buttons of his creased shirt.

'Anna's in her bedroom,' I said uncertainly. 'Asleep.'

'How is she?' he murmured, glancing behind him.

'Fine,' I said, settling my face into a mild expression. The tension in my chest was unbearable. 'Headachy.'

'We've had a quarrel.' He went over to the fridge and took out a fresh bottle of wine. 'And I had a *fucking* frightful drive. Anything to eat?'

It amazed me how readily Bonamy accepted a stranger's presence in his house. I gathered it was a mark of his breeding, how accustomed he was to staff.

'There's some fish pie,' I said, humming slightly as I assumed the role of housekeeper. 'I could make you a plate?'

Bonamy thanked me graciously and sloshed wine into a glass while I made myself busy, boiling peas to go with his food and loading the dishwasher. I enjoyed showing Bonamy that I was acquainted with his home. It seemed to relax him, too. As I bustled about, he drank even more eagerly than Anna. One glass, then two: a man clambering to get under the thick quilt of its sedation.

'Take care. It's hot,' I said eventually, setting down the plate I'd microwaved.

Bonamy sat at the counter and rounded his lips to let cold air into his mouth of mashed potato, just like a schoolboy. I washed dishes, my back to him while he ate.

'Was she okay this evening?' He hesitated. 'It's Gus, isn't it?'

I turned to face him. 'Gus, yes. And a little sad, yes.'

Bonamy's Adam's apple pulsed with emotion. 'You're across what happened, I take it?'

'The sighting?' He nodded. 'I never actually asked,' I said, aware of the shake in my voice. 'How was she?'

'You mean, Mary?' The muscles beneath Bonamy's forehead shifted, like a wave retreating. 'Do you know, you're the first person who has actually asked me that question?' He laughed in a hollow way. My chest felt very tight. 'I can't—' he began to say, then paused to clear his throat. 'I can't tell you how good it was to see her. I was on the escalator. Gliding down, my mind elsewhere, reading something on my phone. And just like that, she floats into view. This husk of a human. My daughter.'

I gazed at him. 'Did you talk to her?'

'I tried. She blanked me entirely. It's so odd, what you do under pressure. I just kept talking. I said, "You should be careful, the air in these stations is very polluted. It's filled with iron filings."' Bonamy chuckled, self-mockingly. I couldn't bring myself to join in.

'She didn't acknowledge you at all?' I pressed him, my chest prickling with sadness.

'No. Not as any normal person would. Her face was this blank window; she just stared at me with these wide, sightless eyes. She gave me absolutely *nothing*. Just clutched this handful of tatty leaflets. So, being me, I carried on like a loon, telling her all sorts of stuff about us and the business and dear Quill and various family friends.' He narrowed his eyes as he relived it. 'For a moment, I thought she'd crumbled. Then she started heckling me, using this foul language, shouting at me to leave her alone. I think the exact phrase she used was "Get the fuck away from me."'

I heard myself gasp. 'I'm so sorry, Bonamy—'

He swallowed a mouthful of wine. 'Now my wife is furious with me for not kidnapping her. Ridiculous, isn't it?'

'But you couldn't possibly have done that!'

'—She's a grown woman.'

'—With her own mind.'

'Precisely.'

Bonamy looked at me kindly. I wondered if, for the first time this evening, he was noticing my age, perhaps even my proximity to Mary. Despite everything, I felt myself bloom.

Then a voice came from behind him. Anna had appeared noiselessly at the glass doors, like a ghost. The back of her dark ponytail was matted from where she'd been lying asleep, and her eyes looked bald and swollen from crying.

'When did you arrive?' she asked sharply. 'You didn't read my email?'

'No,' Bonamy began in a measured tone, opening his arms towards her. 'I didn't read anyone's email. I was driving as fast as I could to get to you.'

She sidestepped him. '*Please* don't start making *me* feel guilty—'

'Please let's not argue in front of Gus,' he warned.

I made for the bathroom. Anna made an apologetic face and tried to keep me close by, lightly linking her arm in mine, but I excused myself firmly, nervous to be caught listening.

Locked inside, I gripped the edges of the basin and pressed my forehead against the cool glass of the mirror. One deep breath. Then two.

This job had to end. It was clear now that I had trespassed much too far into this family nightmare and gained nothing but a terrible proximity to their suffering. My gaze fell on a photograph of Mary on the bathroom wall. A big black-and-white portrait of a gap-toothed girl with her chin in her hands. Again, that preoccupied stare. I wondered, how often were you in this position? A piece of tumbleweed caught between your parents' livid energies? Outside, Anna and Bonamy's voices were rising and falling so quickly in anger, it was hard to catch the precise words.

'You're wasted,' I could just make out Bonamy saying, though his tone was now concerned. 'Have you taken something? What have you had?'

'There it is again,' Anna protested. '*I'm* the fuck-up, am I? What I want to know is, what the hell you were doing in Maida Vale in the middle of the day?'

My stomach turned as I remembered Bonamy's description of Mary in the Tube station. *Blank window, sightless eyes.* I studied my own reflection in the mirror, looking closely into my face for the first time in months. A terrifying recognition dawned. He could have been describing me.

Outside, Anna began ramming plates into the dishwasher, signalling the end of their row. I flushed the chain, but, before going back outside, I reached into my pocket and found the perfume I'd taken weeks ago from the Finbows' dresser drawer. Pasting it on my wrist, I inhaled deeply. Briefly, I was transported by the old scent. Just for a moment, the roaring guilt in my mind dulled. The path ahead was clear now. I had to free myself. I would leave my job this evening and never speak to the Finbows again.

When I rejoined Anna and Bonamy, they were leaning against each other, speaking in quieter voices.

'I'll get out of your hair now,' I said, entering the kitchen breezily and bending down to say goodbye to Quill. My chest hurt to think it would be the last time.

'Why not stay for another drink?' Bonamy suggested, keen to ward off another row. 'You've been taking such good care of that dog.' He smiled softly at Anna. 'Of all my creatures.'

I hurried over to my bag, explaining that it was too late and I had to get the bus. But, in my haste, I stepped on Quill's paw. He yelped, and for some reason, probably the alcohol, my ankle softened when I stepped sideways. I grasped the side of the counter as I tripped, but my body lurched and the little tin of perfume fell out of my pocket.

'Did something just fall?' Bonamy asked.

'Not sure,' I said, scanning the floorboards, my mouth dry with panic.

He got up to look. 'I'm sure I heard something.' The silver tin rolled agonisingly over to his feet.

Anna craned her neck to check the ground. The walls of the room started to collapse inward.

Bonamy's knees cracked as he squatted and picked it up, resting it carelessly on the worktop in full view of Anna. When she noticed the object, she turned and frowned. Blood drained rapidly into my legs.

'That's Mary's perfume! Where on earth did you find that?'

GUEST V FINBOW: DAY ONE

Outside the law courts, the sky is white, the sun half obscured by a fumy haze of smog. I collapse on a bench at a bus stop and rest my head in my hands, replaying the hopeless spectacle of Anna's evidence. A drumming anxiety descends. It has started to seem very possible that the Finbows will lose.

I check my phone. My meeting starts in twenty minutes, and I am about to board the next bus which will take me north, when I become aware of somebody waiting at the pedestrian crossing. At the sight of her, my stomach lurches. Lucy Ayres, the woman who has sat next to me all day. Oriel's mother.

Her head moves side to side as she waits for a sensible moment to cross. I raise a hand in greeting, but she doesn't see me, and crosses over the road. I step away from the shelter, just to check which way she is headed. South, towards Waterloo Station. Did she miss me waving? Or was she ignoring me on purpose? There isn't much time, yet I find myself following her, darting suddenly into the road so that a cyclist almost clips me. The man turns and curses, but I'm walking fast along the pavement now, craning my neck to keep sight of Lucy as she reaches the part where the Strand forks in two.

I go after her, entranced. My fast walk becomes a run. She inches slowly up the right-hand side of the street and, for a while, I am only ten metres behind her. What is it that compels me to follow? After our shared experience in the courtroom today, I have decided we cannot pass each other like strangers. We must discuss what has happened. I wonder what she thinks of Anna's questioning. Perhaps if we go for a walk, she will tell me how Oriel is doing. Perhaps if I buy her a coffee, I can correct the lies I told her this morning. I can tell her who I am; how I am really doing.

We pass office workers and tourists on Waterloo Bridge. I am about to call out her name, when a bus empties its passengers onto the pavement. Caught up in the swarm of people, somehow, I also lose my view of Lucy's coarse, dark hair. I cross the river but Lucy is nowhere to be found, and I don't know why I am pursuing her.

My footsteps slow. I start to feel embarrassed, but why? I have been ghosted countless times before. This is always the pattern of things for me: I crave the company of people who vanish. I don't know why it still makes me feel so foolish. As I turn back, an evening newspaper is thrust into my hands. I tuck it under my arm, making a neat fold between Anna and Bonamy's front-page faces, and walk towards my meeting.

The café where I'm meeting my support worker is north from the courthouse in Clerkenwell. It's the kind of place that has framed photographs of the owner on the wall; the owner's brother and mother, too. The tea comes stewed from a silver urn, and a bottle of vinegar is set out on the surface of every Formica table.

When I greet Bernard, he gives my arm a quick squeeze. Settling opposite, he tells me how troubled I look.

'This is just my face,' I say, tossing the newspaper to the side.

'Well, in court, you'll need to cheer up a bit,' he says, gently. 'Their single aim will be to discredit your character. They barely need to prove or disprove what you say, only to make you sound disgruntled, misguided, angry.'

'What if I'm all of those things?'

He raises his eyebrows. 'You'd have every right to be. But we need you to be calm and objective. Above all, unswervingly truthful. They're going to try and make you look obsessive. Perhaps even a stalker.' Bernard sighs. 'For what it's worth, Augusta, I think what you're going to do is very brave. It's not easy standing up for the truth. Admitting what happened to you; everything you've done.'

A lump appears in my throat. I concentrate on aligning the salt and pepper shakers to repress it. It's his kindness that undoes me.

'It's fine. Honestly,' I say, but my voice cracks. I can barely say the words.

'Not long until all this is over, so just lay low over the next few days. Don't talk to anyone. We have concerns that she may try to approach you. If that happens, remember everything we told you to do: don't engage,' he urges. 'And—'

'—I know, I know. Don't engage. *Ignore her and walk away.*'

Bernard reaches into his pocket, then slips a pamphlet to me: a guide to giving evidence from the Courts and Tribunals Service.

'This is bullshit, fundamentally,' says Bernard. 'It sugar-coats the whole thing. But I'm professionally compelled to give it to you.'

There is a guide to the different oaths I can choose to take. As I read it over and consider the full magnitude of what stands before me, the text grows pixelated. I can hear Bernard's phone ringing, as if I'm emerging from a dark tunnel. Then it's his soft voice excusing himself as he gets up to answer it. He slips out of the café, leaving his file – a blue paper wallet stuffed with documents – on the table beside me.

I toss the pamphlet aside and look through the window. Bernard is still talking on the phone. I bring the file towards me and study what's inside. At the top are the notes of what he is supposed to cover in today's conversation. Beneath that, my evidence: screenshots of emails and text messages, labelled numerically, with other marks alongside them in blue biro. A photo I had taken of Quill and me together, months before. Then, just under those, is a scan of the most recent photograph I'd sent him. It had been the most painful evidence of all to provide. But here it is, scanned and numbered: my favourite photograph.

It's a polaroid, showing a group of girls standing in front of a Renaissance church in the corner of a piazza. The facade of the building is ornately carved in light stone, its surface like gelato, gorgeously whipped and curved. At the top, there is a mosaic in gold and shimmering blue: the Santa Maria Di Trastevere in Rome.

Looming above it, is the square clock tower, the time showing six, so the light is falling, but you can still clearly see the group of girls – five, in total – posing outside it, with arms and wrists intertwined. Their skin and hair vary in colour, but it is all as luminous and creamy as the stonework behind them. Mary Finbow is sat at the front, on the floor, wearing the little red shorts I always liked, her long legs stretched across the cobbled stone ahead of her, a Birkinesque wicker handbag on her lap. And I am there, too, alongside her, my hair sun-bleached and longer. I am crouching there, smiling dreamily, my hand gripping hold of her knee, barely balancing.

PART TWO

ROME, SEPTEMBER

Two years prior

There's a term in ceramics that I love: *quartz inversion*. When clay is fired, there's a moment when all the water is burned off and the molecules become fixed and fused together. It's a point of no return, after which the shape of an object can no longer be altered.

The night I first met Mary in Rome was a Friday in early September. We were outside a crowded bar in Piazza San Calisto in Trastevere. It was a meeting that produced a fusion between us, an inversion of my life from which there was no recovery.

Before Rome, I'd only visited Europe a handful of times, in my early twenties, taking eerily cheap flights that landed miles away from the city I intended to visit. Growing up, I'd fantasised about the trips abroad that would elevate me into a different, better being. Each city – Prague, Amsterdam, Vienna – was carefully selected as a portal to adventure. But I never got it right. The parties that occurred in my hostels – the only places I could afford to stay in – repelled and embarrassed me, but I would end up joining them anyway, because I was lonely. The next morning, disorientated and hungover, I would flock to recognisable food chains to eat lunches; I would get the timings of the galleries and museums wrong.

Part of the reason my trips abroad were so underwhelming was because I was only ever observing a place, never belonging to it. My residency in Rome, I hoped, would change this. I'd have three months to find my feet there, with a stipend and a room of my own.

Ten days in, the first flush of excitement was already starting to waver. I was struggling with the cost of food; I hadn't yet learnt how to source vegetables and dried goods from the street markets and so I was up against the city's bewilderingly expensive supermarkets; those narrow, grey-lit stores where the cost of a can of chickpeas exceeded five euros. The residency would last until Christmas, but I'd begun to worry my savings wouldn't stretch that far.

I'd spent the early part of that Friday evening searching for employment in the winding streets filled with bars, on the left bank of the River Tiber. Unsuccessful and disheartened, I gave up and collapsed into a chair outside the nearest place I could find, exhausted by the rejection and the isolation of feeling poor and hungry in one of Europe's choicest restaurant districts. The bar, I later found out, was a popular spot in Trastevere, but there was nothing special about its interior: an aluminium bar counter lit by strip bulbs, the walls pasted with faded Lazio football memorabilia. People seemed to like the place out of sheer necessity, because it was cheap and Rome was expensive.

I sat there with a beer, engrossed in my book about two young girls in Naples, when a sudden sound interrupted me: cheering from a crowd of men nearby. I looked up. They had become distracted from the football game they were watching and were now applauding the arrival of a group of girls instead.

I liked how the row of girls reacted to the harassment, morphing into a single file, each managing to raise a middle finger at the hooting men, without turning to engage them. When they'd made it through the crowd, they sat down at the empty table next to me.

I stole glances over the pages of my book. One girl was tall and dark blonde, the other even taller, and there were two very fair freckled girls, twins, at the further end of the table. Their long, thick hair and their charismatic, well-bred faces belonged in bewitching online profiles, or perhaps short encounters on the Tube – agonisingly brief, always me staring, never receiving the same interest back.

At the bar, I gazed pointedly at the blurred text of my page, then over at them. My body burned with interest.

'Can I take this?' said the blonde girl. The prettiest. She gestured to the seat I was resting my feet on. Her voice sounded expensively hoarse, like it had been overused and you were lucky to hear it. Mary.

I swung my feet free, and she draped her jacket on the seat: a stiff, red military piece that looked like an heirloom. She thanked me. Our eyes met. Then she turned back around. The skin on her bare shoulders was tanned, but the surface was scaly and dry, in the way the sea dries on skin. I tried to focus on the pages of my book, but something in my attention had awoken. Also in my skin.

I glanced around at the group: the twins chattered to each other, playing with the pug dog that the brown-skinned girl had brought along with her. When, unprompted, the waiter brought over a tray of shots, they knocked them back without any celebration or theatrical fuss. Not how people drank them at home: tongue out, wedge of lemon at the gums, loud grunts of disgust. When the *antipasti* was placed in front of them, they picked at the meat and left the bread, lighting and relighting endless cigarettes.

Their conversation flowed noisily and irreverently. I ordered another beer, then a shot for myself, eventually abandoning my book completely to listen as they teased Mary about someone she was texting.

'Not Vincenzo again? You're *obsessed*.'

I quickly gathered they were going to a party that night. The conversation moved on to whether Vincenzo would be there, if they were too underdressed, about the quality of cocaine that would be provided.

Intermittently, Mary complained about her mother, counting the number of messages that arrived on her phone, asking if she knew the whereabouts of her father.

'Five,' she said, waving her phone screen. 'Six! Fuck me, she's really on one.'

Eventually, they started gossiping about their classes at school. Because of how they were dressed and the way they spoke, I guessed they were artists. My stomach ached with longing;

my peers at CRETA spoke almost no English and I envied this group's casual intimacy. When I heard one of the twins discussing a model casting that was taking place at their school the following day, and that the work was paid, my spirits lifted. Here, finally, was a route into their conversation. For a moment or two, I deliberated, nervous to make the approach, then I drained my bottle and stood up.

'Sorry to interrupt you,' I said, leaning forward and raising a hand in greeting. 'I just overheard your conversation.' All at once, the girls stopped talking and looked at me. The room slowed, the piazza was drained of all noise. The only sound I could hear was my own blood marching in my ears. 'Did you say you were you looking for...' I paused. The phrase itself seemed ridiculous. 'Life models?'

Their gaze flitted over my appearance. Then they exploded with encouragement.

'Oh my God, yes! You must come,' said the girl with the pug.

'Are you English?' one of the twins asked, pulling up a chair. 'You don't have to be.'

'She looks French,' said the other, pouring me wine. 'Are you French? You know, we *urgently* need models like you.'

'Like me?' I replied, half laughing from relief. They beckoned for me to drag my chair closer in, towards their table. 'What does that mean?'

'Different!'

'Pale!'

'Young!'

'Last term, for some reason, we only got these *really old* men to paint,' the tallest girl said, tipping ash from her cigarette with disdain.

Mary shuddered. 'I wonder what was worse,' she said, turning to one of the twins. 'Painting those shrivelled old cocks, or you?'

'Everyone failed last term,' one of them explained.

'Our tutor, Law, was furious,' said Mary. I noticed a squarish brown birthmark near her collarbone as she brought a cigarette to her lips. She offered me one, and I took it.

'Not with you,' said the girl with the pug, teasingly. 'You're his next big project. He's obsessed with you.'

'What's that supposed to mean?' she said.

'Guys,' said one of the twins, gesturing to me. 'Don't scare her.'

I laughed. It felt good, being the object of their attention. Mary rolled a lighter towards me and smiled again. She introduced herself. 'And this is Frida,' she said, pointing to the dog. 'Decca's her owner.'

'I'm Cleo,' said the smaller of the twins. 'This is Bea.'

'Are you sure you have the time to sit for us?' Mary asked, taking her lighter back. I inhaled sharply on my cigarette and let my eyes wander over her face for a moment. She had thick eyebrows, a beautiful wide mouth and that rich-girl skin: pore-less and shiny, as though it were lit from the inside.

'It's paid, isn't it?' I asked, the cigarette curdling my stomach.

'Of course,' she said. 'It's just, kind of a commitment. Like, fifteen or twenty sittings at least.'

'She's lying,' said Decca. 'Mary needs double that.'

'Only because she's a perfectionist,' warned Bea.

'I've got the time,' I said, not wanting to mention how desperately I needed work. 'I'm doing a residency at CRETA. It's not too full on.'

'What's CRETA?' One of the twins asked.

Her sister smiled broadly at me. 'We're very ignorant.'

'Ceramics, right?' Mary said, glancing down at the cover of my book. 'What are you reading?'

'*My Brilliant Friend*,' we both said, simultaneously.

She laughed and I blushed.

Decca tossed her phone down onto the table. 'Our lift's here.' I looked about, wondering who was driving them, whether it might be that guy, Vincenzo. 'You'll need to come in tomorrow morning at ten,' she said, turning to me and scooping up her dog. 'It's the Melrose Academy on Via Renella. Look fabulous.'

'Not fabulous,' Mary corrected, putting on her jacket and stuffing her cigarettes into her handbag. She paused and cocked her head at me. 'Just like this.'

The next morning, I rose early and dressed in the dark corridor of my apartment so as not to wake my room-mate. The coordinator of my residency, Thea, had helped me find my room near Termini station. Although the walls were soft with damp and painted in an inexcusably bright lime-green colour, I had, at first, fallen in love with the space. There were two single beds, and a pair of long windows which opened onto a precarious little iron balcony. I sat there most evenings with a mug of wine, watching the sky change colour and the traffic crawl forward over the ancient cobblestones. But then, at the end of the first week, it transpired that the second bed in the room was to be occupied. My room-mate, Christina, was a plump woman from Poland who had arrived in the city for research purposes. When I asked her what course, she had replied, without further expansion, divinity studies. I excused myself from the conversation after that, not wanting to think about my old school, Kingsfold. She slept early, and guardedly dressed herself in the bathroom. She wore the kind of footwear that made me wonder if she was training to become a nun.

After blagging the bus down to Largo Argentina, I hurried across the Tiber into Trastevere. Via della Renella was a subdued little street. No shops were open and the pavement was shaded by green ivy that hung between the buildings like a dense, low cloud.

Outside the school, I pressed a worn-looking bell.

A voice answered over the intercom, *Pronto?*

Inside, the wooden lift was from a film set, ornate and antiquely charming. As it staggered to the third floor, I squinted at my reflection in the mirror, trying to imagine my features translated by oil paints. My jaw was too pronounced, I thought, and my complexion had never been quite right: pale, but shadowy, at the same time. The fact that I had put myself forward for this was starting to seem ridiculously big-headed. I had never been told I was beautiful before, let alone that I could model. But, as my anxiety built, there was also a thrill. Hadn't I always waited for the giddy newness of an invitation like this? I rearranged my CRETA tote bag, a signal, I hoped, of my own creative legitimacy. Then I remembered Mary's encouraging smile from last night. Her meaningful gaze: *just like this.*

The lift opened onto a large hallway. Sunlight poured through the windows on one side. The Melrose Academy, I'd read this morning, was an old atelier, now transformed into three studios, a small gallery and a lecture theatre. It was overseen by Lawrence Melrose, who came from a long dynasty of eminent portrait artists, a family line which began in the 1500s. Course fees were chokingly high, so I was surprised that the entrance was understated and dingy. Countless pairs of boots and plimsolls had been left outside, and I glanced at them, wondering which pair were Mary's. Beyond the doorway was an atrium, which led onto a long corridor lit by three hanging globe lights. On the wall, immediately on the right, was a corkboard, covered in tatty flyers for Italian lessons, classical music concerts to be held in the Terme di Caracalla, fishing huts available in Sicily, art material suppliers, a schloss for hire in Switzerland. Momentarily enchanted, I grasped at a bunch of flyers and stuffed them into my rucksack. I decided to keep my shoes on, so it would be easier to leave if I found that I'd made the wrong decision in coming.

The sound of voices led me down the corridor to an airy, semi-circular studio filled with light. As I entered, I swallowed down that silvery and rich back-of-the-throat taste of oil paint, then something dryer, more fibrous; what I later came to know was the smell of the unpainted canvases. I paused by the doorway. Sitting in clusters on the floor, draped over each other, were around twenty students; mainly girls, bar one or two boys. In their barefooted state, they looked like scruffy urchins, but that was partly because of how thin they all were. In their short shorts and summer dresses, I noticed how their thighs never became fleshy. They never softened and widened in the feminine way that I despised mine. Their legs just continued their narrow quest upwards and never really became thighs at all.

The would-be-models were older. Some wore elegant, wispy clothes – perhaps they were art teachers themselves – but others looked less conventional, as if they were more used to be being naked. All of us, I noticed, kept our shoes on.

I strolled over to a plastic chair in the corner, slumping down, feigning nonchalance. Then I saw her: Mary, right over in the far corner.

She was sitting cross-legged on the floor, with a grey, tired expression on her face, and earphones plugged into her head. I stared, willing her to look at me, but she was studying something in her hands. She was in the same clothes from the night before, and that realisation triggered a shiver of envy. I fantasised about who Vincenzo might be: tall and blonde and as entitled-looking as she was. I imagined him opening the car passenger door for Mary. Her sliding in, letting him steal a sideways kiss on the mouth.

Watching her now, I wanted to know where she'd stayed, how she'd got to look so ragged. When she glanced at the clock on the wall behind me, I nodded my head to the side, trying to catch her attention. But she looked straight at me, then back down.

My stomach turned to ice. *Cold bitch*, I thought to myself. Had she forgotten meeting me? I thought of the strange way her fingers had curled around mine as she introduced herself. But then, there was also the bar table, crowded with shot glasses, their party that came after. I tried to smile at the twins instead who were slouched in chairs at the back of the room. Cleo was braiding Bea's hair while she lay in her sister's lap, her eyes closed in relaxation.

Decca shuffled into the room minutes later, wearing a leotard, carrying Frida under one arm and sporting a pair of tiny cat-eye sunglasses to shield her eyes. Instead of occupying a chair, she lay horizontally on the floor, holding the dog high above her head and kissing it directly on its mouth.

They regretted inviting me. That's why I was being ignored. Embarrassed, I studied the portraits propped against the wall instead. I was impressed at how life-like and beautiful the faces were; how the artists had rendered the bright sparks of their models' eyes, the quiet secrecy of their postures. I'd read about this last night; it was the precise, realist method of portraiture that the Melrose school was famous for. But they all looked the exactly same, and none of their faces were like mine. Partly, it was the costumes: the female models wore lacy dresses, haughtily pursing their perfect rosebud mouths. No one, I decided, could soften my angles into one of these agreeable, aristocratic faces.

As I was considering this, the classroom door swung open. I turned around and in marched a man in late middle-age. He was handsome but stocky, wearing brown corduroy trousers, plastic blue glasses and a cream paint-splattered smock. Squashed into his left hand was a Diet Coke can.

'Jesus.' He stopped suddenly. 'It looks like *The Virgin* fucking *Suicides* in here. What did you all get up to last night?' His jaw tightened. The room fell quiet. 'And who the fuck left the lift door open? I had to walk up all three fucking flights of stairs.' All of this he delivered in a light Scottish burr, an Edinburgh lilt.

I glanced over his tanned, slightly oily, skin and broad shoulders, which were rising and falling from the exertion of his climb. Lawrence, though Mary had called him Law. He was the great grandson of the female founder of the Melrose Academy. I'd spent my journey here reading an interview with a famous artist he'd taught in London during the early 2000s, a woman who went on to paint a controversial, but adored, portrait of an American president.

His criticism could be stark, apparently, at times even brutally honest. But she was slavishly devoted to him and credited all her successes to his 'foundational' teaching. The current intake studied us nervously, eager to see if his outburst had disturbed us. All except Mary, who lifted her chin towards a beam of light and shut her eyes.

Lawrence turned to us then. His voice marginally softened. 'I get a very bad back, you see. And if I'm injured, I can't teach, so they can't paint and you can't model.' He ran a hand through his floppy brown hair. 'Did you find refreshments?'

No one had, but we nodded.

'Good.' He flicked a piece of paper straight in his hand and studied it. 'Well, thank all of you for coming. Lots of familiar faces,' he said, speaking quickly. 'And for those who haven't done this before, I may as well tell you now, the process is a tad odd. We used to ask models to submit a headshot, but it's better for the students to see you in person before deciding whether you're right for them. It's a big investment of time on their part, so don't get offended if no one wants to use you. We'll pay you for your time today, anyway. Then there's always next term and next term and next term, et cetera. We've been here for over a hundred years.' He gestured towards the idle students and gave a theatrically camp sigh. 'And, as you can see, no one's going anywhere. *Allora*. Let's get to it, shall we? You students know the drill by now. When I call your name out, it'll be your turn to choose. Simple enough.'

Without waiting for a response, Lawrence began reading out the names of the students who, in turn, pointed at the model they wanted to work with. Many of them seemed to know the first names of the models already, while others had to point at or specify their sitter by calling out prominent features like 'red hair, tall'. I pressed my weight down into the plastic chair, smiling faintly as those who stood or sat close to me were selected. Inwardly, I was horrified.

In Her Defence

I glanced from Mary, across to Decca, then back to the twins. Mary hadn't selected yet but nor had she given any reassurance that I would eventually be chosen. I wavered, wondering if it was too late to try and leave the room. One by one, they chose models who weren't me. It was hurtful, the way they scrutinised our faces and whispered to each other.

Decca bagged the best-looking young man early on, in what appeared to be a pre-arranged transaction; the twins chose an older Italian couple who they also seemed friendly with. Suddenly, I didn't want to be chosen. I folded my arms against myself as my hangover from last night's drinks squeezed at my insides.

Mary still hadn't had her turn yet. Now and again, I saw her glancing over. Eventually, there were just two of us left: a neat-looking woman with a polished dark bob haircut, and me. The woman sat with her legs crossed, a self-assured smile pasted across her face. My throat began to feel very dry; the back of my neck heated, as if someone had taken a match to it. I leant over my knees and stared at the ground.

'Mary?' Lawrence called, repeating himself more loudly so she could hear over her headphones. She looked over sulkily, clearly annoyed that she'd come last on his list. Again, he asked her to choose.

Mary removed one earphone and squinted between me and the older woman. I smiled hopefully, aware of a pulse in my stomach.

'I'll go with Gussie,' she said, quietly. Lawrence looked confused. One of the twins turned and muttered something to her, so Mary sat up and spoke a little more loudly. 'I'll have Augusta, please.'

Lawrence turned, stiffly. 'Have you sat before?' he barked.

I gestured to the chair I was sitting on. 'Does this count?'

The students laughed. The other woman, my alternative, beamed between Mary and me, her gaze falling briefly on my tote bag, which she seemed to recognise. I felt awful for being chosen over her, but, at the same time, I also admired the crisp dignity of her outfit: a white button-down shirt tucked into her denim trousers; a red handbag which she gripped; the stacks of blue and green statement rings made from coloured glass. I smiled back over at her to reassure her there were no hard feelings.

Lawrence addressed Mary. 'No one wants a repeat of last term. You held everyone back. You're better off going with someone a bit more experienced, Mary. I believe our other volunteer has sat before?' The woman nodded. 'She'll be more *straightforward*.'

Again, that burning sensation appeared at the back of my neck. But Mary shrugged adamantly.

'It's my choice,' she said flatly. 'She's my choice. I would like to paint her.'

The room quietened. Mary kept staring at Lawrence, daring him, it seemed, to quash her. I thought back to the article I had read on the way over about Lawrence's teaching style. This exchange seemed harsher than that. Personal and pointed. It was obvious that their friction existed before this morning, and I couldn't help enjoying my part in it. Lawrence shifted on his heels and looked again, helplessly, at the other woman, before clearing his throat and pointing at my feet.

'Next time,' he said, 'shoes off.'

The smile I gave Mary next was probably too grateful, but she returned it, half triumphant, tongue in teeth. When Lawrence left the room, trailing behind the other woman, Decca grinned at me, raising Frida, the dog, up above her head so that she resembled a flying pig. As the animal grunted and looked around the room with wet, worried eyes, Decca waggled its paw in my direction. I waved back, unsure if it was a greeting or some joke at my expense. A few of the students laughed. Mary sauntered over.

GUEST V FINBOW: DAY TWO

When I think back to Lawrence's words that day, I can't help admiring him slightly for his reluctance to let us work together. Back then, I thought he was only a snob, but he sensed something dangerous about the combination of Mary and me. And that half impresses me.

I'll take Augusta.

I would like to paint her.

It is a comfort to remember that, at least at one stage, I was her choice. That Mary once possessed the capacity to make her own decisions. Even if that moment seems very long ago.

There had been another girl, back when I was in school, who chose me. Her name was Polly. Her parents were actors in a touring theatre production, and when she arrived in the middle of the year, we were paired together. After our lessons ended, we hung around in town, waiting for her parents to finish their rehearsals. We'd listen to her iPod or take turns jostling the vending machine until it yielded Galaxies or Twirls, which we split between us. I loved her music taste, the elaborate doodles she made on her schoolwork, and the fearlessly affectionate way she'd take my hand in public. No one, not even my mother, had ever done that before.

My parents found out about us when we were caught together in the school toilets. It was the summer – exam term – so our act was referred to as *cheating*. But my parents, who both worked at Kingsfold, understood exactly what Mr Greening meant when we were summoned into his office for questioning. Until only five years ago, this had been a faith school: an institution which frowned upon black bras and that coached us to organise our time so we completed our homework before Sundays. A girl, caught with another girl, was unspeakable.

Sitting beside my parents, who were mute with fury, I apologised through tears. It was explained to me that not only had I risked my education, but also their jobs. We all agreed it would be better if I left Kingsfold after the summer. Mr Greening organised a separate room for me to sit my exams. I was treated like a contaminant.

'The counselling is highly effective,' he said, handing my parents a pamphlet as we stood up to leave. 'We've seen it in the past. There are excellent therapists who are *very* well-trained in this exact *problem*.'

Polly and I kept in touch online for a while, but never saw each other again. In times of intense stress, I still find myself dreaming of her, and the night before Mary's evidence, Polly came back to me again. This time with Mary.

My dream rendered her differently to the girl I knew in school. Her face was older, her body now more regal and voluptuous. Together with Mary, she sat on a white horse, a terrifyingly large creature, like the ones the police use for riots. The two girls were clothed, but with the sleazy, loose-hipped posture of Lady Godiva. I unfurled backwards onto the floor and, in full view of Justice Larkin, the horse trampled over me. The girls took off together without a backwards glance. I woke up clutching my ribs and gasping for air.

There would be no more sleeping, I knew. In my stuffy hotel room, I lay and watched the dawn light creep into the room, thinking of what Mary's cross-examination might bring. There was a time when I wrote my dreams down and analysed them in forensic detail, but there was no point in that now. My night terrors have nothing left to reveal. I am already well aware of my defective parts: the delusional tendencies and petty jealousies. My stubborn inability to let go.

When I enter the courtroom early the next day, my nerves jump alive. Already, Mary is sitting below in quiet conversation with Jean's lawyer.

In Her Defence

Her appearance causes my heart to stop. Mary used to be an inventive, provocative dresser, but now she wears a loose tunic which looks hand-dyed. Her long hair is cropped, with a fringe that hardly meets her forehead. Although she is transformed, the sight of her still takes me back to those Melrose parties in Rome. Strong drugs in abundance. Borrowed antiques worn as fancy dress. Me on the periphery. They happened all over the city: on rooftops, in private courtyards, on the banks of the river or right above the Piazza di Spagna. It is difficult to decide when I'd been lonelier, then or now.

I linger at the back of the gallery, which is slowly starting to fill with observers, resenting all the legal reasons that prevent me from shouting down from the gallery and greeting her. But what would I say to her, anyway? No small talk could bridge the delta that stands between us. All I want is to see her laugh like we used to. To tell her how sorry I am for everything.

The door bangs behind me. It's only some journalists filing in, but Mary startles at the sound and she glances up towards the gallery, then at the clock, and finally, her gaze falls on me. We both freeze.

Slowly, almost imperceptibly, she lifts her chin and an expression of warmth passes over her face. My eyes burn with tears. We gaze at each other, even as doors begin to open around her, with lawyers and clerks filing into the courtroom. We keep on staring. She raises a hand, not high, just near her waist: a wry *what the fuck*. For a short moment, this nightmare is suspended, and we are back in that dusty classroom in Rome where the air is heavy with the smell of oil paints and the musty odour of the students' bare feet.

I'll go with Gussie.

It was during my Roman residency that I learned how to read signals like these; the almost invisible gestures that mattered the most. Time and time again, I learned that affection emanated from those around us. We just had to tune in and raise our awareness to its existence.

Today, I saw it. And for a brief moment, up in that gallery – our eyes locked together, Mary's hand raised in greeting – I felt drenched in happiness.

Someone can say your name a certain way, give a wave, or simply look in your direction, and it's like the sky bursting open.

ROME, SEPTEMBER

It was our fourth sitting. The other students had finished for the day and sloped off to the bar, leaving Mary and me alone. She had placed me in a little leather chair that was balanced on a stack of pallets. Her idea was to raise my body and face so that it was level with her eye as she painted. I lowered my gaze when she leaned over and manoeuvred me, her jewellery clinking as she smoothed the hair by my ears. It was hard to know where to look. The smell of her up close, of cigarettes and the blackberry tang of her perfume, made my face feel hot.

'You're so pale,' Mary said, stepping back, like a hairdresser admiring her creation. 'It's beautiful.'

I smiled. I'd heard those words often enough, but never before as a compliment. I tried to relax my shoulders and settle into my seat, but it felt precarious to me, to be sitting up on those pallets with my ankles crossed. I fidgeted constantly, clasping and unclasping my hands, even though they were supposed to rest effortlessly in my lap. Again and again, Mary would bid me to just let them fall.

'Can I have some of that?' I said, my eyes flitting to the carton of red wine next to Mary's bare foot.

'No wine yet,' she said, firmly.

'Why?' I asked.

'Because you need to concentrate.'

'On what?'

'Looking ethereal.'

We laughed.

'Seriously.' Mary pointed to the back of the room 'Stop looking at me. Over there, please.'

A smile appeared again at the corners of her stained lips. In her right hand, she held her brush in a cramped gesture. She was wearing denim shorts and an oversized pink shirt rolled at the sleeves. Her beautiful blonde hair was pulled up, but scruffily. Thick strands of it were tangled in the gold chains of all the delicate necklaces she wore. I straightened in my chair and bit on my tongue, tried to do as I was told.

As soon as I started sitting for her, it was clear that Mary struggled with portrait painting. I'd seen the way her peers eyed her canvas, watched their faces after they'd packed their own work up, betraying mixed expressions of encouragement and pity. The weak, sisterly smiles were reserved, uniquely, for Mary. Between themselves, they were more furtive. They glanced enviously at each other's paintings, never lingering much longer over it beyond a quick, competitive eye. I hated to see Mary frustrated, but I also liked that she was lagging behind. It gave us opportunities to be together. Left alone in that semi-circular classroom, we talked freely.

'You know, I had this paranoid thought before our first sitting,' I said, interrupting, as Mary ran her brush along the canvas in a fussy swipe. 'What if I'm supposed to be naked?'

'That's in the summer term.' Mischievously, she looked up. 'Would you still have done it?'

'Would you still have chosen me?'

Mary rolled her eyes. 'I told you before. I wasn't ignoring you at that casting. I was concentrating on not being sick.' Our eyes met momentarily, and we smiled at each other. 'You were always my first choice.'

'Over that other woman?'

'Over all of them.'

Her words caused a swimming feeling in my stomach. I had to look away, over towards the window. The light was paler now. It had shifted from the butter yellow of late afternoon towards evening. I could see swarms of birds – hundreds of them, starlings – moving across the sky like a flat spinning disc.

We were quiet for a few moments. My gaze returned to Mary as she walked backwards to her vantage point, which was marked by a little cross on the floor. From that distance, her eyes darted prettily between the canvas and me.

'I don't like it when you go so far away,' I said, teasing. 'I feel like such an object. What would happen if you stood still at the easel instead of moving back there all the time?'

'I can't do that,' Mary said, quietly.

'Why?'

'That's how we do it here. And we have to follow the rules.'

'It's painting.' I laughed. 'How can there be rules? It isn't grammar.'

Mary's expression fell. She put down her brush and bent to drink more wine, the muscles in her neck vibrating as she swallowed. I tried not to look at her tanned, flattish chest as her shirt fell open, revealing the two soft, lace triangles of her bra.

'According to Law, I need strict containment,' she said, straightening and wiping her mouth.

'Law's an old man,' I countered, 'clinging to a family name.' Mary smirked uneasily. 'You could always leave here, you know. Do something else. You could rent your own studio. Just experiment.' I often played this role with her, suggesting a rebelliousness I hadn't achieved in my own life.

Mary shrugged. 'In the future maybe, but I still don't have the right foundations.'

'Says who?'

'Lawrence. And besides, I can't just leave. Mum and Dad would turn the tap off.'

It took a moment to work out that *the tap* meant money. When I suggested she could get a job, she laughed. The only money she'd ever earned for herself, she said, was from modelling.

'Even then, my mother put a stop to all that. She was jealous. It was mental.'

'Ignore me, then,' I said. 'I never went to art school, so I'm probably bitter.'

'Don't,' Mary said, in mock despair. 'I've seen your work. That means you've raw talent, which actually makes me feel worse.'

I felt myself glow, but Mary's smile had faded and I was surprised to find myself pitying her. We hadn't known each other long, but I'd noticed how quickly her mood often shrank from boisterous to insecure.

Eventually, she said, in a flat voice, 'Mum and Dad have paid extra for me to be here.' We locked eyes. Hers had hardened. 'A lot extra.'

'Seriously?'

Mary trained her eyes on the canvas, though her skin was flushed. 'And I'm pretty sure everyone knows. Or has guessed it. He's a friend of the family.'

I looked away, not wanting Mary to see that I'd already discovered this personal connection to her tutor. After the casting, I'd stayed up late online, searching her name. In seconds, Mary's whole existence was arranged in photographic thumbnails, not in any kind of dated order but randomly and chaotically, like panels on a patchwork quilt. Every stage of her life had been documented, and that's where I discovered Lawrence, in a holiday photo. Mary was aged about eleven and pictured somewhere tropical, chlorine-bleached frizz escaping all around her like a halo. Her face was tilted up towards her mother's. Lawrence was in the background, dressed in a black polo shirt. He was slimmer and tanned, but it was him, unmistakably.

'You've moved,' said Mary, bringing my attention back to the room. She came over to adjust my position, bringing the wine against my lips. The liquid was warm, like bathwater, so I grimaced and dribbled. She laughed, put it down, then directed the tilt of my chin, the angle of my shoulders. She fiddled with the strap of my top, which was loose and had floated down my arm.

'Actually, let's leave it down,' Mary said, brushing my shoulder to lower the other strap, too. She stepped back. 'It's very pretty like that. The shadows are interesting.' Again, we locked eyes. 'There's this darkness falling around you.'

A couple of days after that sitting, I was working in the basement studios of CRETA in the Monti neighbourhood of Rome. Compared to the Melrose classrooms, my residency was dusty and cramped. It was below ground and shared with four other ceramicists. We competed for everything: time on the wheel, drying areas by the window, shelf space in the kiln out the back. So, it was a relief, on that occasion, to be working there alone. Sitting at the wheel with my foot pressed down, I was lulled by the sound of its humming and the miraculous way – I have never lost my awe of it – my hands transformed a rough, spherical ball of clay into the graceful cylinder that would become a vase. Something of use and beauty.

When I looked up, there, by the doorway, was the woman from the model casting. My heart skipped.

'Can I help you?' I said.

She beamed widely at me. 'I was looking for Thea,' she said. Her voice was soft; a neutral, British accent.

I lifted my foot from the pedal. 'She just left.'

'Oh,' the woman said, clasping her hands together in thought. Unlike the day at the painting school, she now wore glasses: delicate gold frames which complemented her navy shirt and pleated cream trousers. On her fingers were brightly coloured enamel rings that looked like miniature abstract sculptures, and she carried a tote bag from a recent exhibition at MACRO that had recently ended.

'She literally just left,' I said. 'Should I ask her to come back?'

'No,' the woman interrupted, hastily. 'Not to worry. I'll see her later tonight.'

Thea was the head of the residency. She was Italian, gay, and a successful ceramicist in her own right. I worshipped her. She had emailed me personally to congratulate me for getting on the programme, then she set about finding me my room. The notion that these two women knew each other alerted my interest. I wondered, excitedly, if the woman facing me was a collector.

I let the clay vase I had been throwing weaken in my hands, then went over to the workbench, nearer where she stood, hoping to draw her attention to the other pieces I was developing. The woman kept surveying me, closely.

'That's it,' she said, with a little gasp, bringing her hand lightly to her forehead. 'What a funny coincidence. I knew I recognised you. You were at the Academy weren't you? A couple of weeks ago?

'Yes!'

'You were picked at the end by that lovely girl!'

We introduced ourselves. Her name was so old-fashioned that I had to ask her to repeat it.

'Jean.'

'Like the denim?' She nodded, offering a warm hand, the one with all the interesting rings, and let it linger on me.

We both agreed what an awful experience the casting had been.

'Sorry I stole the job,' I said, shyly.

Jean's laugh tinkled. 'Oh, I have plenty of work to do.' She took a small step towards me. 'How's the modelling going?'

I considered her question for a moment, wanting to downplay how thrilling it was. 'It's actually quite uncomfortable.'

'Uncomfortable? Why?'

'Holding the pose. I get so stiff. And it feels pretty unnatural, being watched all the time.'

Jean paused, as if she wanted me to expand on what I'd said. It was the first time I experienced her prolonged quiet. You fell right into that silence, words spilling everywhere. Sometimes it made you overly frank. Other times, you said things just to fill the gap. Things you didn't mean.

At last, she spoke, tilting her head slightly to the side. 'I sat once before. It was nerve-wracking, I remember. I had this constant fear I might not make a good painting, that I'd let the artist down.'

I smiled. Jean's observation was spot on. She considered me seriously for a moment. 'Don't overthink your pose or try too hard. The body has its own alphabet. Just let your posture speak for you.'

That phrase resonated. I had recently started messing around in the studio, taking casts of my hands as they made those characteristic Italian gestures. I liked Jean's idea that every human posture could be unique. I wondered, again, about her taste in art.

'Do you mind if I sit down for a moment, Gus? I've been walking all day – these Roman hills – when you get to my age, you really feel it.'

I gestured tentatively towards some stools and Jean settled down close to me, leaving her bag on the table. I noticed her smell: tuberose layered over Italian laundry detergent. It calmed me.

'How was the exhibition?' I asked, referring to her bag.

'Magnificent,' she said. 'Did you go?'

'I was dying to. It ended just before I arrived.'

'I've got the catalogue,' she said simply. 'I'll give it to you.'

A warmth passed through me, which quickly shifted into curiosity about who exactly this kind woman was. Her questions kept coming. 'Are you here for a while, Gus?'

'Programme ends at Christmas. So, shortly after then. Or when my cash runs out.'

'Oh,' she tutted, making a long 'O' sound. 'That's not long at all.'

'I know.'

'You want to stay longer, I take it?'

'Desperately.'

'Where are you living?'

'Termini.'

Jean flinched. 'Now that worries me.'

'Well,' I said brightly. 'It's a shared bedroom and we recently found a peephole in the bathroom that we think our landlord uses for his own entertainment. But, apart from that, it's a palace.'

I waited for Jean to laugh, but she only looked concerned. I shrugged away her worry. 'Honestly, it's fine. I'm actually hardly there.'

She blinked at me, unconvinced. 'And what was Gus's life like before?' In the third person, her question seemed less direct, so I found myself telling her about the job at the cinema, the short stints at a studio when I could afford it.

'That sounds extremely varied,' she said, politely.

'Yes,' I said. 'Varied but also...' I trailed off.

'Kind of a struggle?'

'Yes,' I admitted. She smiled knowingly at me. 'It was. Almost always a struggle.'

She told me that she split her time between Rome and her place in Primrose Hill in London. 'For now, it's mainly Rome.'

I hesitated. The woman was living my dream existence. 'How do you know Thea?' I ventured. 'Are you a collector or something?'

'That's perceptive of you,' she murmured. 'I do sometimes support artists in their early careers – those with talent, I mean.' Momentarily, she let her gaze fall on my work and opened her mouth as if to say something. I felt myself stiffen, poised for her comment, perhaps even a compliment. But nothing came. Instead, she looked up at me. Her eyes behind her glasses were searching and direct. 'But that's not my main job. I'm also a therapist.'

'Cool.' It struck me that Jean must not only be rich, but also clever. The way she was dressed, it all now made perfect sense.

'What makes you say that?' she said, with a modest smile. 'I mean, I happen to agree but—'

'—You make people happier.' I wanted to believe this, but I also couldn't help thinking of my parents, and Mr Greening's terrifying conversion pamphlets.

Jean flushed. Her skin was plump and very smooth. Although she complained about her age earlier, her face was youthful and unlined, as if she spent more time reading books than outside. I put her in her early fifties.

She smiled, widely. 'I think it's pretty magical too, Gus. It sounds strange to say, but – like you, I suspect – I really love what I do.'

I was flattered that Jean had noticed this about me. 'What brought you to the model casting then? If you already have a job?' Jean's eyes glittered. 'Sorry if that's a rude question.'

'Not at all.' She touched my arm to reassure me. 'It was an academic interest, really.' She paused, just to make sure I was listening. 'The therapeutic relationship is all about observation. It has been a while since I was watched so closely myself.' Her tone lightened. 'A kind of reverse therapy, I suppose. Which means you'll have to tell me about it.' Playfully, she tapped my arm again. 'Since you took my place.' I groaned with embarrassment. 'Just a joke, Gus. I'm glad I didn't get picked. I'm too busy, really, and I can't stand to be in the same room as that man.'

I assumed Jean meant Lawrence, and her criticism made me like her even more. We smiled at each other, then she checked her watch and announced she had to get off. There was a party at Sotheby's that night and she needed to change.

'Let me know if you fancy coming along,' she said, opening a little Hermes wallet and passing me her card. She used both hands to pass it over. All her movements were careful like that. Every gesture was neat and precise. 'They have this amazing terrace which overlooks Piazza Venezia.'

'I can't,' I said, feeling disappointed. 'I've got a sitting.' I studied the card she had passed me. Written at the top in rounded letters: JEAN GUEST. Underneath it read:

THERAPIST & LIFE COACH

Two phone numbers: one British, one Italian. I also gave her mine.

'She's called Mary, isn't she?' Jean asked. 'The girl you're sitting for?'

'Yes,' I said, getting up from my stool.

'Isn't she the daughter of—'

I nodded, then shrugged. Mary affected a weary bitterness towards her mother that I was also trying to emulate. 'To be honest, we don't talk about her much,' I said.

Jean's mouth opened, then closed again. 'Oh, I'm not at all surprised at that, poor girl. Living in that shadow.' She shook her head. 'What an act to follow.'

I looked away, uneasy about the sense of self-importance I felt, just through the association with Mary. Decca and the twins treated me differently too, and now this woman. As Mary's subject, I was acquiring status. Status and substance.

'I've actually got quite a few of her mother's ceramics at home in London,' Jean said, her soft voice bringing me back to the room. She turned to leave then, and beamed again, her hand lingering on the door. 'I've got one of her first-ever pieces. Her work hasn't dated at all. It's still beautiful. Goodbye, Gus. What a total treat to meet you.'

'Bye, and likewise.'

'Call me anytime.'

There are versions of my story where I gush over the coincidence of meeting this woman again, then I excuse myself politely and get on with my work. There are alternatives where Thea forgets her scooter helmet and comes back to the studio, and I overhear the two women have a conversation and try to gauge the real depth of their relationship. There are contingencies I play out for myself all the time, but do I really believe they would have kept us apart? Deep down, I know Jean would have found a way to me. Or I to her. That might be her chief legacy: to see the universe as fated. To believe that some humans are marked out for collision, no matter what we do.

GUEST V FINBOW: DAY TWO

A cold dread spreads over me as Mary is presented with the oath, vowing, quietly, to tell the truth. Across the aisle, Anna stares, horror-struck, at her daughter. She hasn't seen Mary in a year and a half, and she must be shocked by the sight of her: the mousy hair; how nervously she casts her eyes about the lower well of the court.

'Ms Finbow, in your statement,' Ms Ibrahim begins, 'you say: "The decision to take a healing separation from the harmful relationships that no longer serve me is a choice I have reached of my own accord, without undue influence from the claimant beyond gentle professional support." Is this still your view?'

Mary's chin and gaze are lifted, as if her mind is elsewhere. 'Yes,' she says, solemnly. 'And I want the court to recognise that this is a personal matter. The scrutiny I have endured has been intolerable. I am only here because I felt it was important, to honour my therapist and in honour of the truth.'

'Understood,' says Ms Ibrahim, nodding at Mary to acknowledge the gravity of her appearance. 'We will try and move through this as quickly as possible. I first want to draw attention to an assertion made by Mrs Finbow in the newsletter she published, not about Ms Guest, but about you. She states that, before you met my client, you were "the happiest, brightest girl". You, on the contrary, affirm that your childhood and late adolescence were very difficult times. Which is the truth?'

'The truth is that I suffered. And my upbringing worsened my suffering.'

'Could you expand on that, Ms Finbow?' Ms Ibrahim prompts, gently.

'Where do you want me to start?' Mary asks, darkly.

'Perhaps with your diagnoses?'

'Well, I was twenty-eight kilos when they first took me to a rehabilitation centre, aged fourteen.'

'This was a treatment centre for your—'

'—Bulimia. My parents dropped me off and went on a sailing holiday. I had to make my own way home from Arizona.'

'Did you make a full recovery?'

'I don't think anybody really does. But we manage it.'

My chest aches to think of Mary carefully navigating those huge dinners we ate in Rome. And how that *we* means Jean. But now Ms Ibrahim is asking about other diagnoses that Mary received at different ages: her chronic self-esteem issues, her generalised anxiety disorder. Then, from her late teens, the drug and alcohol addiction; the sexual promiscuity.

'They were all manifestations,' Mary admits, 'of my inner pain.'

'So, when your mother wrote online that you were the happiest child, that was a total misrepresentation?'

Mary's face hardens. 'A complete delusion.'

'Stop!' Anna explodes, addressing Mary, who refuses to look at her. 'Darling, you *know* that isn't true.' Ms Carr hushes her, but Anna claws her shoulder. 'It's lies!' she hisses. 'It's all *her* lies!'

Ms Ibrahim is pleased with the interruption. She blinks, patronisingly, at Anna, while the judge calls for order, then goes on. 'Mrs Finbow claims that during your healing sessions with my client, you are being consciously turned against your parents. To quote her text: "making demons out of those that love her most". Is that also your view?'

'No, it is not my view. Anna and Bonamy made demons out of themselves. Your client is simply giving me the strength to acknowledge my experiences.' Mary pauses. 'And their reaction is quite characteristic. They've always obstructed my relationships with those who loved me.'

'Could you give an example?'

Mary laughs, cynically. 'This whole *spectacle* is an example! They're jealous of Jean. It's pathetic. But there were others who faced her envy. Boyfriends I had. Even a girlfriend in school. Anna always found a way to muscle in and wreck things. Which is ironic.' A flash of anger crosses Mary's face. 'Given that I saw her with other men throughout my childhood—'

'—How dare you!' Anna storms. 'This is *outrageous!*'

Once again, the judge calls for order in his courtroom. There is a brief pause in proceedings as Anna is told once again to calm down. Ms Ibrahim drinks water. Jean's lips twitch with excitement.

'What happened when you witnessed this adulterous behaviour at home, Ms Finbow?' Ms Ibrahim proceeds, sensitively.

'I was told not to say anything.'

'Yesterday, your household was described as *"permissive."* Would you agree?'

Mary's jaw clenches. 'There were drugs around, but that didn't mean it was permissive. What I experienced was actively repressive. I went to my mother about many difficult things that happened to me, on account of the way my parents lived. Her response was always the same: don't make a fuss. Their support came in the form of pills or sending me away to school. They only reacted when my struggles became too inconvenient to ignore. Like I said,' she recounts bitterly. '*Twenty-eight kilos.*'

I hold my breath, wondering if Ms Ibrahim will probe into these loaded allegations, but instead, she offers her sympathies for everything Mary has endured and how she has been misrepresented in the newsletter online. As her argument shifts, her tone sharpens; she is about to argue how Jean has been misrepresented, too. 'To the present day: you state your mental health has improved?'

'Transformed,' Mary answers, but tonelessly.

The lawyer smiles. 'Do you attribute this improvement to my client?'

'Primarily.'

'How long have you been working with her?'

'Coming up two years. We were introduced in Rome.' A proud smile appears at the corner of Mary's mouth. My stomach sinks low into my body. I glance to the left of me. Lucy Ayres and I briefly lock eyes. She smiles at me with encouragement, but I look away. Mary goes on. 'Just before I met Jean, I was in a very low place. Getting wasted all the time. Forging destructive relationships. I had no purpose whatsoever. Jean helped me regain control. I began to see my patterns of behaviour had been inherited; they weren't intrinsic to my personality. After only a few sessions, my life started to change for the better.'

'So when Mrs Finbow wrote that Ms Guest, who had been an enormous force for good in your life, was a "cult leader", did you believe her?'

Mary laughs softly and shakes her head. 'Absolutely not.'

'And when she wrote that Ms Guest inserted false memories during your sessions, did you recognise this?'

'I did not.'

Ms Ibrahim lifts her chin. 'Are the examples about your home life that you provided today false memories or real ones?'

Mary looks offended. 'That's a ridiculous question. I'm speaking the truth. I simply gained the strength to name my experiences now. That's what we do in our therapy: we give voice to impermissible things. Eventually we feel better.'

My skin prickles. That *we* again.

'It sounds as if you are on your way to recovery, Ms Finbow, and I'm pleased for you. Before we conclude, is there anything else you'd like to tell us? For example, are there any other areas of your life which have improved, thanks to the support of my client?'

'My artistic career,' Mary says defiantly, 'has blossomed. I'm making the best paintings of my life.'

Ms Ibrahim beams. 'No longer portraits, is that correct?'

Her smile disappears. 'No. I'll never return to those. I'm actively trying to unlearn everything from that art school.' There is a considered pause, then she continues, bringing her hands to her stomach. 'I'm on a much better path now, in every sense.'

'And where, may I ask, is that path headed?'

Mary delivers a smile that makes my heart kick. I remember how she used to look that way at me, or on the rare occasions that she was satisfied with her work. She looks over towards Jean, who gives her a little nod.

'Towards motherhood.'

A sudden quiet drowns the room. And yet I'm sure that I can't have heard her properly. Or I must have misunderstood; some disturbance through the microphone.

Mary continues. 'I'm actually six months pregnant.'

Anna's head jerks upwards. My gaze falls to Mary's tunic, which is just visible above the witness box. I realise, with creeping horror, that beneath the loose material, her stomach has swollen into a pronounced curve.

'Congratulations, Ms Finbow,' Ms Ibrahim gushes. 'I am sure that everyone in this courtroom wishes you the best for the remainder of your pregnancy.'

There is a rushing sound in my ears as the lawyer announces the closing of her questions, which becomes deafening as Ms Ibrahim walks back to her desk and sits down. That word: *pregnant*. Alien, and yet fat with meaning. My thoughts spiral. Does this mean Mary has a boyfriend now? How is that possible? And how am I the last to know? I glance frantically around the gallery in case he's here, but no one seems young enough. Then I check myself, aghast. He doesn't have to be young. He can be anyone. *I'll have Augusta.* Doesn't Mary always get whoever she wants?

But as she carefully descends from the witness booth, I start to picture Mary's changing body: how warped her stomach will become. Body like a bent spoon. Udder breasts. Stomach drooping into a teardrop, rutted with stretch marks. No longer mine, but belonging to others: the man she's fucked, her unborn child.

And, most worryingly, belonging also to Jean.

ROME, OCTOBER

When we exchanged our first text messages, Jean was gossipy and warm. The Sotheby's party was 'a bit stiff', but it had been nice to meet me, she said.

I'm having a party of my own next week, she wrote. *I'll be sure to call you along. You could bring a friend!*

At the time, the idea excited me: the prospect of showing off an art-world contact to Mary. We were in that stage of early adulthood where it was exciting to have an eccentric, older friend. The girls at the Melrose school collected these characters like currency; they were always being wined and dined by mysterious, childless grown-ups, and I wanted one of my own. The scene at Jean's house was delicious when I conjured it: the glamorous expat bringing fabulous people together in her *salon*. I imagined turning up with Mary, getting drunk and gliding around the room, charming all the guests. But Jean's crowd would impress us, too. Mary would say to me in awe: 'Where on earth did you meet her?'

So when Jean kept up the conversation over text, asking kind questions about how I was settling into the city, I responded enthusiastically.

Just climbed the Palatine! I gushed, sending a photo, thinking of the invite. It was important she didn't forget meeting me.

The hill of broken ceramics. So apt for you! And how's your modelling contract? She followed the question with an emoji of an artist's palette.

I replied with an image of a girl shrugging and an upside-down smiley face. For a few hours, she didn't respond, then, sometime in the middle of the night, when I found myself wide awake, Jean followed up with a single heart.

When the evening of Jean's drinks party came, it turned out that no one from the Melrose could make it. They were all going to some pre-arranged dinner that I hadn't been invited to. Deflated, but still curious, I took the tram over to Jean's apartment in the Ghetto alone. The heavy front door was left ajar, so I entered the building without needing to be buzzed in.

The door led into a shadowy courtyard, which was silent and dark, apart from a few glowing windows which shone from the apartments above. I listened carefully for music or voices. Nothing. I brought out my phone to check Jean's flat number, but then I heard footsteps emerging from a staircase on the left side. Through the portico, a figure of a petite young woman emerged. Her long blonde hair was slightly matted, and her coat was held carelessly in her hand, as if she'd left in a hurry. As she approached me, I noticed her eyes were swollen and her nose was lightly running.

'*Buonasera*,' I said. '*Cerco Signora—*'

'You can speak English,' the girl sniffed impatiently. 'I'm English.'

'Oh, great. I'm looking for a woman called Jean Guest? She's also English.'

The girl stared at me, her expression a mixture of envy and concern, before stepping aside. 'It's up there,' she said, pushing her way past. 'Fifth floor.'

Jean gasped as she opened the door.

'Goodness, what's wrong with you, Gus? You look pale!'

Her white shirt had a stately collar, stiff and risen. She wore it tucked into pleated cream trousers and there were orange velvet house slippers on her feet. In her immaculate presence, I felt instantly grubby, like I needed to change clothes, or slip out of my skin entirely.

'Paler than usual?' I tried to pass it off with a smile, though I could feel myself grimacing. My hips were locked with pain. Earlier that day, my period had started. My cramps had begun as I sat still for Mary, and the climb up to Jean's *piano* hadn't helped.

'Come in, come in,' she said gently, beckoning me into her apartment for the first time.

'I just met an English girl outside,' I said weakly, gesturing behind me. 'Is she coming?'

'Ah,' Jean said. 'Not yet. I thought it would be nice to have a bit of catch-up time together first.'

I took in my surroundings. It was calm and warm inside Jean's apartment. The air smelt of heated butter and pasta starch. Taking my coat, she offered a seat on her pale cream sofa.

'Is it cramps?' she asked as I lowered myself stiffly.

I startled. My family never talked about bodily things; I hadn't even admitted to my mother when I started menstruating. But it was Jean's uncanny insight that took me aback; the fact she had instantly guessed the source of my pain. For a moment there, on the sofa, I felt transparent.

I nodded, shyly. 'Just came on.'

'Nasty business,' she said, going back out into the hallway. 'I don't miss mine.' When she returned, she passed me a thick, chalky tablet and a glass of water. 'Strong enough to knock out a horse,' she joked gently, putting on her gold-rimmed glasses to read from the back of the packet. '*Perfetto.*' She surveyed me for a few moments as I gratefully drank and sat backwards. 'Why don't I run you a quick bath?' she suggested softly. 'That always used to help me.'

I protested, said not to fuss. I was thinking of the drinks party and that it was probably rude of me to accept, but the more she insisted, the stranger it seemed to decline. The shower in my mouldy bathroom in Termini barely produced a drip of water. Suddenly, I felt desperate to submerge myself, get a good hair wash and feel properly clean.

'Are you sure there's time?' I asked meekly.

Jean smiled, happy to have won me over. She left the room, and then a moment later, I heard the volley of water running.

It was relaxing, sitting there in her beautiful living room; a crackling recording of an old aria was playing, bookshelves lined the walls and among the artworks there were framed posters from famous nineties art exhibitions held at the Barbican and the RA that I had once read about. But, apart from a few silver bowls of nuts and olives which had been arranged on side tables, I couldn't see any signs of a larger party happening. I was calmed by this prospect of a smaller, more intimate evening that I had anticipated. I leant backwards on the sofa and closed my eyes, feeling the tiredness and relief wash over me. Then Jean appeared again, touching me lightly on the shoulder. The bath was ready.

Her bathroom was small and tiled with high ceilings; a pink cubicle of Italian kitsch. Candles had been lit. And on the side of the bath, she had arranged a cold flannel, a carafe of iced water, and a glass of red wine.

Half dazed, I thanked her. Jean only smiled and pinched my chin. 'I'll leave you be.'

Years later, I think back to this moment and I want to scream. I see myself lowering my body into the water as if it were a pit of snakes. But, at the time, I wasn't perturbed by the odd intimacy of Jean's offer. I was just grateful for the curative warmth of a good bath. My skin prickled and turned puce as I lay with my knees stuck out of the surface, letting the water lap into the diamond shape between my legs. My body loosening, I stared at the whorls of plaster in the ceiling, replaying the way Mary had spoken about the dinner they were all going to, wondering if Vincenzo would be there, too. I found myself constantly obsessing over the seriousness of their relationship. He was always travelling, so none of the other girls had met him, but Mary seemed preoccupied with his messages. Slipping down further, until the water plugged my ears, I devised my own messages to Mary that

I'd send during the party, once I had a few drinks in me. When I sat up, I rinsed my face with water once, two times. The heat was searing and nice. When I opened my eyes, Jean was there, standing beside the bath.

'Jean!' I shouted in a panic, trying desperately to cover myself with my hands. 'Can you get the fuck out?'

'Oh!' she cried, fleeing from the room. 'Sorry!'

I tried to laugh away my reaction.

'No, I'm sorry,' I called, pulling out the bath plug. 'You made me jump.'

'I didn't mean to shock you,' she said from outside the door, sounding injured. 'I was just letting you know that you can take your time. I called the drinks off.'

'What?' I said, stepping away from the draining bath so that I could hear properly. 'Why?'

'You didn't seem up to it.'

I dried myself off quickly, then dressed in my old clothes and the spare underwear she'd left behind for me in a little pile by the sink. It was such an absurdly kind gesture, I thought, to find fresh things to wear. I began to feel terrible that Jean had changed all her arrangements for me; for the fact that I had then snapped at her.

When I went out into the kitchen, Jean was preparing a meal. She gestured towards a round glass table, and I sat down.

'What about the party?' I protested again. 'You know, I can just leave. Or stay. Just let them come. I'll try not to be the spectre at the feast.'

Jean explained that she had only invited her neighbours. They were, in her words, 'relaxed, simple people' and 'very authentic' and that they didn't mind the sudden change. However much I insisted, Jean was adamant. So, instead, I overcompensated, speaking rapidly, complimenting her house, the smell of her cooking. I thanked her for the clothes she had lent me and made a joke about my prudishness in the bath, blaming my upbringing. Jean blinked when I said that, looking at me with interest, the candle flames reflecting in the lenses of her glasses.

'In what way, repressed?'

I reflected on her question. 'Maybe not repressed but disembodied. Anything physical was completely avoided.'

Jean blinked again, more gravely. 'I'm guessing they were religious?'

'Ha,' I said, impressed. 'Once upon a time, yes, very religious. They got out of the church sometime after I was born. I often feel guilty about that.'

'That's understandable.'

'Though I'm not sure why I should.'

'No.'

'They still sent me to an ex-religious school, partly because it was the best free one in the area, but also because they were employed there. Dad worked in the grounds, Mum worked in one of the science labs which was—'

'Awkward?'

'Exactly,' I said, and smiled.

Jean chewed her food for a few moments. There was the nutty sound of her back teeth meeting together. I sipped my wine and reflected on Jean's profession; the mode of her exchange made me wonder if she ever switched off.

'And what do you believe in now, Gus?' she asked.

'I believe in pasta,' I said, making a show of pressing my fork against a flat parcel of ravioli so that a white sauce bloomed out of it. 'What's in this?'

'Nothing fancy.' Jean glanced from side to side. 'Gorgonzola. Pear.'

'To me, that's fancy.'

Jean chuckled which, after the mention of my childhood, made me feel good again. I took another mouthful of wine, then leaned back in my chair. The cramps were much better, and my body throbbed a low pulse of wellbeing.

'Not just pasta. I also believe in the beauty of Rome. I think Rome is my religion.'

'Oh good.' Jean clapped her hands together. 'So you like it here in *la bella citta?*'

I couldn't admit how lost I still felt. Nor how confused Mary was making me feel. The low mood I sunk into on the days I texted her and she didn't reply. So, instead, I told Jean Rome was paradise. I rhapsodised about my favourite parts of the city: the marble fountain that looked like a ship; the Spanish Steps that spilled down towards it; the perfect symmetry of the Farnese palace. I explained that, for me, Rome radiated a beauty that was almost abusive. 'As in, it actually hurts my eyes.'

Jean said she still felt the same, even though she'd been coming here for years, since she was about my age. For a while she wrote down all her insider tips to the city: hidden chapels on the Palatine Hill, murky crypts near the Tiber, a French church with secret murals that had been painted by Caravaggio. There were three different gelaterias I must try, she said, before I could make an educated decision on which was my favourite.

'When do you next have a free afternoon?' she asked, casually. 'I'll show you around.'

I told her I'd love that, but in my mind, there was a single snare: *Mary. Mary. Mary.* I was imagining going to these places with her, not Jean, and seeming worldly as I did so. I was hoping there were still parts of the city that we could explore together.

'And how's the portrait coming along?' Jean said, putting away her map and guidebooks and returning to the table with two bowls of tinned peaches and mascarpone cheese. My cheeks coloured at the question, as if those thoughts of Mary were written across my forehead.

'No idea,' I said. 'Mary won't let me see it yet. It's a weird place, that school. The whole style of painting is so technical and restrictive. Plus, Lawrence is horrible to her.'

Jean had been crumbling biscuits over her dessert, but she stopped when I said this. 'How so?'

I frowned. 'There's just this weird friction between them. And he puts her down all the time. Makes these snide jokes at her expense. I hate it.'

'So the rumours are true, then,' Jean murmured in a censorious tone. 'The man's a bully, is he? Poor girl.'

'I know.'

'Well, Gus, do tell her, if she ever needs someone to talk to, someone impartial, I'm always here.'

We were quiet for a moment then, and I began to copy the way Jean was breaking biscuits into her bowl. When I told her how good the food was, her expression lifted.

'One of my clients just brought these biscuits as a gift,' she said, wiping her mouth. 'She's a little bit devoted to me.'

'Must be heavy,' I said, trying not to spray crumbs, 'hearing everyone's problems all the time.'

'Sometimes,' Jean said. 'But it's the only way we can transform ourselves.' For a while she stared straight ahead, lost in the thought. Then she turned to me. 'People say I give too much of myself. Today was hard. I had an extremely difficult client. Her name's Oriel, she's quite resistant.' She brightened. 'But then you came.'

I laughed modestly, ignoring the twinge of unease I felt at the way Jean revealed her client's name. Was she referring to the frightened girl from outside?

'But I made you cancel your party!'

'You *are* the party,' Jean countered, laughing.

Flattered, I struggled to respond. The thought of being a positive force in Jean's day felt so unexpectedly good that I needed to banish it. Instead, I concentrated on spooning up the peach syrup, and we fell into an uneasy silence. Then I felt Jean's eyes watching me. I had the feeling she wanted to ask something.

'It's actually handy, that it's just us. I need your help with a little task.'

'Sure,' I said.

'Just a little favour. You don't have to say yes.'

I laughed. 'I know I don't. What is it?'

Jean rose from the table and took out a folder from a tote bag which hung on the back of a chair. She opened it and an excited look flickered across her face. 'I just have a little homework to do. Well, it's more of a game.' She had to go through a refresher course so that she could continue practising in Italy as well as the UK. The homework was just a formality, she said. 'An informal formality.'

Jean directed me back into the living room and brought out tea. What she needed to do, she explained, was conduct a word association exercise. It was very simple. She'd read a word and I would respond with the first word that came into my head. It could be anything at all. *Window* could trigger *cow* and that would be perfectly fine. There was no wrong answer. She just needed the data.

'What if I get you into trouble?' I joked, though I was feeling excited. 'Or myself in trouble?'

Jean sat on the sofa, bringing out her notebook and a tape recorder. 'Whatever comes out is totally fine. Now, why don't you sit over there?'

I got up and settled giddily into a tightly sprung armchair that faced away from where she was sitting.

'Eyes closed,' she instructed. 'I'll be recording you, is that okay?' I glanced back over at her. Her legs were crossed now, her hands steepled on a knee. Soon, she began reading in a crisp, clear voice:

'Ship.'

'Boat.'

A silence and then again that clear, calm voice:

'Father.'

'Sin.'

'Needle,' Jean said.

'Free.'

I answered as quickly as I could, worrying at times that my responses were too obvious and that Jean would think me shallow-minded. As with the portrait, I wanted to be compliant. I wanted to come up with interesting answers for her, not to let her down in any way. But, as she spoke, the words began to carry a hypnotic rhythm. I felt my mind softening as the words kept coming.

'Insect?'

'Shell.'

'Abuse?'

'Study.'

'Work?'

'Utility.'

Some words felt more freighted with meaning than others. Though I tried to speak confidently, my throat began to narrow as the session wore on. I looked down and noticed how my hands shone with sweat.

'Good,' Jean said, 'very good. Do you need a break? Or some water?' she asked. I shook my head, so she continued until her voice became soporific and my own began to sound hazy and thick. At times, my answers came so naturally, I couldn't even hear them.

'Cry?' Jean asked. 'Woman? Grass? Dear? Sleep?'

Ten minutes later, we were finally done. Jean set down her pen, went over to the window and opened it. A quietness had fallen over her. As she lingered by the window, seemingly lost in thought, I began to worry that she might have divined something terrible in me.

'Did I pass?' I said to break the silence. I smiled cheerfully, though my mouth was dry with thirst. I was fearful that my inner world had no texture and there was nothing to analyse.

Without turning to face me, Jean asked, 'Was that something that your parents taught you, that your work had to be useful?'

The question startled me. I wondered what else she'd perceived. I lowered myself carefully onto the sofa again, propping the cushions around me. Quietly, I said, 'I have no idea.'

'It's a difficult relationship with them, isn't it?' said Jean, sitting back down.

'How could you tell?'

Jean surveyed me with pity. The muscles in my throat started to feel tight. I noticed the box of tissues resting there on the table next to her, and the bouquet of white roses beside it. I thought back to Mr Greening's office. The threat of those pamphlets. Now, sitting across from Jean, I wondered: was she the kind of person who might help me? Who might seek and exorcise the damaged parts inside?

'I usually just speak to my parents on the phone,' I said, feeling a wave of guilt at how dysfunctional I had let things become.

'How often?'

'Not often.'

'Let me guess. It's you calling them?'

'Yes,' I said, my voice breaking with emotion. 'You're right.'

'And they don't ask about what you're doing, do they? About your life?'

I shook my head and wiped my face quickly with the back of my hand. I hadn't permitted myself to cry in Rome yet. When I was frightened about money, or frustrated by the standard of my work, I bit down and told myself: *you wanted this*. When I was sad to find my spirit was still lonely, I told myself: *this is just who you are*. Now, here I was, in front of a woman I barely knew, freely weeping. I was amazed at how quickly my defences had fallen.

'Do you feel that they don't approve of what you do?' Her directness was affectionate, even maternal.

'It's more the fact of what I don't do. Getting a proper job, that kind of thing. That, and, well.' I gestured sadly to myself. 'Who I am.'

She let me cry on for a moment or two, my shoulders jolting. Then I apologised, which she said I had no need to do. She handed me a tissue and I collected myself, blowing my nose.

'You're carrying such a lot with you, Gus, aren't you?' she said, finally. Then her eyes glinted. 'Because there's something else, isn't there? Mary?'

My stomach lurched. 'Is it that obvious?'

I tried to treat her comment lightly, but it was the first time I had admitted my feelings for Mary, for any girl, to someone of my parents' age. On the one hand, I felt exhilarated, but on the other, I felt frighteningly exposed.

'But aren't you getting on pretty well?' she said.

'I'm not sure. I hope so.'

'I'm sure she adores you.' Jean smiled, then got up from her chair and led me out of the room. Moments before, she had pointedly checked her watch. It was now time for me to go. 'But do *you* adore you? That's the bigger question. That's the part that needs work.'

By the front door, she kissed me on both cheeks. As she clasped me warmly, Jean apologised for going so deep.

'That game can be quite confronting. And I can be such a nosy parker. You must tell me to back off sometimes.'

'Don't apologise. I actually enjoyed myself. Thank you.'

'Well, that's encouraging.' She beamed at me. 'I'm looking at so much potential here, Gus.'

I smiled back. Then she slipped me some cash for the taxi home. A fifty.

I asked the cab to stop once we'd got onto Piazza Venezia so that I could walk and keep most of the money. Standing by a late-night pizza stand, with traffic thundering over the cobbles, I texted Mary. I was exhausted from my evening with Jean, but also desperate to see her. Looking back, I wonder if there was something already troubling me, on a bodily level. Some nervous energy I needed to release or numb out.

Just out of drinks party – so nice, I wrote.

I made out to Mary like I'd spent the night with a bigger crowd.

Jean is such an eccentric, I wrote. *You'd love her.*

Mary replied effusively, which made it clear she was drunk. Excited, I asked for her location, which after a minute or two she managed to share. She was near Piazza del Popolo in some nightclub.

Gussie babe, she wrote, as I hurried up Via del Corso. *I need you!*

The devotion to Mary that Jean had just observed was rearing up in me now. I told her to stay exactly where she was and that I'd be there really soon. My phone buzzed. Mary, again. I felt a twist of joy at the sight of her name on my home screen.

Come find meeeeeee! Xxxxxx

The seasons turn quickly in Rome. By October, it was too cold to spend hours sitting idly outside in the piazzas. With the money I had earned from the Melrose school – a merciful ten euros an hour, which came in envelopes of coins after the Friday sitting – I began to immerse myself in the galleries and museums that Jean had recommended I visit, using her pass, which got me a discount. Gradually, Rome started to feel like a friendlier place; no longer an expensive antagonist, but a glorious host.

Whole afternoons disappeared as I studied the sculptures in the Vatican Museums, or the Villa Borghese, in a hungover or dumbfounded state, notebook in hand, seized by competing emotions of wonder and fear. Often Rome seemed a crazy place for a residency, because the works I saw were so intimidating. To visit those galleries and then return to my cramped studio to work on my own pieces – vases, bowls – homogenous, mainly useful objects, as Jean had already identified, was humbling.

Sometimes it helped to affect an inner nonchalance to the wonders I was seeing: that cosmic portal in the roof of the Pantheon, Nero's marble bathtub, Michelangelo's little turtles on the fountain near Jean's place in the Ghetto. Jean had a checklist for me – she called it the *foundation*, and I was gradually working my way through it.

Since I had taken the bath at her apartment, Jean would send me text messages to check in, and sometimes, only if she had the time, she'd arrange for us to visit some of the sites together. Each time I met her, I was struck, not only by her kindness, but also her worldly access. She was eager, even adamant, that I experienced it all and had the best of everything: the highest views, the creamiest gelato, the most abundant *aperitivo*.

'You should bring Mary with you, next time,' she said. 'I'm sure she'd love this, too.'

But Mary was often coolly indifferent to her surroundings. She'd only lived in the city for a year, but I noticed that when she ambled past the Pantheon, she barely looked up at it; when I showed her the secret Caravaggio frescoes in the French church – a tip from Jean – she had yawned noisily like a bear. Piazza Navona – a place, for me, that was so dazzlingly baroque I practically shielded my eyes – was, for Mary, merely a venue for a coffee, or someone's flat for the late-night, post-nightclub binges she called *afters*.

I couldn't do it. I couldn't be cool. I was starting to love the city with an intensity that was becoming inseparable from my fixation on Mary. She was there in all my favourite works: the smooth marble of the Bernini sculptures reminded me of the pale underside of her arms; Apollo's indents on Daphne's flesh made me think of how my fingers might dig into Mary's hips. That golden afternoon light which filled the naves of every chapel I visited reflected her waterfall of hair; the smells of the pizza restaurants in Trastevere, salt and yeast, might also be the taste of her mouth.

When I couldn't see Mary, or talk to her, I wanted to talk about her. This wasn't something I could discuss with my Italian peers on the residency who spoke poor English. It was obviously impossible to broach this subject with my roommate; she had recently adhered a crucifix to the wall nearest her bed and I was certain she was still a virgin.

So it was that Jean, who had so easily perceived my crush, became my confidante.

When she passed by Monti, I'd take a work break and meet her for a coffee – Jean usually arriving on her old Dutch bicycle in some fabulously structural black coat – and I'd lean against the mirrored bar and tell her about my conversations with Mary and the little frissons of attraction that were passing between us during our sittings. Jean never let me forget that not only was she an expert on Rome, and on the works of art and sculpture that we both enjoyed, but she also had a professional understanding of the human mind.

'This is what Mary's actually thinking,' was how she often began her sentences. Her analysis, frequently, was informed by the 'crushing' weight of wealth that must have been bequeathed to Mary. That, and her famous parents, who, Jean was adamant, had clearly been 'very absent'.

But, along with her academic interest in my blossoming friendship, I could also tell that Jean liked the whole lovelorn drama of it all. With no one else to turn to, I was grateful that she indulged me. The more openly we spoke, the more normal I began to feel. Not only that, but a richer, warmer sensation I hadn't known in myself before had begun, too. An excitement, like an itch.

Looking back, I see that speaking openly with Jean not only brought me huge relief, but also, for the first time in my life, a sense of hope.

It therefore seemed natural that I confided in Jean straight after my tenth sitting together; the one where I saw Lawrence touch Mary.

We'd started out in high spirits.

'You're early,' Mary had said, skipping out of Lawrence's study. She was barefoot and dressed in her painting shorts – ripped denim, cut high on the thigh, which showed off her slender figure – and a powder blue shirt made from one of her mother's famous prints. A matching ribbon was plaited into her hair. I had been waiting for her in the corridor, talking to Decca. She'd leaned in and kissed me on the cheek in front of everyone. It was the first time she had done that. Briefly, I was transported; the air was full of the smell of her perfume, the tropical scent of her shampoo. Keeping a firm hand on the small of my back, she steered me, playfully, towards the classroom.

Once I was in position, Mary put on music, then began to make bold, confident strokes on her canvas, skipping back and forth from her vantage point. She'd lost that expression that I'd noticed in previous sittings; that frightened look. Kind smiles escaped from her pretty mouth, and little sounds of encouragement. She no longer seemed so at war with herself.

When I remarked that her feedback session with Law must have gone well, she told me it had.

'I'm blaming it on you,' she said, giddily. 'He's quite happy with how this is going,' she said, pointing her brush at the painting. 'It's a miracle.'

I smiled. 'You seem to care a lot about what he thinks.'

'Because he's brilliant.'

'He seems so tough on you, though.'

She thought this over, then she looked back at me, a wry smile spread across her face. She began to tell me about what he'd said in the crit, that Mary was starting to remind him of his most famous student. 'Just before she got picked up by a gallery. He's only tough on me because I've got potential.'

We painted in silence a while longer, until Mary granted me a bathroom break. On my way there, I met Lawrence in the corridor. He was wearing his usual cords and a black painting smock, carrying that perpetual soda can in his hand.

'Still here?' he grunted, as though I was a party guest who had overstayed my welcome. I hurried on past him, my eyes trained to the floor.

As I walked towards the bathroom, I peered into the other classrooms, enchanted by their grand proportions and casual privilege. The traditional materials the students used could only be bought from specific, exclusive suppliers. Yet the oil paints were dried out and wasted; brushes were left out in turps overnight and destroyed. At the Melrose, the first-year students learned draughtsmanship from actual classical-era busts. These were strewn about the classrooms, along with other fragments of ancient sculpture, as carelessly as children's toys.

It was the same with the students' own expensive possessions that I encountered in the bathroom. Beautiful designer clothes were draped everywhere; oversized cashmere jumpers in bright colours, balled up and left behind. I put on an orange jumper and studied myself in the mirror, running my fingertips along my arms in amazement at its softness. When I slipped it into my bag, the theft was easy to justify. I'd take much better care of it.

As I approached the classroom again, Lawrence's voice floated towards me. I wondered, at first, if he was speaking Italian. But then I realised that his voice sounded agitated because he was upset. I hung back at the door and saw them there together. Lawrence standing behind Mary at the canvas, his blue glasses raised and resting on the middle of his forehead. The room was darker now; it was lit by a pale globe light which hung down from a heavy chain. Dead insects had collected along the bottom of it.

'Tell me, Mary,' I heard him say. 'Why the fuck are you so afraid of paint?'

He was close, too close, behind her. Even from the doorframe, I heard his laboured breathing. I felt a painful connection to her then, as if the heat of his breath was on the back of my own neck. Mary lowered the brush that she held in her left hand and stared at the portrait. She brought the other lightly to her cheek. Her voice wavered.

'I'm not sure,' she said.

Lawrence sighed and reached for her left wrist, snatching the paintbrush from her. 'You can lay it on much thicker – here – that's it.' He pushed the brush into her palette, so hard that I could hear its hairs scraping through the thick oils. '*Fucking* roll it around. Really cover it. Much thicker.'

Mary grasped her own forearms as she nodded and followed his movements. She took the brush back from him and tried dabbing at the painting. Lawrence remained behind her, his crotch pressed against the seat of her shorts, watching her carefully. Several moments passed, then he reached forward and took her wrist in his hand once more.

'You need to work into this area, make it more prominent,' he said. He shook her wrist. 'Why are you so stiff here?' he said. 'You've got to relax.'

I held on to the doorway, unable to breathe, as he guided her movements against the canvas, seemingly to correct the tension in her arm. They were standing so close together that her ponytail was pressed against his open mouth.

I checked up and down the hallway, in case anyone else was left at the school. I knew I had to re-enter the room, but I needed to choose the right moment. So, again, I held back. I didn't want to embarrass Mary, catching her like this. Yet, at the same time, I had no idea whether this kind of thing was usual. There was something routine about the way he stood practically astride her, something accepting in her response to him that prevented me from speaking up.

Eventually, he sighed and let go of her arm. But then he stood to the right of her and touched her face. With two fingers, he pressed and massaged her temples.

'Look at me,' he said, acting as if he was coaxing her. 'Fucking look at me.'

Mary was directly facing the open door now. I stepped back but it was too late, she'd seen me. Her eyes were lifeless. She glanced from me and met his gaze again.

'You're tired, I can see it,' he said. 'But you need stamina.' His tone grew kinder, but I could see that Mary was still uncomfortable. The toes of her bare feet were wriggling; her knee twitched involuntarily.

Now she'd seen me, I had to go in. As I entered noisily, he jumped back from her.

'Don't forget to use your mirror,' he said, his voice much louder than before. He picked one up from a nearby easel and passed it to Mary. I went over to my chair on the platform, careful not to disturb the folds in the black curtain behind me.

Law watched me get back into position. Then he called over to Mary. 'Are you sure we can afford for her to stay this late?' He turned to me, grinning. 'At this rate, you cost more than a prostitute!'

Then, just before he left the room, he patted Mary's shoulder. 'Sweetheart,' he said, in a falsely pally tone. 'I should have also said, your shadow lines are spot on. What you've done beneath those cheekbones, it's very good. Our practice last term paid off.'

I wrung my hands in my seat, wondering exactly what strange intimacy last term's practice might have entailed. I tried to ask Mary if she was okay, but she just stared at the canvas, biting on the insides of her cheeks. Then she tossed down her paintbrush.

'Let's leave it there, shall we?' she said, throwing a sheet over the canvas before I could see it. 'Good to leave on a high.'

Her mouth was still twitching as she tidied her things away, and there were blotches of colour visible on her neck above the collar of her mother's shirt. For a second, they looked almost like the marks of someone's fingers.

Then they faded.

'How did she seem afterwards?' Jean asked calmly, when I rang her the next morning.

I remember feeling glad to have someone older and more responsible to talk to about it. Wriggling free of the duvet, pressing my feet against the damp cool of my bedroom wall, I told her all about how Lawrence had handled her and taken it *way too far*.

'Mary was very subdued all evening. We went for dinner with some of the others. Or rather, *we* ate dinner. Mary ordered this giant plate of truffles and didn't touch her food. She just drank and smoked and then got up and paid for everyone. She said she couldn't be bothered to split the bill, she just wanted to get out of there. We were about ten people. Can you imagine being that rich?'

'I told you before,' Jean corrected. 'Her money's a trap. But did you talk to her? Did you acknowledge what you saw?'

I sighed. 'We talked around it on the way to the restaurant. I tried to see if she was okay, but—'

'—But what?'

'She didn't want me to press her. She made me feel really lame for thinking it was unusual.'

'Did she say it had happened before?'

'Nothing pervy like this. It's weird. I was sure she said he was gay.'

'He sounds like a bully,' Jean murmured. 'Abusive.'

'I know,' I said, noting the confusing hint of triumph in my voice. It unnerved me, how good it felt to gossip with Jean about the whole episode. Another experience that my own mother and I had never shared.

She kept on at me for more information. 'So, what did you get up to afterwards? Did anything else happen between you two?'

The handset heated my earlobes. I liked the sensation of it, the hot phone, one leg scissoring the duvet, Jean's voice close in my ear. My mind darted back to images of Mary and me dancing in the club, green lasers bouncing off her clothes, her hair, her exposed clavicle.

'Nothing *happened* happened,' I said, with regret. 'We went on to some club in Pigneto. Circus themed place. It was really fun, but she was absolutely *gone*. By the end of the night, she could hardly stand.'

'Traumatised, most probably,' Jean said, with a sigh. 'Be patient. Mary's going through a tough time. She needs you.' There was a pause. 'And I also think she wants you.'

'Really?' I was smiling against the phone.

'Oh yes,' she said, gently. 'I'm sure of it. She just hasn't acknowledged it to herself yet. But as with any relationship, first, we must open up to ourselves. I wish I could talk to her, because it's the first step of what I teach in my sessions. The next stage is then *much* easier.'

'What happens then?'

'That's when you open up to each other. Allow yourselves to be *truly* vulnerable.'

GUEST V FINBOW: DAY TWO

In cross-examination, Ms Carr uses Mary's history of poor mental health against her. It's proof, she argues, that Mary is susceptible and can be easily exploited.

'Like many of those who are victimised by charismatic cult leaders, aren't you desperate for a solution to the chaos inside your head?'

Mary places a protective hand on her stomach and I feel a shiver of envy. Her response is coldly emphatic. 'Not at all. We don't *impose* solutions. We embrace the chaos. That's how Jean's coaching has rescued me.'

'I just want to check, Ms Finbow, that you do mean rescued and not *recruited*?'

'Ms Carr, that is commentary,' Justice Larkin warns. The lawyer raises an apologetic hand, then points her pen in Mary's direction. 'How often do you meet each other, Ms Finbow? How many times a week are you and Ms Guest *embracing the chaos*?'

Mary cowers. She glances towards Jean. 'It depends; three or four times. On the weekends, we do reading.'

Ms Carr cocks her head to one side. 'And on average, how long are these sessions?'

'It depends.'

'Try to guess?' There is a pause. 'At a minimum?'

'Two.'

'Two hours?' Ms Carr gives a theatrical sigh, as if fatigued by the very idea of it. 'Are you aware that the traditional analytic hour typically runs no longer than fifty minutes? And that, much like cross-examination, it is broadly understood that excessive lengths of time under questioning can be destructive?'

'I'm aware,' Mary says coolly. 'But, in the past, traditional methods have not served me.'

'What else is untraditional in your sessions? Would you describe regression therapy and memory retrieval therapy as untraditional?'

'Yes.'

'Would you describe them as unconventional?'

'Yes.'

'Dangerous?'

'No.'

My palms dampen. For a moment, I close my eyes and I am wandering dizzily around Jean's flat: the stench of lilies is heavy in the air, the kettle whistles, and the pink tiles in the bathroom where I rest after our conversations are cool beneath my feet.

'So, I'm a total novice,' Ms Carr's voice echoes below. 'What is "memory retrieval therapy"? Is it as simple as remembering someone's name? Or recalling what you scribbled on a shopping list at home?'

Mary straightens. 'It's simple. We conjure scenes from my past, then replay them. Jean monitors my bodily reactions. After that, we discuss them.'

'What comes up in those discussions? Typically?'

She glances over at Jean and they exchange smiles. My stomach curls. 'How I might have felt at the time. How I feel today about whatever has happened. It helps me to release things.'

'Release what?'

'The anger,' Mary answers, without hesitation.

Ms Carr pauses, allowing us to reflect on the bitterness of Mary's response. 'Could you expand on what you mean when you say, "conjure scenes from my past"?'

Mary pauses, then gives a blissed-out smile, like a religious believer. 'There are so many episodes or memories we repress. All the difficult things we have shut down in order to function. First, we must access them. Then excise them. And it's vital now that I have another life growing inside me. I can't let her inherit them.'

Ms Carr frowns. 'So, we go around, having absolutely no recollection of these nasty episodes until when?'

'Until we remember the buried trauma.'

'And we keep these memories in some kind of lumber room of the psyche, like bulky, ugly furniture that we don't want to look at?'

Mary's chest lifts. 'That's it,' she says.

'It's got to be a pretty big basement, don't you think?' Ms Carr snaps. 'Because we're not just talking minor injuries, are we? A dropped ice cream, or not making the netball team? And we're not really talking about the usual bread and butter of therapy, which explores inconvenient or painful bits of our lives; the facets of our relationships that we choose to ignore. No, regression therapy requires its participants to recover memories of major personal trauma, many of which have far-reaching, even criminal, consequences for those involved.'

The judge cautions Ms Carr again for commentary. Chastised, Ms Carr lowers her voice. 'What I want to know, Ms Finbow, is whether you ever felt pressurised in these sessions to fabricate things that didn't happen?'

Mary fixes her gaze downwards, almost as though she is trying to suppress a laugh. It gives her an eerie aspect. She looks bitter and unhinged, eaten up with it. 'Nothing is fabricated. My family has given me enough material, thank you.'

Ms Carr's cheeks turn pink with frustration. She carelessly flips the page of her notebook. 'Then let's turn elsewhere.' She reads aloud. '"No alcohol, no drugs, no reading outside of the set reading list. No music. And no contraception." Are any of these rather restrictive ground rules familiar to you, Ms Finbow? Because they have been relayed to us by some of Ms Guest's ex-clients.'

'Some of them are,' Mary says, blinking. There's a tugging in my chest as I stare at her stomach again and think of the pills she might have flushed. 'Like I said, I feel better for it.'

Ms Carr looks gravely at her. 'When did it become "no friends, no family"?' She leaves a heavy pause. 'How soon after your sessions commenced, did the claimant begin advocating for a permanent severance from those you once loved?'

'We don't think of it as severance,' says Mary, an expression of grace spreading across her face. She's unaware that she is conceding the point that Jean encourages the isolation. 'It's a healing separation.'

Ms Carr shakes her head, disbelievingly. 'My Lord, the ostracisation of susceptible individuals from their social milieu is a common characteristic of cultic organisations.' She turns back to Mary. 'So, no books, no music, and no pill. When did it become "no home"?' Ms Carr pauses theatrically and Mary's face clouds over. 'We have a report which states you have recently moved to an outdoor camp a short way off the M1. Do you confirm this?'

For a moment, there is quiet. An awful, exposing silence. Mary looks stricken.

'It's a unique community,' she stammers.

'Do you pay to camp there?' Ms Carr enquires.

'We have evolved beyond monetary transactions.'

'Are you sleeping *rough*, Ms Finbow?'

The knowledge comes suddenly – borne in a second. Jean has made her homeless. Because of their restraining order, Anna and Bonamy are not allowed within a certain radius of the properties Mary owns. But it was understood she still moved between them. I start to feel sick as I consider it – I always believed Mary had autonomy there; places she could escape to.

'I refuse to comment on some spy report my parents have commissioned.' Mary's voice trembles.

'How about a neighbour from the camp?' Ms Carr presses. 'She has stated that your temporary home is unsanitary and,' she reads from a slip of paper on her desk, 'full of slugs. We've had reports that you, now in your second trimester, sleep on a dirty mattress on the floor.'

'I like living there,' Mary says, avoiding Anna's sad gaze. 'It's simpler.'

Ms Carr nods facetiously. 'These are unconventional choices, Your Honour, and it's perhaps not uncommon for those afforded privileged backgrounds to favour alternative existences. The issue here is that Ms Guest is now a *direct beneficiary* of these life choices.' She lists the different components of Mary's wealth portfolio. There had been quarterly trust payments made to Mary, but Anna managed to get them stopped last year. Ms Carr explains how Mary existed instead on the income from the properties she owns: a mews house in Notting Hill, a block of flats in Hampstead, other developments overseas in France and Corfu.

'You became increasingly reliant on this income, so what was the reason behind signing these properties over to Ms Guest last month? It's an illogical thing to do. Were you being manipulated, Ms Finbow?'

Mary swallows, aware that she's been backed into a corner. 'I needed help. I couldn't manage it all. It was distracting me from my real work.'

Ms Carr throws her a sympathetic look. 'Has Ms Guest told you that your financial assets obstructed your healing journey?'

I bite my lip when I see tears fill Mary's eyes. Vehemently, she shakes her head, but she has fallen into Ms Carr's well-laid trap. Mary's severance from her friends and family members was sad, but excusable. But no well-meaning person would isolate Mary from her money.

'I wanted Jean to have the income,' she croaks. 'It's only fair if she's managing them. And the legal fees. Since I am responsible—'

'—I'll take your word for it, Mary. To me, it sounds as if you are being defrauded. Though that may be a matter for the court to decide.'

A ripple of scandal rises above the rows of spectators. Ms Carr pauses to allow Mary time to blow her nose, then proceeds softly. 'We learned earlier today that your baby is due in three months' time, is that correct?'

'Yes.' Mary's voice is cracked now. So small and sad that my own eyes fill with tears.

'Are you aware that if you remain at the camp when the baby is born, then you will most likely be reported to Child Protection Services?'

Mary's face twitches as she looks about. 'I'll move back then, I think.'

'To one of your properties that Jean Guest now manages? That would make her your landlord, wouldn't it?'

'It will be safer for my daughter that way,' Mary says, choking. 'I can't do it without Jean.'

'Why not?' Ms Carr asks, gently.

'I'm too *weak*.'

'Our view, Mary, is that you are not weak, but that you have been targeted, and consciously weakened, by a calculating individual who seeks not only your financial assets but now your offspring. Do you agree?'

'No!' Mary bursts out, rattled now.

'Let me put this differently. Do you affirm, as you did in your previous cross-examination, that the claimant was treating you for issues relating to sexual promiscuity?'

Mary flinches. 'Partly.'

'And when did the claimant advise you to stop taking contraception?'

Mary falters. 'I don't remember.'

'But it was her wish?'

'It was my decision, too. I was gaining so much weight. And it was sending me crazy. You don't understand how unhinged I was. It made me completely blocked. And angry. I was going completely off my head.'

In the front row of the gallery, Bonamy covers his eyes with his hands. I picture his grief over his multiple losses. If she succeeds, Jean will not only have stolen their child, but also their only grandchild.

This is what makes my legs shake as the cross-examination closes and the judge announces an adjournment for the rest of the afternoon. This is what frightens me even more than the harrowing thought of Mary defrauded and sleeping rough: Mary referred to *her daughter*. In three months' time, she will be having a little girl.

Jean has always longed for a daughter of her own.

ROME, NOVEMBER

As we became closer friends, Mary occasionally referred to previous issues she'd faced growing up. Sometimes I worried about the occasional skipped meal or the complaints Mary made about her parents, but it was all outshone by her dazzling wealth, which I couldn't imagine would be imprisoning. During my teens, I'd been obsessed with Andy Warhol and all the beautifully elfin heiresses that had decorated his world. So, I saw Mary as my Edie; I misread her damage as glamorous dishevelment. Half friend, half fantasy figure, I couldn't stand the greyscale boredom of the days when I didn't get to see her.

By the start of November we were going out almost every night, though often in a group rather than alone. After the sittings, we'd go to the spots around Campo de' Fiori with the fake flame patio heaters. I'd sit in the corner, quietly proud to bask in the company of Decca, Mary, and the twins, who had embraced me now I was Mary's model. At the time, I worshipped their exuberance, the garrulous way they glided from bar to bar, attracting attention, getting drinks for free. Back then, I read their behaviour as confidence, a wild and mysterious energy that I was lucky to witness. Now I can see that their behaviour emerged from egregious entitlement. Nothing else.

My own lack of confidence was something that Jean often brought up. We started to go for lunch together on the Mondays and Fridays before my sittings with Mary. Over amatriciana and wine – in restaurants I never normally could have afforded – she referred to the different ways I was blocking myself. It was a shame, she used to say, how low my self-esteem was, when everyone else could see what a bright spirit I had.

'You're getting in your own way,' she'd warn, sipping her glass of Frascati. 'You're obscuring your own light.'

Jean knew I'd dropped out of art school by then, but she blamed that on my parents' failure to take my work seriously, rather than my chronic inability to see anything through. According to her, it all stemmed back to my parents' rejection of who I was. That was why I couldn't conceive of myself fully as an artist. I was afraid to open up; to act as a channel for my true creativity.

'I see it all the time with my clients,' she'd say, glancing carefully at me. 'And it's just *incredible* how my treatment benefits them. One day, we really should dedicate some time to it, Gus.'

Whenever Jean mentioned her clients, I felt a shiver of envy towards them, these girls with glamorous names like Oriel, who seemed to phone Jean all the time. Therapy, I had already concluded, was a rich person's privilege that I couldn't afford. The girls from the Melrose often talked about their shrinks' analyses of their thoughts and actions: why they drank so much, painted badly, fought with their parents or slept around. They were given a narrative framework for their lives. A better story to tell themselves.

When I listened to their accounts of what they had learnt, I felt a deep longing. How badly I wanted a story, a way of making sense of all the muddled patterns I had fallen into. How I craved a container for the unmanageable feelings which flowed towards Mary. But also in those moments, I felt a giddy gratitude towards Jean. That such a generous and worldly woman would take an interest in me seemed an insane stroke of luck. She knew I couldn't afford to have proper sessions with her and was kind about it, joking that one day, she hoped, she'd get me on her couch. She often reminded me that she had a special payment structure for students.

'But I can't even afford a haircut, Jean.'

'Well, perhaps there are other ways. Think it over. I just want to see you shine.'

One of the things that Jean was adamant about, was bringing Mary into my own creative practice. In her view, the Melrose school was making Mary miserable, teaching her nothing but paint-by-numbers. 'You could be the one to set her free from that,' she suggested.

Once or twice a month, our residency hosted evenings where alumni and current members of the programme sold pieces of work. Jean insisted that I invite Mary, instead of following her moonily from bar to bar. Not only that, but Jean announced she might try to come along, too. She was *dying* to meet Mary, especially after everything I'd told her.

The next event was the second week of November. Jean got very involved in the whole evening, helping me plan what we'd do afterwards, and even lending me money for a new outfit. But when the event began and I stood around in my new clothes, I grew agitated. If Mary didn't appear, I'd have nothing to show for Jean's investment in my clothes, for all her goading and coaching. She wanted me to text her as soon as Mary arrived, and that made me uneasy, too: the sense that Mary's no-show might upset Jean even more than me.

As I waited, I tried to quieten that fear by drinking a lot of wine. The exhibition space at CRETA was an echoey place that had once served as a storage room for grain. Although our basement studio was crowded, I loved the area upstairs, and was proud to show it off. Its walls were pale blue, but the paint was starting to crack and peel like eggshells. I liked that about the room – the way its rough walls underlined the solidity of all the exhibited pieces. Supporters of the programme, and friends of the artists gathered in circles, drinking wine and eating cheese and fried artichokes. They were well-dressed in that typical Roman way: the men wore wide, soft loafers on their feet. The women wore belted puffa jackets with fur hoods.

I milled around for about an hour, trying to keep up with conversations I couldn't understand. There were a couple of trips outside for anxious cigarettes. More wine. Some staring at the wall. Then, just as I was about to text Jean to say there was no point coming because Mary hadn't arrived, I felt a hand on my shoulder.

'Look at you!' Mary said, playfully flicking the silver trousers Jean helped me buy. As Mary rotated and admired me, I inwardly blessed Jean's generosity.

We hugged. Mary's own outfit was all black, and tougher than normal: dark jeans and a leather jacket which rested on her shoulders like a cape. Her hair was drawn up to the top of head in a tight bun. As I held her, I could feel the notches of her shoulders through her clothes, bird-like and fragile beneath all that leather armoury. For a sad moment, I thought of Lawrence. Had he detected that, too?

We collected drinks, then I led Mary over to where my work was. I'd just finished my first sculpture, the only piece of work I'd made that wasn't, as Jean put it, *functional*. It was a modest-sized sculpture of a gymnast, a work that Jean had helped me source the materials for, covering the costs, she promised, until someone had the sense to buy it. The idea had come to me over the summer, inspired by an American gymnast I'd grown obsessed with during the previous year's Olympics. I was moved by her physical freedom; her flight as she sprung over the vaulting horse, the thud as she shifted her weight between her hands, the brown beans of muscle in her arms. There was a hypnotic rhythm to the flow of her body that made me want to try and sculpt her. Or, something in her power that eventually dared me to. Although I was proud of how it had come out, and happy, too, to hear the praise of my peers at CRETA, it was Mary's approval that actually made my work feel interesting.

'*Beautiful*,' she said, smoothing the gymnast's flanks and abdomen admiringly, like a trainer with a racehorse. She listened as I explained how I'd modelled the piece, the steel wool I'd used to polish it. My heart soared.

'Is he falling or what?' Mary interrupted, cocking her head to the side.

'Falling?' I laughed. I pointed to the surface at the base of the sculpture, which the gymnast held on to with a single hand, her legs pressed together neatly as a knife. 'No, look,' I said, then hesitated. 'It's also a she.'

'Wow, I didn't get that.' Mary paused, turned her head again. 'Quite butch, isn't she?' I said nothing. She went on. 'I see it more like she's desperate, like she's gripping onto an edge with only one hand. Like she's fallen and is about to let go.'

I squeezed my lower lip and glanced over Mary's shoulder to where a woman was feeding bits of food to the dog she held in her arms. What I wanted to portray was the gymnast's control over the horse, her mastery of gravity. Mary had got it wrong, though there was no point in correcting her.

'I wish I could do hands as well as you,' she murmured, gripping mine and bringing them next to the sculpture. 'They're perfect.' For a moment, the room fell quiet. There was nothing around except the feeling of her hands on mine, the flood of excitement this caused me. Then she burst out laughing and the spell was broken. We moved away.

'Can we go soon?' she whispered loudly, swiping drinks. 'I'm getting museum legs.'

Outside, the streets and bars were busy, but we managed to find a table somewhere on the Piazza di Santa Maria. My studio was across the river from the Melrose school, only a five-minute walk from the Colosseum but in a far cheaper and younger part of the city. To me, Trastevere was an ossified place, a tourist trap, whereas Monti had its own realness. It was past ten, and the streets were full of spirited drinkers, either spilling out of bars or squatting along the pavement kerb. Over near the fountain in the middle of the square, a female busker was singing jazz covers that Mary kept singing along with. I smiled happily as I watched her approach the busker with a handful of scrunched-up euro notes. Now that I was with Mary, I felt no inclination to text Jean.

'I still find it weird seeing you out,' Mary said, sitting back down. There was an empty bottle on the table between us and we'd just called for another. 'I spend so much time observing you that I forget sometimes you're actually this real person, moving about the world, making stuff. It's cool.'

I smiled and sipped my wine, but it hurt. Mary was a constant presence in my mind. When she was quiet over text, I was wracked with unease. Earlier this week, she had gone silent for a few days because she was in London, dealing with some family drama. Jean had tried her best to calm me down, but I'd barely slept.

'I was on damage-control duty,' Mary said, when I asked her what had happened. 'Mum got photographed in Annabel's with some MP. Dad's devastated. She's such a cow.'

'Fuck,' I said, though my stomach swam with excitement at the scandal; the fact I'd been trusted enough to be told. Mary assured me that it was fine, that it happened all the time.

'The first time I saw my Mum with another man I was, what, eight?'

'Wow, actually?'

'They just carted me off to therapy.' Her hands trembled slightly as she lit her cigarette.

'Did it work?'

Mary gestured to the table around her, scattered with bottles, and looked doubtful. 'Nope!' We both laughed.

'I guess, on one level, I admire how my parents didn't stop their lives when they had me,' she said. 'I made no difference to how they lived. They just partied on. I've always been the third wheel in their relationship, which is why they spoil me.'

'Same,' I said, leaning back in my chair and exhaling smoke. In what felt like a pathetically dishonest way of levelling with her, I heard myself say, 'Dad spoiled me, too.'

'Ugh,' Mary sighed.

'It was oppressive.'

'Precisely,' she exclaimed, then she leaned forward and rapped the table. 'I just needed things to be normal.'

'Right—'

'I was so jealous of the children I saw in films who had yellow school buses and lunch boxes and homework. You wouldn't believe how badly I craved an ordinary life. You should see all my doodles from my childhood – it's all drawn on hotel stationery. Like, here's my home, and my imaginary pet dog, and our car, but it's all scrawled over a pad of paper from the Chateau Marmont, you know?' For a moment, she turned away and asked the waiter for something in Italian.

'Your parents took you around with them?'

'Everywhere. Until I was about thirteen. India, Méribel, Kenya. Wherever they were seeking inspiration.'

'Amazing.'

'I guess so. I only know about it from photos.' She scratched at her face. 'Large parts of my childhood, I honestly just can't remember.'

I asked her if she had been homeschooled. She asked me if could tell and I said, 'Sorry, but yes.' That made her laugh, and she regaled me with stories about her useless tutors who mainly took her skiing or to the beach.

'All bigger wasters than my parents. They did whatever they wanted with me. It took them fifteen fucking years to figure out I was dyslexic.'

She went on like that, listing all the ways her privilege had constrained her. I nodded along, embarrassed to think of my own background. If Mary was going to want me, she'd need to think there were parallels between our lives. So I made my childhood sound, if not as glamorous as hers, then eccentric in its own way. When we talked during our portrait sessions, I made out that my parents were members of a made-up intelligentsia: teachers, rather than classroom assistants. Then, perhaps most inventively of all, I made out that my parents were devoted to me. I was the apple of their eye, their life's focus, and not the source of an awkward problem they wanted to tidy away.

We had just ordered a third bottle of wine, when Mary's phone flashed on the table in front of us. She snatched up the handset and swore. It was Vincenzo. I panicked. 'I'm supposed to be going over,' she said, looking conflicted.

I swallowed down a tight knot of envy. 'To his?'

'Yeah. He just got back from a work trip in Milan.'

'But it's late,' I said, taking in the polished sheen on her face, all the studs and hoops that were stacked along her earlobes. She hadn't dressed up for me, then – it was all for him.

'Do you think it's too late?' Mary asked, biting her lip guiltily.

'That depends.' I tried to keep my voice even. 'Do you actually like him?'

She grimaced. 'I'm not sure. Is feeling flattered the same as liking someone?' She paused. 'He can be weird.'

'What do you mean?'

Mary adjusted her position in the chair, took a large mouthful of wine, and described in detail the strange ways that Vincenzo liked to fuck her. Of course, he tied her up. That was, she said, pretty standard. The worst bit was how he finished: holding on to her head and staring blankly at the middle of her forehead, moving forcefully, with the rhythm of a man coldly ducking his enemy under the sea. She gave a pitying laugh, like it was all a game.

'And sometimes, when he's not concentrating, he kisses with all of his teeth, like he's eating an apple.'

'Gross,' I said, trying to wrinkle my nose. My face felt rigid.

'And if he doesn't want proper sex,' she said, in mock-outrage, 'then he just pushes your head down towards his crotch. Like this.' She clasped her fingers together. 'Like I'm a cafetière!'

Mary giggled as she told me about it. I produced a laugh, too, but the images of Mary together with this man made my insides feel stale, like I'd smoked too many cigarettes. That phrase kept tormenting me: *proper sex*.

I managed to stall her by drinking slowly. By the time the bar closed, there were three empty wine bottles on the table, and other glasses which contained remnants of grappa and limoncello. Mary seemed wasted enough to have forgotten about Vincenzo. Then the bill arrived, which Mary grabbed off me in a gesture of secrecy.

'There's another present in the loo for you,' she said, her eyes glinting. 'Go. Quickly.'

'I can't,' I began. Then I stopped. Inexperienced as I was, it occurred to me that if Mary had already taken drugs, then pretty soon, she'd want to do more of them. And that if I did them, too, she'd stay with me and not go to Vincenzo. I stopped protesting.

The line of cocaine she had left on the cistern of the toilet was as fat as a slug, and lay alongside a rolled-up note. I inspected it for a while, inexpertly took what I could manage, pocketed the money, then swept the rest away. When I came out, our table was gone. Mary was standing in the piazza, twirling a rose that she'd bought from a street hawker.

'Where should we go now?' I said, squaring up to her. The inside of my nose dripped and burned, and everything suddenly felt very urgent. She placed the rose between her teeth and brought my face next to hers, levelling her gaze with mine. Our jaws were identically stiffened. 'Afters at your place?'

Her face softened and she leaned her chin towards me, passing the rose into my open mouth. She used her fingers to seal my lips around it. 'Heaven,' she said. There was the sharp sensation of thorns puncturing my lip. When I squealed in pain, she dropped the flower and waltzed away, laughing.

We snaked our way through the streets of Monti towards the Forum, talking rapidly about our surroundings. We loved that smell of night jasmine which could descend on you suddenly, drenching you like a thundercloud; we loved the crumbling plaster on the front of each building; every shut-up restaurant we passed, we vowed to visit later because it looked delicious. Every so often, we stopped and pointed upwards to large, lit-up apartment windows that displayed far-away adult worlds. We speculated about their stuffy adult lives with rotating bookshelves, discerning artworks and decanters of wine. We laughed if we managed to glimpse the owners: the men wore gilets and had slicked-back hair; the women were in various stages of pregnancy. Mary said that she'd rather die than be any of those people. I disagreed and said I'd happily wear a gilet for life, if I owned an apartment like that.

We kept on walking and talking about what it felt like to live here. There were times, I said, when I found the city to be so beautiful, I felt the need to make a fist and punch through the air to check it moved, that I wasn't standing against some theatrical stage set. Mary told me she used to feel the same, but she worried sometimes if she was taking it all for granted.

I joked that Mary took everything for granted, 'including me.' But she didn't seem to hear. So I grabbed hold of her hand and we did it together. We made a fist and swiped it so fast that it left behind a whirl of pink light like a comet. I screwed my eyes shut and opened them again. What Mary had lain out for us in that bathroom was strong. I dropped her hand and we laughed. It became a game. I knocked the air, and she knocked at the apartment building to one side of her. I knocked a car. She bashed a window. I pushed at a pair of bikes that were propped against a lamppost. When they both fell, unlocked, Mary laughed in surprise, then raised an eyebrow.

'This means we can take them, right?'

I assured her, yes. I would have agreed to anything that prevented her from going to see Vincenzo. But she didn't need my approval. Mary often appropriated minor objects with the carelessness of someone who had been given everything she wanted. *India, the Alps, Chateau Marmont.*

Soon, we were barrelling through the Forum towards Piazza Venezia. Behind us, the Colosseum loomed, bone white. We powered fast away from it and down over the cobbles towards the busy roundabout of Piazza Venezia. Mary raced ahead, tantalisingly lifted from the seat, her calf muscles flashing in the lamplight as she pedalled. By the time we'd turned left and onto Campo di Fiori, she was looping all over the place, shrieking and laughing.

'Where are we going?' I called as she almost took out an old man. '*Mi dispiace, signor!*' Suddenly, as I said this, I was jolted into a flashback of Mr Greening, regarding me with disgust. My parents to the side of me, white with fury.

I'm sorry, sir. I said I was sorry.

I squeezed my brakes in protest. 'I thought we were going back to yours?' I shouted breathlessly. She began to weave her way over to me, making little circles on her bicycle.

'Can't you tell what I'm spelling out?' She was standing up on her pedals, yanking the handles of her bike like a dog chasing after its own tail. 'I'm saying your name. Look. G-U-S.' She wheeled around and grinned at me. 'Have a go at mine.'

I smiled back at her, then pushed downwards on the pedals, exhilarated, steering jerkily through the letters of her name.

M-A-R-Y.

She clapped her hands with encouragement, following my movements.

'*Brava*,' she yelled.

I did it again – this time more confidently. I raised myself up from my saddle:

M-A-R-Y.

Those were the letters I traced on her skin later that night, right along her shoulder blades. Mary's apartment on the Lungotevere was magnificent: grand, frescoed rooms full of antiques, dirty ashtrays, and unfinished canvases from previous terms. The kitchen off to the side was more compact, with shiny white cupboard doors and a chrome coffee machine.

Mary snorted what was left in her baggie from a plate in the kitchen, then staggered into the bedroom, collapsing on her bed which jutted into the centre of the room. Wriggling free of all her clothes except for her knickers, she lay prettily on her side.

'You look like a model,' I couldn't help saying.

'*You're* the model,' she slurred. 'And I'm so glad you're here.' She leaned in and kissed me softly on the cheek. Our eyes met, then she turned over and asked me to rub her back. 'I'm too wired to sleep,' she mumbled.

Her body was very brown and narrow, her spine protruding out of her lean flesh as she turned away from me. I reached out to touch her, breathing shallowly. To prevent my hands from trembling, I concentrated on pressing the letters of her name into skin, all the while paying close attention to the little sighing noises she made. After a few minutes, Mary ordered me to take off my clothes, too.

'I'm a really hot sleeper,' she whispered drowsily.

I turned out the lamp and undressed, then climbed back in. She inched herself towards me. For a while we lay there, tucked close to each other like apostrophes on her wide, princessy bed. I concentrated on quietening my breathing. Then I pulled the eiderdown up from our knees, to cover us both. When I brought my hand underneath it, I let it fall on the warm outside of Mary's thigh.

A shock of adrenalin at this act. Then fear over what to do next. My excitement of touching her was tempered by dark shades of shame. At first, my hand felt disembodied; I could scarcely feel her skin at all, only its warmth. I waited for her to move me, but Mary carried on breathing steadily through her mouth. For a few moments, I left it there while I watched the car headlights from outside cast long shadows on the opposite wall. Then, my heart hammering, I inched closer again. Her hair smelt of smoke and sweat, mixed in with the detergent of her bedsheets. I raised one finger, then two, then, feeling myself flood with fear, my whole hand upwards to her waist.

My nerves were alert, electric. But she never protested. She let me keep my hand there, even when my fingers trailed up and down the smooth curve of her side. Several minutes passed as we lay like that: Mary making little contented sounds, while I could barely take in air. Then, from outside, came the sound of an ambulance, its blue lights filling the room through the gaps in her window shutters. Mary stirred towards consciousness; her body stiffened. The vehicle passed and she turned away from me, to pass the rest of the night, lying like a baby, flat on her front.

Mary was still lying in that position when I got up the next day to get her a glass of water. It was morning. I'd barely slept.

'Where's my phone?' she mumbled drowsily, slapping her hand around the bedside table.

'I put it on charge for you,' I said, collecting it from the sideboard. 'Hold on,'

Mary guzzled the water and called me an angel, then dropped her head back on the pillow, making indiscriminate sounds of regret about her hangover and all the coke and the property we had stolen. Simultaneously, a peal of church bells nearby filled the room.

'I need confession!' Mary groaned. 'I need a celibate priest,' she said, and laughed. 'I demand a very hot but celibate priest.'

I laughed, too, and climbed back into bed. Mary's phone remained loosely in my hand, but I didn't want her to look at it yet. I wanted to retain the intimacy of our space. It was impossible to know if she thought what had happened in the early hours was a big deal. Was she masking her eyes for her headache, or to avoid me?

'Hold on,' I said as I became aware of her phone vibrating. I squinted at the screen. 'He's calling. Finally, your holy father!'

Mary sat up. 'Vincenzo? Give it to me.'

She reached up for the phone, breasts unfurling flat as I playfully lifted it away from her.

'Shall I answer it?' I teased. 'Let him know you're unavailable?'

'Gussie...' she warned.

'I could say you're a little *tied up*?'

Mary didn't get the joke. Her face was thunder. She swiped once more for the phone. I withheld it.

'For fuck's sake, Gussie!' She sprung angrily out of bed, grabbing my wrist and snatching it from my hands. 'Seriously! Could you just stop being such a *fucking freak*?'

I laughed shakily, but her words hurt. Mary threw on a robe and went over towards the balcony. 'Where are you going?' I asked. She ignored me.

I lay there for a moment, heart racing, as I recovered from the heat of our exchange. But then, as my gaze wandered around her room, at the books on her bedside table, the piles of jewellery alongside it, I began to reflect on something else I'd seen on Mary's home-screen, late last night when I put it on charge. Her background was an old photo of her parents, but layered above that was a message notification: a direct message from some artists' mentoring scheme.

Sorry for the DM, but I just had the strangest dream about you!

I registered the exclamation mark with a stroke of unease, but I couldn't place the source of it. I was probably jealous at the assumed intimacy of the exchange, just as I resented the conversation Mary was conducting with Vincenzo in Italian on the balcony.

I realise now: those misgivings were tiny jolts of recognition. Whoever was writing to Mary shared the same gushy cadence of a woman I also regularly corresponded with. And yet, this knowledge was too deeply buried, too early to name. For months, years, I forgot about it.

In Her Defence

Here it is now: the memory retrieved. I see Jean's predatory text message overlaying Mary's family snapshot on her home screen like a blot of dark ink: the scribble of someone demented as they go back through old photograph albums, desperate to redact the past. A black stain obscuring the Finbows' faces, spreading slowly outwards, gradually erasing them.

PART THREE

ROME, NOVEMBER

If you asked me, why did I let her in? How did I let Jean control my life so intimately? My answers would be embarrassingly naïve.

Because she worried about me.

Because her apartment was nice.

By November, Jean was offering her home as a sanctuary *whenever things got a bit much,* providing me each time with freshly pressed pyjamas, a carafe of lemon water, and stacks of good reading material. I had been the kind of child who was expected to make her own breakfast, so it was a novelty when she greeted me in bed with a cup of coffee, soothing the perpetual hangovers and comedowns I was sustaining from trying to keep up with Mary. But, as I let her lavish all sorts of maternal comforts on me, was there also an uneasy twinge inside? A strained note which might have warned: this woman is kind, but is she too interested in me? What is it that she wants?

If there was, I chose to ignore it. I had found, for the first time in my life, someone to lean on.

Jean's memory for the mundane logistics of my existence was astounding. She remembered when my deadlines were, and niggling bits of admin to do with my course. She tested me on the verbs I was learning during the Italian lessons I'd started taking from Bea, often sprinkling them into conversation so they'd cement in my mind. Economising was easier when she helped me source art materials and plan meals. Nights out were much cheaper, because she gave me the password to her taxi account. There were promises, too, of introductions to collectors back in London, other courses she'd heard about that she might help me get onto. Then, in perhaps the most irresistible of her offers, a place to stay in London when my course was done. 'You'd love my house in Primrose Hill,' Jean boasted, 'it's very seventies, very airy. To be honest, I rattle around it. There's a bed for you next year for as long as you need.'

At that point, I began to obsess over the creative freedom that living with Jean would bring. Without the obligation to pay rent, I could make ceramics full-time, become unblocked in the way Jean wanted me to. Become an *artist*. And that dream twinned with another: a future in London with Mary, who was due to return home next June. I knew she wouldn't want to be with someone who took depressing day jobs just to make rent. No, if Mary was going to want me, I needed to commit to my creative work full-time. If I was successful, things might level out between us. It might disguise how painfully I needed her.

But since the night I stayed over, Mary sometimes acted coldly towards me. We were still meeting twice a week for the painting sessions and going out with Cleo, Bea, and Decca, but instead of inviting me back at the end of the night, Mary would disappear off. I'd search helplessly for her in the smoking areas, on the dance-floors, or in the toilet cubicles of whichever nightclub we'd fallen into. How bitterly I swallowed Decca's shrugging appraisal each time: Mary had probably gone off to be with Vincenzo.

The thought of it made me act in ways I wasn't comfortable with. I was aware that I was becoming hopelessly addicted to those confusing, push-pull forces that underpinned our interactions, but I was powerless to stop the pattern. On the days I texted Mary and didn't get a reply, I gripped my phone, hawk-eyed, to check when she was online. Every time she opened the app and didn't respond, I sunk into a lower mood. If her silences lasted longer than forty-eight hours, I'd find myself going round to her apartment, just to see if her lights were on, though I never admitted that to Mary, and not even to Jean.

And then, just as my heart was hardening and I was growing used to the coolness, Mary's behaviour towards me would change.

In Her Defence

She'd insist that I come over to her apartment on the nights she was detoxing. Or drinking less, because we agreed that wine at home didn't really count. Often when I arrived, she'd seem in a shaky mood, biting her fingernails and distracted by her phone, so I would bustle around and help her to relax. We'd curl up together under blankets, and I'd select a Paolo Sorrentino film to watch on her projector and pull-down screen. My tastes in cinema impressed her, but also that I knew how to talk about the films in a critical way.

'I just watch it,' she said one rainy Monday evening, standing up from the sofa and tying a lime-green scrunchie in her hair. Her legs were like long, brown poles, extending from the baggy white t-shirt she liked to wear when she was at home. The black lace of her underwear flashed at me as she raised her arms.

'You actually understand the mechanics of what's going on.'

Not long after that movie night, Mary messaged to invite me for a drink that evening with her godfather. Jean was delighted for me, suggesting it showed that she was perhaps more serious about me than I thought.

Meeting the family! Such a good sign! Keep in touch, won't you? she wrote. *I'll be waiting to hear...*

Mary had referred to her godfather by his nickname, Beaker, but when I found the two of them in the terrace bar of a hotel near Piazza di Spagna, I was so shocked at his celebrity I couldn't speak. He was an American actor, famous for his role in a big-budget gangster trilogy and rich from his own brand of whisky, which he'd launched shortly afterwards. I slid mutely into my seat, trying to catch Mary's attention to communicate *what the fuck,* but she just smiled with squiffy eyes and carried on talking.

The air was full of paraffin from the patio heaters and the cloying blanket of Beaker's cigar smoke. Nearby, a waiter hovered, our champagne bottle crooked in his arm, trying to maintain the fiction that Beaker hadn't been recognised. This was pointless, since he and Mary were speaking in drunk, boisterous voices. They were also dressed up in conspicuously elegant clothes, like characters from the fifties: he wore a tux, and Mary had pinned her hair up, and was wearing a lot of Bulgari jewellery, which they had picked up together earlier that day. It was all just for a joke, apparently. Everything that evening seemed to be a joke. They laughed loudly at everything.

'Perfect,' Beaker said, beaming, after I'd explained that I'd not been sent to a British boarding school. He fixed me in a twinkly stare. 'I always said Mary's needed a normal friend. Someone – unlike her – who is sane.'

Mary laughed and said, 'There's nothing normal about Gus,' to which I replied, 'I'm right here, you know,' and they both laughed.

Mary continued addressing him about me. 'I swear she's making me a better artist,' she said, her voice slurring to a slight lisp. She squeezed my arm. 'Light works in this amazing way on her.'

'In what way?' I interjected, leaning away from the table because the stench of Beaker's cigar was burning my nostrils. I preferred this conversation topic. The portrait connected us. It was my only real source of social legitimacy.

'You hold your pose really well,' Mary said, 'but somehow you change all the time.'

'What do you mean?'

'Yesterday, a cloud went over the sun, and as I looked along the canvas back to your face, it had completely changed. You reflected all these different shadows.'

Beneath the table, her foot clipped mine: a spiked heel against my trainer. I kicked back. We smiled at each other. Then she glanced down towards her lap and adjusted her napkin. More quietly, she said, 'Suddenly, you were this whole other person.'

When the food arrived, Beaker and Mary spoke for a long time about people I didn't know. I drank glass after glass of champagne, smiling along and laughing at their jokes, but it was hard to join in.

In Her Defence

Mary's mother was frequently mentioned. She was hoping to branch out into some acting and Beaker had been helping her with it. She was on the form of her life, apparently, though as he spoke, Mary's attention drifted. She began to look at her phone. The table shook against her fidgeting knee.

'You guys not talking again?' Beaker asked, sensing the shift.

Mary shrugged and folded a thin slice of grilled courgette into her mouth. 'Anna's been busy. So have I.'

'Ah,' he said, pinching the stem of his wine glass and bringing it towards his mouth. 'You girls. Too similar. She said you'd been quiet. She's worried you might be in love.'

'Worried?' Mary's skin flushed. 'What kind of mother worries when her daughter's in love?'

'So, it's true!' Beaker cuffed his arm around her shoulders and brought her close to his chest. I thought briefly of my own mother. When I had fallen love with Polly, she worried herself to the point of open disgust.

'Do we get to hear about the lucky guy?' Beaker asked.

There was a pause then. How long did it take Mary to respond? I stared over the balcony towards the Spanish Steps and the row of designer boutiques facing the bottom of it. The streetlights were white and round, packed tightly against each other like a string of pearls. My foot searched for Mary's again under the table. She looked at me and smiled. A frisky glance. My heart raced as I tried to interpret what it meant. Between my legs, I felt a bead of pleasure.

'Not yet,' Mary said, turning back to Beaker, withdrawing a cigarette and lighting it. 'We're keeping it a secret for now. A secret because it's precious.'

At the end of the evening, just after Beaker had stumbled off to bed, blaming jet lag, a waiter arrived and placed a thick cream envelope on the table. I panicked that it was the bill, but it contained a plastic key card.

'The mad bastard,' Mary shrieked. 'He's got us a room.' She gripped my hands with excitement, clunking her emerald bracelets against the table.

'For me, too?' I was incredulous.

'Let's go!'

We charged downstairs together. Mary in the lift, me racing her down the stairs. Inside the quiet hotel corridors, I soon realised how saturated I was with alcohol. My limbs felt dangerously light, and the carpeted floor slanted upwards as I ran towards the lift and waited for Mary at the doors. When they opened, she was striking a pose, one long leg propped on the railing, her black evening dress pulled down and a tanned left breast exposed in her hand. I burst out laughing and called her a complete whore, even though my mind was fixed on the jam-brown colour of her nipple. She kissed my cheek then skipped past me, bashing the key card impatiently against the bedroom door.

It wasn't a bedroom, but a suite, spread over many floors: a series of rooms so decadently furnished, I had to remind myself to breathe. I went around, running my hands over the marble mantlepiece and its soft white beds, not wanting to think of my own shared bedroom in Termini, with its lime-green walls and concrete floors. What would Mary say, if I ever let her see it?

While I explored, Mary fiddled with the speaker and rang reception to ask for a corkscrew. On the wall was a silver button, which made me laugh with surprise. Of course, there was a lift. It brought me upwards to the top floor, a roof terrace with a view towards St Peter's, and a vast tiled bathroom with a sunken bath.

I rested on the lid of the toilet for a while and squinted, drunkenly, at my phone screen. There were three messages from Jean.

I just had a dream about you! she had written about thirty minutes before. I felt a sudden tightness in my chest. Then she texted again. *Mary was in it too!*

I exited the chat, but it was too late. Jean had already seen that I'd read it, so I would be expected to respond. Placing the phone face down by the sink, I caught sight of myself in the mirror: flushed cheeks and dopey-eyed with drink. Why was Jean's concern making me feel so irritated? I thought of what Mary said earlier: *suddenly you were this whole other person*. Part of me knew that Jean was at the root of that quiet transformation; I was growing more confident, I knew, from the sense of safety she provided. But I resented Jean for being the source of it. Ever since I'd left home, I'd prided myself on the art of self-reliance, an independence which prevented me from owing anybody anything. So, when yet another message arrived from Jean, asking if everything was okay, my response was curt:

All fine. Thanks! X

When I went back down to the living room, Mary had fixed the speaker, and was trying to get a cork out of a bottle of wine by placing it in her shoe and slapping it against the wall. It made us hysterical. I filmed her first using her stiletto, then my trainer, to make two blurry films which I considered sending to Jean. But I resisted doing so, knowing it would be smoothing over an irritation she wasn't even aware of. When Mary succeeded in removing the cork, we screamed with laughter and toasted ourselves, drinking the wine straight from the bottle. It delighted us, just how disgusting we were being.

'I can actually taste your foot,' Mary said, gargling it like a wine snob. She filmed that, too, sending a video to Beaker. 'Thank you, baby,' she cooed, turning up the music and adjusting her breasts in her reflected image as she recorded herself.

'Why is he called Beaker?' I shouted over the music. It struck me as odd that she called a man thirty years her senior, *baby*.

'Because of this.' She crouched at the glass coffee table in front of the fireplace and tapped a heap of white powder from a little bag. 'He's a fiend. Mummy named him after his nose.'

'Oh, right,' I said, joining her on the ground. 'Does he still do it?'

Mary laughed as if that was a stupid question, and retrieved more paper wraps from her clutch bag. As we knelt closely together, I suddenly saw how wasted she was. Her blue eyes were cloudy now, like beach glass. 'He left me all these.'

The hours vanished in the way they do when you're on that kind of trajectory. We drank more. Mary tipped line after line of cocaine onto the coffee table. I followed her lead, even though it was starting to have the opposite effect and I felt I was becoming more sober. Still, there was that urgent feeling. We talked earnestly about nothing I can remember. We danced, separately, and then together. With the lights on, with the lights off. We smoked, hanging out of the window, and played a demented game where you had to wear everything in the room that you could find. Mary hung a kettle from her wrist and a hairdryer round her neck, which made me cry with laughter. I wore the free condoms as ankle socks. Afterwards, we put on the bathrobes and shower caps and went down into the bath.

The sunken tub was filled dangerously high. Mary was lying fully outstretched in the scented avalanche of suds, her feet next to my ears, and her hair stuck to her face. She was spitting water at me. Swigging wine and spitting that, too. Then she praised my naked body, saying that I had the perfect female form. She told me off, when I climbed out of the water and tried to cover myself up.

'Stay for next term,' she said, watching me stretch upwards to take a towel, running the tip of her finger down the front of my thigh. 'I want to paint all of you.'

'What about Law? He won't have it.'

'Fuck Law,' she slurred. '*Hate* Law.'

There were two double beds, though Mary wanted me in hers. Together, we lay in our towels, both trying to ignore the grey daylight which was seeping into the room beneath the blinds. I closed my eyes. My body was throbbing from the heat of the bath and from every bad substance I had consumed. Next to me, Mary twitched and changed positions, turning her back against my body. I lay there, breathing deeply, driven wild by her nearness. I thought of Jean's advice, her certainty that Mary wanted me. I just had to love myself enough. I had to let myself be vulnerable.

I dared to move closer, burying my face against Mary's shoulder and reaching around to rest my hand on her warm stomach. A moment passed. Fireworks across my skin; shoots of fear through my mind as I tried to gauge Mary's thoughts. For a moment, she stiffened and I wondered if she didn't want my hand there. Was she afraid of this? Or was it me? Did she want this, but not with me? I held my breath, willing her to turn. My thumb at her navel, the rough nub of an old piercing. Much more than vulnerable; I was utterly exposed.

'Hi,' I whispered as she slowly shifted her body around to face me.

'It's you,' she said, inching closer so that our lips touched and our smiles reflected each other.

'It's me.' Trembling with uncertainty, I placed both hands on the indents of her lower back. Then she held my chin with her hand and kissed me. For several moments, she kissed me. I wanted to cry from pleasure, from sheer gratitude of it. I only pulled away when I became too afraid of making a sound.

'Wouldn't Vincenzo mind about this?' I whispered.

Her tongue ran playfully across my lips. We kissed again. Mary wriggled down and kissed my neck. 'We're casual,' she replied, her voice sleepy and close. 'He won't care.'

I hesitated, confused, but still glad she hadn't disputed my use of *this*.

'You shouldn't do it if you don't actually want to.' I meant Vincenzo but Mary misunderstood me.

'Shhh,' she said soothingly, reaching towards my stomach. 'I want to.'

My heart kept on with its jumpy rhythm. Partly from the drugs, but partly also from the panicky arrival of everything I had wanted. My throat narrowed with a swell of relief that was hard to control.

I heard myself talking quickly and nervously. 'You should stop worrying about what people think, Mary. You have so much freedom. Sometimes, I imagine I had your life—'

'—Freeness,' she whispered, drowsily, still intoxicated. There was a sad pause. She was very still in my arms, her face now resting by my ear, where my pulse was racing. The hair at the back of her neck felt wet from our bath. 'Not freedom. I don't have freedom.'

I pressed a finger to her lips, then pushed inside it. My stomach coiled in pleasure as she sucked it lightly. She told me her mouth felt numb from the coke. I brought her close to me again and kissed her for a long time, just to check how numb it was. Then we laughed.

'Mine, too, a bit,' I said.

She pushed her tongue over my teeth, my gums.

'Can you feel that?' she whispered.

Yes, yes, I could feel that. For me, nothing was numb; my nerves were drawn tight across my skin. As she placed her hands on me, every touch left an almost unbearable imprint. Too much. I was frightened of crying out again or seeming too eager. Enough now. I climbed up onto her so that she was lying flat on her back.

Could she feel that? I asked, wanting her to feel it at last. Freedom. However fleetingly. Could she feel that, I asked again, as I listened for her sighing sounds. Did she like that?

I woke up late the next day to find our bed was empty. Venturing downstairs, there was Mary in the breakfast room, barefoot, and wearing the hotel dressing gown over her evening dress. She barely acknowledged me as I joined her at the table, where she was talking with someone she knew from London. She remained sitting there, laughing and drinking coffee, when I told her I was leaving for my afternoon class. Or that's where I told Mary I was going. Instead, I went straight to Jean's.

Over text, she'd invited me for tea, promising to cook me something restorative and healthy but also – she admitted it in a jokey way – because she *just had* to know everything. By the time I finished telling Jean the story of our night, there were tears in her eyes.

'But I don't understand why Mary's ignoring me now,' I said, a little disconcerted by how moved Jean was. I showed her all the messages I had written Mary after I left the hotel. They had been read, but ignored. 'It's starting to feel like nothing actually happened,' I said. 'Like we didn't sleep together. That I imagined the whole thing.'

'Except, you didn't,' Jean replied, suddenly grave. We were sitting on her cream sofa and she wore an apron to protect her silk shirt and crepe trousers. A tray of jasmine tea and Sicilian lemon biscuits was arranged on the ottoman ahead of us. 'Don't doubt yourself,' she said, squeezing my hand. 'It absolutely happened. I believe you.'

'I feel so stupid, like I pushed her too far. I wasn't really sure what to do. She must regret it now—'

'—She doesn't regret it,' Jean said, sharply.

'How do you know?'

Jean shrugged. 'Don't forget, Gus, humans are my thing. Mary has a lot of stuff to work through. Accepting that she wants to be in a same-sex relationship will be a big deal for her. Families like hers are more conservative than they look.' She paused. 'Poor girl. I've seen this problem time and again.'

'Really?'

She told me she'd often worked with closeted girls, who'd felt trapped within aristocratic families. 'They seem permissive, but their families are *always* the problem. You could always bring her to talk to me, you do know that, don't you?'

I thought of how sadly Mary had spoken last night: *freeness, not freedom*, but when I considered introducing Mary to Jean, I felt deeply jealous. It was the idea of no longer being Jean's favourite. I thought of Mary stretching out on her sofa as I did; the pair of them eating together. I wanted that intimacy with each of them, but separately. Alone.

'So, you don't think Mary regrets it, then?' I said. 'What we did?'

Jean shook her head. 'Didn't she say your body was beautiful?' Dazed still at the memory, I nodded. 'Didn't she ask you back for next term?' Jean's mouth made a wet sound as she smiled. 'Then it sounds like we're in love!'

'Do you think so?' There were strawberries along the trim of Jean's apron. I stared at the print until the fruits jigged and blurred. She beamed at me.

'I do! And you know what else I think?'

She reached towards my chin and tilted it upwards. Her eyes were travelling all over my face and she was smiling at me proudly.

'What?'

'I think it's just what we deserve.'

GUEST V FINBOW: DAY THREE

On the day of Jean's testimony, I am early. Even now, after everything that has happened, I can't bear the thought of Jean noticing me come in late. That sickening feeling of having let her down.

But as I reach Courtroom Six, I discover that the order of the day has been slightly delayed. We are not yet allowed in because the judge has granted someone permission to give evidence privately. I must have missed the announcement yesterday amid my shock at Mary's news.

'I see you're taking such detailed notes,' Mrs Ayres comments shyly as she finds me by the locked gallery door.

'Oh,' I say, startled. 'For Anna.'

'Of course.' She hesitates, then eyes me carefully. 'And how are the Finbows getting on?'

My voice wobbles. 'Frightened,' I say. 'Mary. The baby.' Lucy continues staring at me, but tenderly now. Across her face, an expression of gentle disbelief grows. I keep on talking, speculating about who the father might be. Lucy shrugs.

'The important thing is, there's now a *he*, and not just a *she*. It's a positive sign. A crack of light in the tomb.'

'What do you mean by that?'

'Mary's got someone else in her life besides the witch. When Oriel was working with Jean, all relationships were prohibited. She wasn't allowed any social contact, boy or girl.'

'And now?' I ask, hearing hope in my voice. I want to hear of her daughter's career; of rapid recovery. I am desperate to hear the story I always heard of Oriel: *she's thriving.* Lucy gazes warily at me, her lower lip quivering. But before she can answer, the door to the gallery opens and we are ushered in.

As Jean reads the oath, a nervous hush falls over the gallery. Her appearance is altered from those elegant Roman outfits. Now, she is drab high street, wearing a navy long-sleeved cotton top with a key-hole feature at her neck. Her bob is more severe as well, though the ends of it are still neatly curled under. With a jolt of revulsion, I see how frumpish her jewellery really is: at her neck is a string of orange beads, the kind of resinous material that might trap a fly.

Then Jean glances upwards, her eyes scanning the gallery, before her attention is called away again. Although she has not seen me, my view of the witness box wobbles, and a hot lump moves up and down my throat. I lean forward to conceal the tears that are now streaking down my face and which fall onto the wiry carpet below. The mere presence of Jean in the stand has dissolved me. Almost instantly, a knot of anxious longing has formed in my stomach. I try to fix my mind on the lies she has told and the homes she has taken over. I conjure images of Mary, pregnant and sleeping on the floor.

But I am far from comfortable with this public execution. Now, as I observe her in the courtroom below, I still desperately miss the beam of Jean's attention. Her tender acceptance of who I am. All the comfort she once stood for. It shames me how much I still love her. How, despite all her false promises and everything she used me for, there is still a part of me who wants her to love me, too.

ROME, NOVEMBER

Towards the middle of November, my parents came out to visit. Fearing international call charges, they had written to me about their plan on Facebook, which I never checked, so when I finished late one night in the studio and received a long text containing the logistics of their arrival, I almost collapsed. They were due to arrive the following day.

I studied the message for signs of an ulterior motive. My parents hadn't visited me in London, let alone Rome. They never flew anywhere. I panicked, imagining that one of them might have a disease. When I met them from the airport bus, I discovered that they had won flight vouchers in the school staff raffle.

That weekend, it rained almost constantly. As I guided my parents through the different neighbourhoods I had fallen in love with, they trudged wearily alongside me, in plastic cagoules and hiking boots. Their presence made me feel painfully exposed, as if my new life was a fiction. Rome seemed more like a film set than ever, but uglier, too, as I absorbed their critical stance on what I was showing them: the tapestries by Raphael in the Vatican Museum were too dark to see. The treasure I showed them in the vaults was simply more evidence of papal corruption. Trastevere was a 'bit of a mess', thanks to the graffiti that was daubed onto the walls of its apartment blocks and restaurants. I didn't show them my apartment, for fear of their hostile assumptions once they worked out I was sharing a room with a girl.

I did my best to steer them out of Trastevere as quickly as possible, in dread of bumping into Mary or someone from the Melrose. In the Colosseum, my dad kept asking, 'Where are the lions then?' until eventually I snapped and stalked off to wait for them in a café nearby. At dinner, which we ate early, I told them that I was sitting for a portrait. They pulled confused faces at this, before changing the subject to the volume of Chinese people they'd seen that day and where their money might have come from. Then my mum tuned her narrow gaze into mine.

'Speaking of money, does this course you're on get you an actual job?' She was gripping her rucksack nervously in her lap.

'No,' I said quietly. Behind her shoulder, the Colosseum was garishly lit up in the colours of the Italian flag. 'It doesn't work like that. And it's not a course, it's a residency.'

'When's it finish?'

'Christmas,' I said, feeling a shoot of pain as I acknowledged this. Hardly six weeks away.

'And then what?' my dad interjected.

'I don't know.' I shrugged. 'Maybe I'll try and stay here. As long as my money lasts.'

'What?' said my mother. 'Live here in Italy? Why?'

My parents were suspicious of anyone who emigrated from their home country. It was running away; failing to face down your problems. I thought of Mary's offer to stay another term. The fantasy had evolved into a life where I lived in Mary's apartment. I brought us breakfast, focaccia from the bakery on Via del Moro, and we cycled to work together in the warm sunshine of a Roman spring. At the day's end, we'd sink wine and eat spaghetti with artichokes, discussing what we had made, debating every creative decision. Then my parents would be proved wrong. I wasn't running away from life. I was running towards it.

'It feels too soon to go back,' I said. 'I'm only just settling in.'

My mum delivered a slanted smile. 'It's not a special someone keeping you here, is it?'

I felt myself flush. Any attempt to discuss my feelings for Polly after the saga at school had been immediately shut down. Then I had given up trying, fearful of Mr Greening's therapy leaflets. That was years ago now, and as I studied my parents' faces, I tried to summon the self-acceptance that Jean was encouraging in me. For a moment, the world stilled. I took a breath.

'Actually, Mum, since you mention it—'

But then Dad interrupted loudly, folding his arms. '—No Italian boyfriend?'

The world animated again. Our Diet Cokes arrived. 'No, Dad,' I said, swallowing away the tightness in my throat and focusing on the menu. My parents' flat-out denial of who I was never failed to wound me, and I felt stupid for even considering a frank conversation with them. They weren't interested in the reality of who I was. They much preferred to hide.

I ordered Roman tripe that night, knowing it would freak my mum out, which it did. When the bill arrived, I calculated the figures on my phone, but my dad surprised us by offering to pay. As we left the restaurant, my parents identified which were the most expensive items on the menu. It was noted that they were mine.

On the Sunday morning, I took my parents to my studio in Monti to show them some of the pieces I was making. They nodded along as I talked, though I might as well have been speaking in Neapolitan dialect.

'This I like. This I can actually see in someone's kitchen,' my mum said.

I looked up and noticed that the jug she was holding came from a different shelf. 'Not one of mine, Mum,' I said. 'Sadly.'

It wasn't necessary to leave as early for the airport as they did, but we decided to part ways just after lunch. At Monday's sitting, when Mary asked how the weekend had gone, I maintained the fiction of their scrappy bohemianism. I said that it was *so nice* and heard myself tell lies about the restaurants we ate at, the galleries my father insisted I visit, that I so wished she'd been around to meet them.

'Lucky you,' Mary said.

When I arrived at Jean's later that week for dinner, the flat was full of lit candles. Jean was freshly showered and smelling of face cream, her hair still damp and elegantly combed back from her face. I felt a strong urge to cling onto her soft neck when she greeted me at the door, enveloping me in her warm tuberose scent.

'Oh!' Jean said, releasing me and hardening a little. 'So you didn't bring her?'

She knew that I had stayed the previous night at Mary's, and that we had spent the day together, warding off comedowns in her flat. Jean had extended the dinner invitation to us both, but I didn't feel ready to introduce them yet. I was too shaky from staying up all night and, besides, when I left Mary, she was walking towards the bathroom with a glass of wine, perky again, and heading over to Vincenzo's.

We ate pasta with lemon and olive oil alongside some pale slices of veal. Jean listened patiently as I tucked into her wine and wittered on about Mary's relationship with Vincenzo.

'I don't get why I haven't met him yet. Do you think she's afraid I'll say something?' Jean shrugged, a little stonily, but I carried on. 'This evening was the *worst*. She does this thing of trying on all her outfits in front of me. Like she enjoys me watching her get changed. It's total agony.'

I looked up to see Jean watching me carefully, a dark look on her face. 'Don't you think it's time you were just honest with Mary?'

Her sharp tone wrong-footed me. 'I thought you said I should be patient with her. Not push her into anything.' I trailed off, nervously.

Jean sighed and put down her cutlery. A sudden clatter of steel on ceramic. The darkness on her face was spreading. 'I asked you to bring her tonight so I could help the two of you. Then you overruled me. You thought better of it—'

'—She was tired—'

'—Well, *I'm* getting tired of this, Gus.' Her eyelids twitched with anger. The way she said my name caused a flood of fear. 'I can't help you both.' She pressed her palms together, tipping them in a prayer gesture. 'Not so informally. No. You're asking way too much of me.'

My cheeks burned. Jean had never spoken to me so roughly before. I stared at her, desperately trying to read her face, to understand what I had done, but she was illegible. I whispered an apology but Jean ignored it. She wiped her mouth, then picked up her fork again with purpose, stabbing it into her food.

'You have to understand, all the coaching I give you. All the support. It's my *profession*.'

Only a handful of seconds passed, but the silence felt terrible. I stared into the candle until my eyes hurt. 'Sorry,' I said, my voice croaking again. 'I thought we were friends. I was just asking as a friend.'

Jean grunted an acknowledgement. There was a slight softening in her face now; she looked thoughtful as she curled a hive of spaghetti around her fork. Sad, even.

'Correct. We are friends. I care a great deal about you. But there are also boundaries.'

'I'm sorry—'

'And people pay for my expertise. It's not something I can just keep giving away.'

'I know—'

She jabbed a thumb towards the bottle of wine that I'd drained. 'And I'm not like Mary, or those other girls,' she said, raising her eyebrows with mock-authority. 'I don't have endless reserves for you to sponge off of.'

I sat there, stunned. How wrong of me to cross Jean, to abuse her confidence and all her smoothing, consolatory words that I had started to rely so much on. I thought back to the irritation I felt on nights out when she texted me, and felt sick with guilt. I had been taking her for granted. And I must have been boring her, I realised, sitting there, eating her food and going on about Mary.

If I wasn't careful, I would push her away. Jean said I was always pushing people away.

I watched Jean's face closely, to see what she would say next. I felt a hopeless tremor in my face as I tried to smile. Our eyes met. She tried to return it but her face was too tense. She stabbed again at the food on her plate. I drew my cutlery together, unable to stomach eating. It seemed a risk to take anything more from her. To exploit her goodwill more than I already had.

Finally, she said, 'Why don't we set some time together instead, when you're a bit less over-tired? We could have some proper sessions, instead of circling these points so informally.' She managed a tight smile. 'Don't you think that would be helpful to you?'

I hesitated. In recent weeks, Jean had been suggesting how much both Mary and I would benefit from seeing her more formally. I had always registered the gifts that Jean's clients sometimes left for her on the hallway table: cartons of white roses, bottles of wine, little envelopes which I thought must contain notes of gratitude. I knew that she was transforming their lives, and I envied them for it, but the main issue was, I couldn't pay her. I'd wanted to use my small savings to extend my stay in Rome for a month or two beyond Christmas. By then, the situation with Mary might be clearer; things might have progressed into something more concrete and defined.

My voice wobbled. 'How much would it be?'

'Why don't you sleep on it?' Jean said, ignoring my question and moving abruptly to clear our plates. I tried to get up and help, but I was moving too slowly and clumsily to be of any use. 'Give it some proper thought,' she said, glancing towards the door. 'That would give me my evening back, anyway. I have work to do.'

Jean didn't respond to any of my messages or calls until the following Saturday. I spent the interceding days in a state of restless regret. It was the first time, apart from my parents, that I felt I had truly hurt someone. I sent a written note of apology and multiple texts. Once or twice, I buzzed her door, desperate to make amends. When she didn't reply, I felt frantic. Jean had been my compass in Rome, and without her, I was lost. Finally, as a last resort, I mentioned Mary, a subject that always engaged her.

A lot's happening with Mary & I miss talking to you! We could go for lunch, my treat? I really am so sorry.

Then – relief – on Saturday morning, a few messages arrived. She had been in London, tied up with the problematic client she'd mentioned before: Oriel.

You sound troubled, Gus. Is everything ok? x
Not really.

We arranged to meet later that afternoon on the Ponte Sisto.
Don't be late x

Jean claimed her obsession with lateness stemmed from the fact she was a worrier. Five minutes late, and she'd convince herself that something had occurred. It was all thanks to her avid imagination, she admitted. The intrusive thoughts she suffered from, which led her to believe that bad things had happened to me. So I arrived at the Ponte Sisto early that afternoon with a full fifteen minutes to spare.

The bridge was filled with Saturday shoppers: Roman couples wearing metallic puffy coats and smart boots gripping each other's gloved hands. I envied all of them; the contents of their thick paper shopping bags and the warmth of the homes they were returning to. I leaned over the side of the bridge and looked out at the Tiber: the river was high, its grey surface swirling and unreflective. Then I squinted further off towards Mary's apartment building, trying to see if her lights were on or not.

Jean drew up alongside me and nudged my elbow. The damp air had flattened her hair and she was dressed in a navy trench coat. Her lips were lightly painted red, in the way she sometimes fixed her face when she left the house.

'I'm so sorry, Jean, for making you feel used,' I said, staring straight ahead. 'I can't stop thinking about it. It's horrible.'

Jean reached over and smoothed a strand of my hair. 'Can I tell you what I don't like feeling, Gus?' Her warm hand lingered by my ear.

I turned to her and sniffed. 'Go ahead.'

'I don't like feeling that I can't fully help you. It makes me feel hamstrung.' Her hand drew around to my chin, lifting my face upward. 'I want to help you, Gus,' she went on. 'You've been through such a lot.'

'Have I?'

She stared at me with concern. 'Think of what you've faced: parental abandonment, heartbreak, professional disappointments, financial precarity.' I looked away, though as she spoke, I was surprised that I didn't feel bad, I only felt seen. 'But it's actually your relationship with Mary that I'm most concerned about. You're getting in your own way. You're letting her hurt you, instead of love you.'

I laughed a little, though this idea stung. I didn't want to push Mary away. I wanted a relationship with her, and for my life to be a success. Suddenly, I was determined. I'd use my overdraft to pay Jean. It was a small price to improve myself; to become worthy of a relationship with Mary.

Jean nodded towards the apartment buildings that ran along the Lungotevere. 'Which building is hers, then?'

I showed her the balcony and the metal gate which allowed you to enter the colonnade by her front door. Then, suddenly, from behind us there was a loud cry: *Guarda!* Someone near us on the bridge pointed up, and above us, in the lilac grey sky, a huge black shape appeared: thousands of tiny birds flying together, warping and shifting like moving clouds.

'Oh, look!' Jean gasped, reaching into her bag and removing a pair of binoculars. 'Look,' she said, gazing upwards. 'Look, they've come!'

The sky above us was thick with little birds. Standing alongside each other, we watched them flying, marvelling at the miraculous synchrony of it and the different shapes the swarms made: helix ladders which curved into spheres, then neat columns which warped into zig-zag shapes.

I smiled up at the sky in astonishment. 'How do they know where to go? How to follow each other?'

Jean lowered her binoculars and let her eyes linger affectionately on my face. 'Somehow, they just do,' she said. 'They communicate with each other, somehow.'

We stayed watching as the birds swooped lower in the sky, now making the shape of a flat, spinning disc. As neatly and tightly as they flew, I still couldn't help noticing the few birds that fell out of sync as the shape shifted. They flew off, dizzy and bewildered, alone. It was as if they'd just got it wrong, or they were distracted by something, a beam of light, perhaps, a different sound, another rhythm. For whatever reason, they had lost their place in the swarm, in the pattern of things.

I rested my head on Jean's shoulder as we watched the birds. It was a huge relief that things were fine between us again. She must have felt it, too, because she let her head rock lightly against mine.

'When do we start, then?' I asked, quietly.

She made a satisfied sound. 'If you're ready, tonight.'

'What do I pay you?' I asked, feeling my heart race at the expense of what I was signing up for.

Jean hushed me, placing an arm over my shoulder and bringing me close. 'We don't have to discuss that now.'

'I mean it,' I said, glancing up at her. 'I'll pay.'

'We'll sort it out,' she said. 'Nothing right away. I know you'll make it up to me somehow.' I felt a puzzling twinge again at this, nervous that it would open me up to another accusation of abusing her time, but Jean seemed more relaxed now. 'Pay me back by spreading the word. When you're a famous artist back in London, you can tell everyone about me.' This time I laughed, and she kissed the top of my head. 'No, Gus, I'm only asking for you to be happy.'

'Then you've got a deal,' I joked.

She squeezed my hand. 'I'm only asking for that. That and your dedication.'

GUEST V FINBOW: DAY FOUR

Your dedication. My dedication. Jean's dedication.

As she opens her questioning, Ms Ibrahim paints a deeply loyal portrait of her client.

'You are a committed practitioner,' she announces. 'Many of your clients attest to the miraculous impact that your specialism, hypnotic regression therapy, has had on their lives.'

'Thank you,' Jean says, using a deeper voice than normal.

'Will you explain how your sessions work?'

She straightens and smiles. 'It's a broad church. We use the term to encompass hypnotic methods of accessing the past. As we proceed backwards, we revisit and re-evaluate certain events. I monitor my client's bodily reactions as we liberate what the subconscious has repressed. This might be what we call "trauma with a big T", such as abuse or neglect. It could equally be "trauma with a little t": moments of humiliation, shame; micro-events of cruelty that have a profound impact on us as adults.'

I listen, appalled. When we began our work together in Rome, there was no talk of trauma, no big T or little t. I wasn't aware that Jean had a specialism. Even by the third or fourth session, the names of formal methodologies were never mentioned; Jean made no oblique references to hypnosis or repressed memories. We simply talked. And, as we talked, Jean listened to the parts of me that I couldn't hear myself. The parts, she explained, that I had chosen not to hear.

'In your statement, you acknowledge that regression therapy has, in the past, attracted some controversy,' Ms Ibrahim goes on, the corners of her mouth turned down, to show that this is not a concession of much significance. 'Is that still the case?'

'It is,' Jean says. 'Some members of our community have not witnessed its beautifully liberating impact.'

'Would you say that there is any methodology within psychotherapy which is free from controversy?'

Jean shakes her head. She lists other disciplines that she is an expert in. Reiki, emotional tapping, somatic coaching, EDMR. internal family systems therapy. 'It's hard to think of one which is not criticised by someone on the peripheries.'

Her statement triggers a hum of discontent from around the gallery. Anna shakes her head and whispers, cynically, in Ms Carr's ear.

'Methodologies such as mine, which are, at the vanguard, so to speak, will always receive criticism. Regression therapy is a beautiful, powerful, sometimes horrifying mess of ideas. The same as any academic discipline.'

Ms Ibrahim raises her voice. 'Is it your view that Mrs Finbow has exploited its controversy in order to defame your reputation?'

Jean's face hardens. She is unequivocal. 'Yes.'

'And why is that?'

'Because the issues that have arisen in her daughter's sessions were not acceptable to her.'

'And these were issues that Mary Finbow approached you about, of her own accord. Correct?'

'Correct. Mary Finbow came to me for the same reason my other clients come to me. She was facing grave difficulties and seeking guidance.'

My pulse quickens. The hardness in my throat reappears.

'Yet, it is Mrs Finbow's absolute view that you actively seek your clients out; that you "recruit" victims to proliferate your network. The programme in Rome, where some of your previous clients happened to have studied, was a feeding ground for you.' Ms Ibrahim tips her head to the side to show she is playing devil's advocate. 'The actions, so to speak, of a cult leader. What is your response to this?'

It pains me to think of how I misconstrued Jean as a slightly tragic figure at the model casting. Then again, when I admired her quiet grace, as she stood in the doorway at CRETA and asked me all those flattering questions about my work. At the time, I thought she was interested in me; cared for my potential. Had she pinpointed Mary as early as then?

'The defendant's notion is absurd,' Jean says sharply. 'I don't seek out clients on a financial basis. I have always generated good income from my practice, but I use that to support those on harder incomes.' There is a pause, as if Jean's lawyer wants us all to witness her client's act of great charity. Then Jean makes a gulping sound. 'I'm sorry,' she says, picking tears from her eyes with a fingernail, 'to get emotional. It's just that, designing courses of treatment for my clients requires a great deal of thought and expertise. What I discuss with the defendant's daughter is confidential; her business, or *our* business, only. I don't follow a particular schema or framework, I just try to make things work for my girls on an individual basis. All I have ever wanted was to give them freedom.' Jean's voice wobbles and I feel a wave of revulsion at the clumsy way she has admitted *girls*; a concession her lawyer ignores.

'You mention your own personal physical and emotional struggles as a result of the stress of these proceedings,' Ms Ibrahim asks gently, a sympathetic expression on her face. 'Could you expand on that?'

Jean shudders. 'I cannot overstate how the stress has affected me. To suddenly have your motives treated with suspicion. I have struggles sleeping. I suffer frequently from panic attacks, nightmares, hypervigilant episodes. I can't even go out for a walk because I am being followed by private detectives. The only thing that helps me is working.' Jean gives a little gasp. 'And Mrs Finbow has taken that from me.'

'How would you describe the emotional impact, as these clients, regular clients, began to cancel their work with you?' Ms Ibrahim asks with pity.

'Severe,' says Jean. She blinks, takes a deep breath. 'It was hard not to take their actions personally.'

'Could you expand on that?'

'It's not just the time I clear in my diary,' Jean says. 'It's not simply about the loss of income or cancelled appointments.' Again, she gulps, and her shoulders hunch over. I look away. Jean may be suffering, or this may simply be acting. Either way, I can't bear to watch.

'You see,' Jean says, then hiccups. 'When I begin working with a client,' she says, gesturing to her heart, 'she takes up residence in here. She enters me. We live within each other.' Jean pauses and looks towards Anna. A slight smirk crosses her face. 'Like a Russian doll.'

My chest beats wildly as I hear her use Anna's phrase: such a neat gesture of intimidation. Cruel. Scarcely detectable. And I hate her.

ROME, NOVEMBER

Jean assured me that the anxiety and restlessness I felt, once we began our formal coaching, was perfectly normal. I was feeling compromised, apparently, because I was letting someone in.

'You've never done that before,' she said. 'Or, no one has ever *permitted* you to do that before.'

Jean called our sessions my *healing time* and her plush, white living room was my *healing space*. We met in the middle of the day and talked until mid-afternoon. Often, she took audio recordings of our conversations and shared them with me afterwards. After we were done, I'd walk back to the studio, or over to the Melrose school, playing them back to myself; something that Jean insisted I do, as a way of sealing our observations into my subconscious mind. This was the first of a series of rules she later came to insist upon. But, of course, she didn't call these rules at the time. Like the homework she asked me to do, and the books I was to read, they were presented like common principles or *terms of our engagement*.

Here was one: *don't tell anyone about our sessions, Gus, not yet. Keep it sacred.*

And another: *There's no right or wrong in this room. No true or false. My only role is to listen and reflect back what I hear.*

What Jean reflected back was the idea that most of my troubles were caused by other people: my parents, my teachers, my earliest friendships. Such a seductive concept, or so it seemed at the time, to believe all my issues were not intrinsic to me, but had an external cause. Finally, I thought, I could crawl out from under the weight of my own mind and look outwards. Initially, that felt brighter. For a while, my brain felt flossed clean.

Not only clean, but my mind developed a heightened sensitivity to everything around me. I became hyper-aware to the beating heart of everything, and everyone, I encountered. Tripping along Corso Vittorio Emanuele after our sessions, the colours of Rome were never more vivid: the ice blue of the winter sky wrestled with the bright yellow facades of the stately government buildings; the suffering of everyone I witnessed was painfully evident, but also solvable. When I went to galleries, the artworks acted like a narcotic, transmitting new meanings, bringing me to higher planes of understanding. It was a fallacy, I realised, when people said therapy made you self-centred or too introspective. For the first time in my life, I felt capable of looking outwards. And it was stark how others had treated me; how I had treated myself. And it was lightness: the root of my issues was *them*, not *me*.

Before long, the injustices began to accumulate. I found it hard to take responsibility for anything I did. Instead of feeling liberated, as Jean suggested I should, I began to feel defensive.

My peers on the residency were generally complimentary about my pieces, but, as the pressure built, I grew hotly aware of their criticism. After one feedback session, where Thea and my classmates had criticised the handle on a vase I had made, I found myself colouring and turning away from them all, unable to face the brute truth that it just wasn't good enough. That evening, while I was trying to fix it, Thea approached me.

'Don't take it so personally, Gus,' Thea said, clutching her scratched Vespa helmet. 'I know it can feel a little raw, but we trust each other here. Honesty is part of the deal. It helps us improve.'

'Their negativity,' I said, through gritted teeth. 'It's blocking me.'

Thea zipped up her leather jacket and looked at me with concern. 'I don't understand what you mean.' Still sulking, I mumbled that it didn't matter, and turned back to my work. Thea continued, in the Italian accent I used to admire, 'We're here to play, Gus. Not to be perfect. Before, you were braver. You had a thicker skin. Is something the matter?'

I shrugged and said nothing, hating how fractiously I was acting, the resentment that was growing, just because Thea wasn't indulging me in the way I had grown accustomed to from Jean.

'*A domani,*' I said in a flat voice.

Rebuffed, Thea wished me goodnight. I listened for the sound of her bike starting up, and then, only when I was certain that she wasn't coming back, I picked up the vase. I turned it over in my hand for a moment, feeling the innate failure in it; the lumps in its base, how unbalanced it was. The sound of the bike died away. I threw the vase – the faulty, ugly thing – so that it smashed into pieces across my studio floor. It made a chiming sound as it fell, a brief howl, then I stepped on the fragments, grinding them into smaller and smaller pieces under my feet until they turned to nothing, to dust.

I didn't tell Jean about breaking my work. Although our conversations were far-reaching, some things I still held back. Time and again, she brought up my tendency to self-sabotage, not only with work, but also with Mary. I couldn't admit that I wasn't evolving out of that mindset. Unless I showed progress, I worried that Jean might feel she was wasting her energy and lose interest in me.

As I feared a day when Jean might grow impatient, I tried to chase those thoughts away by telling myself that she needed me as much as I needed her. I loved it when she explained that the patient-therapist relationship was reciprocal, and that we were in a healing cycle together.

'We're a waltzing couple, Gus. You're helping me as much as I'm helping you,' she insisted, whenever I expressed gratitude for her insight, for her time, for her generosity.

Jean had often hinted about her frustrated desire for children, though I always felt hesitant to ask her why it hadn't happened. Then, one afternoon, she opened up about it. We were in her living room, as usual. On the ottoman between us were Jean's infinite supply of tissues and a warm teapot. There had been a miscarriage in her thirties, she explained, devastatingly late term. In a half-sedated state, she'd been forced to deliver the foetus.

'It was my one real chance of a family. And I was going to have a girl.' Her gaze lifted over my shoulder towards the window, then back at me. The plump look of her skin was gone, her under-eyes looked hollow and grey. 'Then, the strangest thing. The night after I met you, I began dreaming of my lost daughter again.'

I gasped, touched by the connection. It made me feel powerful, the fact that I could influence her dreams like that. I leaned forward. 'You know,' I began, gently, 'I read somewhere that when you have a baby, even if you never bring it to term, their genes stay inside you.' There was a pause. The sound of the refrigerator in the kitchen, the jerking hands of her mantlepiece clock. 'So, whatever happened to your ... daughter. You'll carry that genetic code inside you forever.'

'Oh,' said Jean, removing her glasses. 'Like a Russian doll.'

'I don't know if it's my place to say, or if it helps to think of it like that.'

'It does, Gus, thank you. Goodness.' She dabbed at the corners of her eyes with a fingertip. 'Look at me, blubbing. I do apologise. That's not the way it's meant to go.'

'It's okay,' I said, smiling. 'I'm so happy to help—'

'—It should be me making you cry.'

I hesitated, feeling a stab of worry that I wasn't producing enough tears for Jean. Next time, I would try harder, I decided. Next time, I would break down.

'How do you get over something like that? With the baby, I mean.'

'For years, I didn't. I was so blocked by it. Not unlike you.'

I felt a shiver. 'Then what happened?'

Jean's eyelids flickered. 'I underwent some very deep therapy,' she said. 'It prevented me looping over the memories of what had occurred. Being so haunted by the trauma.'

There was a pause while I considered how that might go. 'Was it like this?' I asked.

'A little more intense, perhaps,' she said, chuckling. Then she fell serious. 'A little more productive.'

Jean explained it occurred under hypnosis, and that following her own successful treatment, she practised it with others. 'Those who are ready, I mean.'

'And it helped?'

Jean spoke quietly. 'It has changed my life.'

I brought my legs up onto the sofa and crossed them beneath me. I wondered if I should be going deeper, revealing more of the thoughts I was holding back.

'How does it work?'

'Well, initially you relax. Then you go right back to your earliest memories. The things that first made you really unhappy. Our original traumas, if you like. You go over and over them.'

'Isn't that hard?'

'At first, yes. Then you release it. You rewire them in a way that causes you less pain.'

'What if it's not the past that's troubling you, what if it's just today?' My brain was swimming with all the things that worried me: my bank balance, the sitting later on with Mary, and the Melrose School Christmas party, which was fast approaching.

Jean shook her head, gently. 'It's always about the past.'

I leaned back in the sofa and crossed my arms. 'What if you've managed to forget all the bad stuff? What's the point in dragging it back up again?'

Jean studied me with a serious expression. Her lips were making the small, trembling movements that occurred occasionally when something had captured her attention. Then she broke into a smile.

'How funny, Gus. This is precisely what Oriel used to say! And gosh, you should see how she's flourishing now, back in Britain. I'm so proud of her! She's carved a completely new life for herself.

Unrecognisable. New career path, a brand-new set of friends. She's *untethered.*' I swallowed a stone of envy. She went on, 'We never actually forget, Gus. We just can't bear to remember. There's so much we actively repress, but, in the end, this coping mechanism hinders us. We're blocked by it.' Her lips twitched and pressed together. 'If you like, we could try it today? I think you're ready. We've made such brilliant progress together.'

There was a pause. As I stared up at the chandelier that hung overhead, I thought about how often Jean described me as '*blocked*'. Then my mind reached towards my earliest memories: there was the soothing separateness of the art block at school; the starched collar of my father's shirt I wore backwards as my painting smock; the first time I held clay. The memories from home were hazier. Had my mind made it that way? I conjured images from my childhood bedroom. The floral pattern of my wallpaper and curtains, a taunting crack of summer-evening light beneath it. Down the hallway, our plastic bathroom, and the jar of bath pearls that I would squeeze between my thumb and index finger until they burst, covering my hand in an exciting, sticky fluid. My childhood home was a downcast place, subdued with things unspoken. When I thought of it now, my memories were hazy. Was that because nothing had happened, or had my mind suppressed other things?

Then I had met Polly. My memories of that moment in Mr Greening's office were not hidden; they haunted my waking thoughts. How often, I asked myself, as I watched the chandelier above reflect flecks of winter sunlight around the room, did those memories flash back? Too often. Was this the source of my shame, I wondered? If I went back to that moment now, could it be remoulded, or perhaps cut out?

'How do you put me under?' I asked Jean, in a voice which already sounded different from my own. 'It doesn't hurt or anything, does it?'

Jean chuckled. 'It actually starts with a massage. Just on the head.' She hesitated, and then she uttered the words which I have played and replayed in my mind ever since.

Jean sought my permission. 'Are you sure you're comfortable with this?'

And because I trusted Jean, I told her: yes.

Jean made me shimmy down the sofa and lie flat so that my feet were hanging off the other end. Then I was to shut my eyes and let everything soften. She knelt behind me and then, for a number of minutes, she ran her fingertips over my scalp. Right away, I fell into a deep sleep, my head and neck falling slack like a puppet's. When she shook me awake, I was groggy.

'I've dribbled everywhere,' I said, wiping my mouth, grateful to feel my bladder still full.

Jean sighed deeply, and went back over to her chair. 'Yes, but how do you feel?'

'Dead,' I said. 'What time is it?'

I'd slept for over twenty minutes, but Jean assured me that didn't matter, she had plenty of time. She suggested I stay in that position, with my neck relaxed and my eyes closed. The first game was to walk her through my favourite rooms.

'A guided tour of your happy places,' she said. 'Just talk. Don't think.'

I spoke first about Mary's bedroom, the cathedral proportions of it, the scenes depicted in pastel blues and pinks on her ceiling frescoes. Then I mentioned Jean's own apartment, and how safe I found it here. My breathing was deep, I noticed, as I described those places. I was making involuntary sounds, in and out of my nose, as if I wasn't quite conscious. When we moved further back in time, to rooms from my childhood, I started speaking without thinking. I recalled tiny details from the church hall where I'd played during the summer holidays: the blue bean bags I curled up on; the brightly coloured hula hoops I spun around my waist; the shelves of tatty books in the corner. The words were falling fast out of me. It was astonishing, how much detail my mind had preserved, and that Jean was unlocking.

'Keep taking deep breaths,' she instructed. Then, in a low, suggestive voice, she asked me to describe my unhappy places. Instantly, there was a slow, sinking feeling. I began to describe Mr Greening's study.

'What does it smell like?'

'Dusty bibles,' I stammered. 'And gas, too, I think there's a gas fire.'

Jean went deeper into the scene. 'You're in uniform, aren't you?'

'Yes.'

'What does it feel like?' I hesitated. 'Is it scratchy?'

'Very,' I said. 'Woollen. Too warm. Heavy.'

'And who is next to you now?'

There was a pain in my chest, as though someone was trying to force it open. 'My mum,' I heard myself say. 'She looks so disappointed. She even asks for help. She says, "is there anything I can do?"' Tears were racing down my cheeks, the only part of me that moved. My body was paralysed.

'That's cruel of her.' Jean whispered. 'She's letting you down. Both of your parents are betraying you in this moment.' I opened my mouth and gulped. No words came. 'What would you say to that girl today, Gus? What would you say to yourself?'

My voice choked. 'Not to worry.' There was silence. Eventually, I tried again, a little louder. 'That what you did with Polly was okay. It wasn't a crime.'

'Good. Again, please.' Jean's voice seemed to be everywhere.

My jaw clenched. I felt the muscles in my stomach curl inwards. 'It wasn't a crime.'

Jean's voice was kind. 'It was love and love is good.' Her tone turned insistent. 'Repeat it again, please.'

I hesitated. I opened my eyes. The light was altered now. The room had brightened and the chandelier crystals were refracting rainbows on the opposite wall. I tried it again. Jean's eyes were still closed, as if we were praying together.

It wasn't a crime. We chanted it like a mantra. *It was love and love is good.*

We went through several rounds of this before Jean announced that she would be closing the session.

'You see, Gus.' Her voice was louder now, more matter-of-fact. 'Our memory functions a bit like a roll of film or my tape recorder here. It's all in there, we just have to spool backwards to the difficult parts.'

There was a pause. I hadn't noticed her recorder on the side table. The idea that she had copied any of what I had just uttered, tied a knot in my stomach. Before I could ask her about it, Jean rose and came over to me. Kneeling by the sofa, she held me in an embrace so close it brought me back to consciousness.

'Well done,' she whispered, her voice warm in my ear. 'It's hard, but we can't love unless we release this.'

My mind turned to Mary. I closed my eyes and opened them again, blinking away tears as Jean cradled me tightly.

'Thank you, Jean,' I said, between gulps.

'Your parents let you down,' Jean said, clasping my head to her lips. 'They were cruel.'

'I hate them for it.'

'So let's rewind the tape, Gus. Who is teaching you love now?' Over her shoulder, the chandelier cast flecks of light: red, yellow and violet, swerving, dancing around the room.

'You are,' I whispered.

GUEST V FINBOW: DAY FOUR

'In the United Kingdom, anyone can claim to be a therapist,' Ms Carr announces to Justice Larkin as she commences her cross-examination of Jean. 'There are regulatory bodies, such as the BACP but one is not obliged to belong to them in order to establish a practice. The qualifications that Ms Guest uses as evidence of her training can be purchased on the internet this evening for under five hundred pounds.' The judge watches her thoughtfully, his pen lifted. 'Truly, in twenty-four hours, Your Lordship could claim to be a healer, life coach and *even* a therapist, giving you direct access to extremely vulnerable people.' Ms Carr then turns back to Jean, who regards her stonily. 'Which brings me, Ms Guest, to my first question, if I may. If anyone can claim to be a therapist, can any type of interaction be excused as a therapeutic session?'

'Of course not,' Jean quips.

'Enlighten me. What differentiates an interaction – say, this exchange – from a therapeutic session?'

'Therapists proceed from a source of healing. Whereas you are here with an agenda: to interrogate me and, with respect, make me out to be something that I'm not.'

Ms Carr raises her eyebrows. 'You have no agenda with your clients?'

'My only agenda is to alleviate their suffering.'

Ms Carr scoffs. 'If you were only alleviating suffering, we wouldn't be in this courtroom, would we?' She turns and addresses the public gallery as if we are a jury. 'Look at them up there,' she booms. 'Look these people in the eyes. You can't claim that your work *saves* people. On the contrary, it breaks up families. Your clients may, in a legal sense, be adults when they commence work with you, but they are eventually reduced to missing children:

isolated, lost in the world, dependent on only you, their charismatic leader. So tell me, Ms Guest, how precisely do you do it? What happens in your sessions?'

'There are few parameters. I listen to my clients. That is my primary role. To listen and reflect back what I hear.'

'Do you seek your patients' consent for the methods you use?'

Jean tilts her chin upwards, as if summoning the higher powers she claimed to channel. 'I'm not sure I understand the question.'

'You said yourself that your methods are controversial. It would make sense to gain consent, wouldn't it? Especially in view of the complaints that have been made against you?'

'It's not really my role to keep a record of things.'

'Are you sure? That's certainly not what some of your ex-clients attest. They say the exact opposite, and that they witnessed you recording their private sessions. Do you confirm this?

'I have, on occasion, recorded a session with a client for the purposes of later analysis. Or for them to return back to.'

'Is this why you ban your clients from listening to music? So they can hear themselves on repeat?'

'I don't ban anything. I suggest improvements. And if my clients didn't like how we worked, they wouldn't come back to me, or recommend me to their friends. It's as simple as that.'

Ms Carr frowns. 'Yet we have statements from ex-clients of yours who wouldn't recommend you at all. They were, in fact, very disturbed by the treatment they received from you. Some claim you performed hypnotherapy on them without their express permission.' Jean's face colours, as the lawyer studies her notes. 'According to Temerlin's definition that we agreed in pre-hearing, hypnosis reduces the individual to a highly suggestible state, allowing any newly formed conclusions or beliefs they may hold upon waking to be easily tainted or corrupted. Ms Guest, in your sessions, it is clear that your clients don't access memories that really occurred. Under your manipulation, they fabricate them. Ms Guest, allow me to just confirm with you some of the *memories* your ex-clients have uncovered during the last two decades. Across pages 670-725, we have statements from two ex-clients, who began to recall memories that suggested their parents participated in paedophile rings, committing deplorably violent and sickening acts. From page 800 onwards, we have a statement from another client who, after only one or two sessions, suddenly began to recall histories of sexual abuse from within the close family network. When these clients terminate sessions with you – as some of the lucky ones do – and are rehabilitated, they realise that these events did not actually occur at all. They all attest to how excruciatingly painful this realisation is.' She pauses for a moment, staring meaningfully at Jean. 'Some never recover.'

Jean glances, nervously, towards Ms Ibrahim. 'I don't— I don't think I am obliged to comment on specific cases.'

'Then can you confirm the following dates upon which you received letters threatening legal action?' Ms Carr then reads out a long sequence of dates, spanning the last twenty years. Jean confirms each one, looking as if she is having to swallow something that is spiked.

'One ex-client, who cannot be named, even lodged a statement with the Metropolitan Police, claiming that you were blackmailing her with the material you recorded. Can you confirm that you were brought in for questioning on three separate occasions?'

'Yes, but they found nothing against me,' says Jean, with her head bowed.

'And how could they?' Ms Carr cries with exasperation. 'You're not bound to any code of conduct, are you?'

This comment provokes a hum of excitement in the gallery, though down in the courtroom, Justice Larkin issues a final warning to Ms Carr for her commentary. She apologises, then changes course, to confirm the details of Mary's property management. I bunch my fists to hear how much rent this is earning her. Then a far darker thought occurs: Jean, living in one of these London residences with Mary's child. It cannot be allowed to happen, I decide. I must not let that happen.

'I do not control what Ms Finbow chooses to do with her financial assets. Ms Finbow felt responsible for the loss of my other clients, thanks to her mother's vicious campaign. She has chosen, temporarily, to support me through her property, because that is more efficient. I am grateful for her support, but she is not duty bound to do so.'

Ms Carr sighs and folds her arms. 'Why did you continue working with Ms Finbow, if the relationship impacted your earnings to the degree you have accounted for? Why keep going, if, as you say, your professional standing is being shredded?'

Jean's lips tremble. 'Because my clients come to me with deeply embedded trauma, and I make a commitment to them. This was the case with the defendant's daughter. When we began working together, she was extremely damaged. There was a huge amount to unravel throughout her childhood.'

Jean presses her palms together. I glance at the back of Bonamy's head and imagine, queasily, what many in the courtroom might be thinking: that he is the cause. My heart aches for him.

'All I want, all I have ever wanted, is to help Ms Finbow,' Jean continues. 'The same goes for everyone I work with.'

There is a pause and Jean looks upwards towards the gallery. I try to look away but Jean's gaze latches on to mine. My pulse races. Her smile is one of mutual recognition: *I know you know.* Then another, perhaps worse look, crosses her face.

It is a different smile, broader and threatening: *I forgive you.*

ROME, DECEMBER

As we entered December, it wasn't the end of my residency, but the date of the Melrose School Christmas party that loomed pathetically large in my mind. It was the twelfth of December, and soon after it, the students would be going home. In bars and at dinners, I overheard them discussing their glamorously full Christmas diaries: the big dinners they had planned, then Boxing Day departures for the West Indies, or to Scotland for Hogmanay. It stung me to realise that the holidays signified no severance at all to the students' relations. Life in London, or beyond, would continue as it did here, only with a slightly wider social set, which accommodated the siblings, cousins, and friends that they often talked about.

During our sittings, I often asked Mary about whether I could model again next year, but she remained vague. She still needed to check with Lawrence. So, I tried to be flexible and act like it wasn't a big deal. I didn't want her to know the truth: that my staying on in Rome to be near her and Jean – what was starting to feel like my future happiness – depended on the work, and, of course, the payment, she could give me.

When the day of the party came, I lay weakly in bed, studying the invite: a thick tablet of embossed cardboard. There were no concrete details printed on it, only the theme. This year, it was the age of the Roman emperor Nero. I thought that it was a pretentious thing, getting your guests to google the dress code. That was back when I thought the worst thing about Lawrence was that he was pretentious.

I texted Mary for more information. We hadn't spoken much that week. There had been a break in our sittings, while she flew to New York to look around a design school for the next academic year that I desperately hoped she wouldn't get into.

Bourgeois question but do you know time, place etc? I'm coming as a centaur by the way.

She responded, though not until the afternoon.

It's in the old hospital on the island in the middle of the Tiber. Easy to find. Big yellow building. Will be lit up.

A minute later, she added:

Etc

Over the phone, Jean advised me how to get there. I was to cross over the river at the Ponte Cestio. Then, at the tower of St Bartholomew's church, turn right.

'You know, there's a great story about that hospital,' she said. The phone was propped on the side while I changed outfits to show her what I would be wearing. 'During the war, this heroic doctor managed to protect a group of Jews by pretending they were very sick when the Nazis arrived. He got them to present with all these symptoms, coughing like lepers, and claiming all these ailments. He diagnosed them with a made-up illness called Syndrome K, so the Nazis were afraid and wouldn't have anything to do with them. He saved hundreds of lives,' she murmured. 'What a good man.'

I was half listening, worrying about my outfit, when Jean interrupted my thoughts.

'Don't wear that,' she suddenly said sharply, pointing through the screen at a tunic I'd got in a tourist shop.

'What's wrong with it?'

'It's a *costume party*,' she said, and her lips twitched. 'Not fancy dress. There's a difference. Plus, I don't think Mary will like it.'

How do you know? I thought with a shiver of resentment. *You haven't met her yet.*

The large yellow building with the green shutters was lit up in the darkness, exactly as Mary had said. Flares in the grass marked the wooden doors at the hospital's entrance. I crossed the threshold, wielding my invite like a passport, but no one stopped me. Instead, a tall waitress took my coat, then another one smiled and passed me a glass of cold, clear alcohol.

The reception was held in the old apothecary. The space was huge, but the guests filled it easily. It smelt of damp stone, sweetened with the same fig scent that Lawrence used in the bathrooms at the school. And Jean was right: the dress code had been interpreted immaculately. The guests were all wearing ornate costumes that looked more like museum pieces or antiques than fancy dress.

I adjusted the laurel crown that I had sprayed with gold paint, and looked around for Mary. She was hard to find. Most of the guests were blonde and almost all were as tall as she was. But none were as beautiful. It was strange to see so many adults present. The only parties I'd ever attended were designed to escape them, but here, I noticed, there was no generational divide. The younger students interacted seamlessly with older guests, calling them nicknames, taking photos and sharing cigarettes.

Someone touched me on the shoulder. It was Mary. I beamed as I took in her blue toga, the braids in her hair, the jewel in the centre of her forehead. I drew her in for a hug. She smelt like an Italian hair salon, of cigarettes and hairspray.

'I missed you,' I whispered, not daring to ask about New York yet.

When we pulled apart, Mary kissed me on the cheek, then glanced anxiously over my shoulder. 'I have to go,' she murmured. 'Find me later.'

I turned. There, approaching, at long last, was the famous Anna Finbow. She was shorter than she looked on TV and her skin, in person, was a richer pale. Her dark hair was piled onto the top of her head and decorated with lots of little paper butterflies, which were also fastened to her plump chest and the tips of her eyelashes. I stood aside as she waltzed up to Mary, brought her cheek against hers in the performative guise of a kiss, then pointed down at some mark on her toga. Hastily, Mary attended to it, while I lingered there, hopeful for an introduction. But Lawrence swooped in.

'It's the love of my life!' he said to Anna. Looking straight into her face, he shook his head in wonder. 'Is it possible you're actually getting *better* with age?'

Anna laughed and hit him playfully with the back of her hand. In response, he Hollywood-dipped her and pretended to kiss her neck. Everyone around them laughed. Everyone, except Mary, who gave a disgusted look, turned, and downed her glass of champagne. I tried to catch her eye, to signal that I also saw how excruciating this was, but she wouldn't look at me. Her cheeks were flushed red and her eyes were wide with an emotion – embarrassment, maybe, or anger – that I couldn't quite identify.

As I moved around the room, I took every drink, impatiently waiting for the tipping point to happen, when I'd get to find Mary again. I wanted the stuffy atmosphere to lift, and for the party chaos to descend. I wanted the adults to leave so that we could take charge.

First, though, there was the meal to get through. The man sitting next to me asked where I had gone to school. Uninterested in my answer, he turned away from me and spent most of the meal speaking to his female neighbour on the other side. The chair next to mine was empty, so I had no other choice but to listen into their conversation. At one point during the pasta course, I heard them discussing, a student from here. Her name, when I picked it up, was familiar to me. Oriel.

'Seriously talented girl,' the woman was saying. 'I sat in on her interview. She should have been at one of the London schools, really. She was quite brilliant. Very, you know, *intense*. And then, one day, she just stopped coming. Went completely AWOL.'

'Do you know,' the man said, 'I heard about this from someone else. Wasn't some guru involved?'

My wine turned sour. Rattled, I waited for a break in their exchange, wanting to ask what Oriel's surname was, but then there was a sudden tapping on the microphone from the stage: Lawrence's speech was about to begin. What was the point in delving further? I had no clue about Oriel's full name, and it couldn't be the same girl. Jean had said her client was thriving.

'Can you hear me at the back?'

A painful reverberation announced Lawrence's speech. He stood before us in a maroon toga that showed off wide shoulders and thick forearms. Beneath the heat of the spotlights, his eyeliner began to seep towards his high cheekbones. This would only be a short interlude, he assured us, quoting something in Latin. We had no excuse, he joked, for not giving him our full attention.

The speech felt long to me, lasting well over twenty minutes, though the audience leaned back in their chairs and remained attentive throughout. Lawrence discussed the school's founding by his Scots great-grandmother, before going on to thank the donors who managed to keep the spirit of the place alive. The Finbow family had recently made a generous donation, apparently, ensuring that the Academy could remain in its current premises for many years to come. There was hearty applause. With a sincere smile, he encouraged other parents to dig deep in their pockets and support the school in the same way. More applause. The man next to me cheered loudly. I glanced over at Anna throughout the bursts of clapping. She smiled, gripping tightly on to her wine glass, then whispering thanks to those around her. In the opposite corner, Mary was not clapping. She was looking down at her phone. As I tried to catch her eye, I recalled the spitting cruelty in Lawrence's voice from before.

Tell me, Mary, why are you so afraid of paint?
Look at me. Look at me.
My heart hurt as I studied her.
Please, I thought. *Please, just look at me.*

When the meal ended, we were shepherded into a larger garden which had a sloping lawn that jutted out into the Tiber. A display of meticulously choreographed fireworks shot into the sky. The crowd craned their necks and cooed as green, white and red rockets exploded, their coloured sparks vanishing gracefully on the surface of the river. I hung back from the group and watched alone, but standing nearby was Lawrence, his fist clenching and loosening in time with the explosions. I thought about how fluently the evening was going for him: his speech was complete, the crowd had hooted at every joke, and now they cheered over each rocket. All he had left to do – all any of us needed to do now – was to go back inside and dance.

If he'd only left it there, things might have been different.

Inside, the band started up. The guests moved towards the dancefloor where it would be warmer. I followed them, feeling a rush of relief that the formal part of the evening was almost over. But where was Mary? As we inched up one stone stair and then another, I heard loud laughter erupt from behind me. I swivelled round, searching for her, but, as I turned, my eye caught another figure, further off, far beyond the crowd. Towards the end of the garden, standing close to the iron railings that protected us from the river, was Jean.

My chest went cold. I struggled against the movement of people to get a better look. Could that really be her? She hadn't been invited, so did she follow me here? The woman far ahead of me was dressed in a toga like everyone else, and had her back turned, but I was certain it was Jean. There was her dark bob, neatly blown smooth; there was the prim inward lean of her pigeon-toed stance. Standing opposite her was someone else from the school. They were talking intently. It looked as if Jean was holding her hands.

Then the crowd moved forwards. For a moment, I lost sight of her. Back inside the party, I rushed over to the dining tables to get my phone.

Are you here? I wrote, stepping back outside. I searched around the garden but was unable to find her anywhere. I called twice. I messaged again.

Or am I suffering from delusions?!

Shivering, I leaned over the railing where I thought Jean had been standing. I checked my phone again. Strangely, she wasn't online. I looked out over the river while I waited for a response. On the Lungotevere, car headlights flashed through the trees as the traffic moved steadily forward. I closed the app and reopened it, but Jean still wasn't online.

A minute or two passed. Beneath me, the river parted as it passed the island, then each stream met again, and the water flowed down over a steep weir. It was calming to think of how ancient it was. The river would outlive every obnoxious guest at this party. I imagined regaling Jean with that thought during our session tomorrow, when I told her all about the event. Because it surely couldn't have been her that I saw. I must have been influenced by that conversation I overheard at the table during dinner. It couldn't have been her. We would have discussed it. And she would have made a point of finding me here and checking if I was alright. Surely. Again, I checked my phone. Still offline.

She would have let me know. She definitely would have let me know.

As I weaved my way back towards the party, I caught sight of Mary's mother ahead of me on the crowded gravel pathway. She was standing beneath a large patio heater and speaking to another woman about the same age who – like her – wore a beautiful fur cape. I went over there in the hope I might find Mary. Then – still shaken from my vision of Jean – I hung back near Anna, slipping a cigarette from someone so that I could listen to her conversation.

'I used to visit your shop all the time,' the woman was saying. 'The one on the Kings Road. And your memoir, your second. Well, it helped us through an enormously tricky time. We could only have one child, too.'

Anna smiled, without showing her teeth, and squeezed the woman's arm.

'How's Bonamy?' The woman asked.

'Oh, sick of me, I expect.'

'Where is he tonight?'

Again, Anna smiled sweetly, but her facial muscles had hardened. 'Do you know, I have *absolutely* no idea.'

The woman paused, briefly, at the candour of this admission, then continued asking Anna questions about the school. Apparently, she wanted her daughter to attend, too.

'Mary loves it,' Anna was saying. 'She's totally absorbed. I hardly hear a peep from her.'

I listened to them talk for a few moments longer, then I interrupted and asked for a lighter.

'I just wanted to say hi,' I said, addressing Anna. 'I'm Mary's friend.'

'Not another one!' She laughed, briefly glancing at me then around the garden. 'Where is she? Probably doing something naughty.' She flicked away her cigarette, hitched up her toga, and climbed the sloping steps back towards the party. 'Where's my daughter?' she called in the way a queen addresses a court, assuming that everyone was listening. It was clear that I had been dismissed.

I eventually found Mary on the dance floor, right in front of the band. They were playing covers of The Velvet Underground and The Kinks. I brought her a negroni, but she smiled and gestured I should drink it instead. Then I saw the twins: both of them were dancing witchily in their long dresses, waving cigarettes, and spinning slowly, with their eyes closed. For a long while, I joined in with them, unselfconscious in my movement because I was so cocooned in alcohol. Then the band started playing disco songs and we danced harder. An old woman in a toga covered with feathers fell over and had to be helped up by a trio of men. When the band eventually stopped, they were petitioned to play for longer by the adults, who threw fistfuls of euros onto the stage.

Before long, the DJ took over and a bag of speckled pills was passed around. The room got darker and hotter. Condensation crept down the old stone walls, and I began to sweat uncomfortably, which I felt nervous about, but then there was Mary. She leaned in close and I felt the muscles in my face turn to jelly. There was so much I wanted to communicate to her, so much gratitude. I was desperate to tell her how beautiful she was, how lucky I was to know her, how certain I was that the portrait would be brilliant because she was so gifted, she just couldn't acknowledge it to herself.

We smiled at each other. Her pupils were wide, black discs. I moved my hand to her waist, feeling earnest and clumsy in my movements, but it didn't matter, because my pleasure was in my proximity to her, in the fabric of the slip dress she'd changed into, in the feeling of her ribs expanding and contracting against mine. Still, I knew I couldn't kiss her, not here, with everyone watching. Instead, I let her hold my hand, to take puffs of my cigarette.

At one point, she cupped my ear and yelled, 'I met someone you know.'

'Who?' I mouthed over the music.

Mary frowned theatrically, and gestured clumsily towards her neck. '*Amazing* jewellery.'

I laughed, though my chest felt tight. 'Who?'

Mary grabbed my hand again for the cigarette. 'Jane?' she mouthed, exhaling. 'Jenny?'

The sparkling sensation in my skin turned to cold lead, but Mary was speaking to someone else now and becoming distracted. I shook her wrist.

'Where?' I asked.

Mary waved, vaguely. She could have meant the back of the room, or Rome, more generally. I pointed to the floor, then shook her shoulder. Again, her attention was waning. The music seemed impossibly loud. 'You mean, here?' My heart started to beat, uncontrollably. I was too high to hear this. 'I need water,' I said. 'Come to the bar with me?' I tried to lead Mary away from the dance floor but she was transfixed by her phone.

'Wait,' she said, texting with one eye closed so that she could focus. 'Shit.'

I looked down. A text had arrived from Vincenzo.

'Is he here?' I asked, my paranoia doubling. *By the cloakroom,* his message said. 'Mary, did you invite him, too?'

'I've got to go.'

Mary stumbled away and I began to search, hopelessly, for my bag. Away from the dance floor, the party was thinning out. A few groups were still lingering outside by the heaters, but almost everyone that remained was dancing. The euphoria I had been feeling only minutes ago had vanished. Now, I felt only urgent dread as I considered Mary's words. Did that mean my vision of Jean by the river had been real? Why would Jean come here of her own accord and not say hello? I must have upset her. Why else would she avoid me?

I found my bag behind a speaker, though with no phone in it. Then, abruptly, the music cut out. Suddenly, there was only the sound of protesting voices and a ringing howl in my ears. As they struggled to resurrect the speakers, the other guests collapsed back into the circular tables. I searched for my scattered belongings and found my phone on a nearby table, face down, the battery dead. I glanced, anxiously, around the dying party. No sign of Jean. No sign of Mary either.

I had to find her. The fact she'd invited Vincenzo here, to a party her mother was also attending, seemed significant. I imagined the three of them heading off for a cosy nightcap together, laughing over events of the evening, laughing at me. I needed to see what he looked like. I had to try and understand exactly who Mary was choosing over me. I checked outside, scanned the other groups sitting at the tables and figured she might still be upstairs, where the bathroom and cloakroom were.

The stairway was dark and curved, and the far corners of my field of vision were warped and slightly glittering. I gripped the banister hard, feeling struck for a moment by its beautiful S-shape. I walked upwards, calmer now that I was away from the party, as if I had taken refuge in a cool church. I traced my fingers across the corners of the large picture frames that lined the stairway, which contained oil portraits of eminent doctors. Then, from the cloakroom, I heard a shuffling sound, a tiny cry. I looked up. I wasn't alone.

Two figures were clambering out of the tiny cloakroom space. My breath caught on itself. I knew, instantly, the shape of her. I retraced my steps on the stairs so I could watch, unseen. Mary was gripping the railing, but leaning backwards from it. Her hair had come loose and it rested in thick strands on her shoulders. Her eyes were either half dead or rolling backwards in pleasure.

Stood behind her was a man, kissing her neck and pawing at her breasts with his broad hands. My heart collapsed. There was the red toga. His moon-pale skin. The muscle of his upper arm was tensed. No, not Vincenzo. It was Lawrence.

I can still see the image of them, even now. It plays and replays beneath my days endlessly, like a video tape on a loop. I remember hearing a choking sound, then a loud cry. I was moving blindly. I recall the reflex to turn, protectively, away. I hurried back down the stairs and ran from the party, in the direction of Jean's apartment, my hand clamped to my mouth, utterly bewildered.

'Did you enjoy the feast then?' Mary glanced up at me mischievously. It was our final sitting of the term. Her music was playing softly through the speaker and we had the classroom to ourselves. 'Those pills were strong.' There had been an after-party at her flat, she said.

Lawrence had been there. Even the dealer had come inside and stayed up with them. 'I didn't sleep for about two days.'

'Me neither,' was all I could manage to say.

We were both quiet for a while. Whenever she was at her canvas, Mary lost the boisterousness she exuded outside of the school. Now, I hated her painstaking process; how tentatively she mixed pigments in an old pesto jar. I'd once believed, stupidly, that she took such care over the portrait because of me. It was agony to realise that it had only ever been to impress Lawrence.

'When do you fly back?' Mary asked, referring to Christmas,

'I actually think I'll head up to Venice.' I made it sound as if I'd be avoiding a big, flamboyant family event at home, but I'd been saving up carefully for the trip. Jean had given me pointers on which *scuole* to visit and where to eat; all the tourist traps I had to avoid.

'And then it's London, right?' Mary asked. 'Is that the plan?'

'Maybe here for a month or two longer.' I hesitated. 'Have you heard anything more about next term?'

'Gussie, please,' Mary said shortly. 'You can't keep asking me.'

'But have you actually asked Lawrence?'

'I'm waiting for the right time. He says he's already got someone in mind.'

Of course he does, I thought bitterly. There was a pause as I waited for the heat of our exchange to dissipate. 'What are your Christmas movements?'

She pulled a face. 'We've got filming at home.'

Every year, cameras were invited into Mary's house to film the drinks parties and the festive meals that her mother pretended to prepare. Mary had spoken about it before, describing it as an awful intrusion.

'I'm dreading it.' She puffed out her cheeks. 'Playing happy families while Mum and Dad are hardly talking. Plus, I'm so fat at the moment.'

'Don't be mad,' I said, quietly. The memory of her brown nipple, the small mole that lay alongside it, made my legs tense. 'Will Vincenzo be with you?'

Mary gave no impression that this had touched a nerve. 'No,' she said softly. 'He's got work.'

It was shattering, how easy Mary found it to lie. I lowered my eyes and kept quiet, hoping she'd address the coldness between us, but she seemed lost in thought, humming along to the song lyrics, smiling at what was taking shape in front of her. Mary always liked to listen to Joni Mitchell while she painted.

I won't, can't, listen to her now.

After I fled the costume party, Jean had found me shivering and sobbing at on her doorstep. Seeing Jean in her dressing gown convinced me that she couldn't have been there. She seemed to have been asleep: no make-up on, no glasses, either. Without them, her eyes looked narrow and dark, like pellets. She bundled me inside. Next came her tea, the warm bath. So sweet she was; so deft and caring as she spun that tight cocoon. She sat patiently with me while I soaked in the water and told her the story.

'I just wish I could get that image of them out of my head,' I said, screwing my eyes shut. 'She must be so fucked up to be with him. To want to do that. It's fucking *gross*.'

Jean's face was grave. 'No, Gus. Mary's the one who we need to help. She's been exploited.'

My stomach clenched. There was a flannel in my hands. I twisted it between my fingers like a rosary.

'He's a close friend of the Finbows, isn't he?'

'Practically her godfather.'

Jean flinched. 'I wonder when it all started? When someone abuses their position of power,' she continued calmly, 'the victim rarely has any choice over whether they really consent to a relationship. We get mixed up, confusing our desire for acceptance with something more meaningful.'

I shrugged miserably, uninterested in Jean's excuses for Mary, who I had decided was a slut. A vain slut with a weak personality.

'Will you go to the school tomorrow?'

'The school?' I said, aghast.

'Another adult *must* know,' she urged.

I hesitated, unwilling to admit that I couldn't upset things at the Melrose when I hadn't been paid for my last month of sittings. Without that, I couldn't afford to go to Venice, or pay my debts to Jean, which were starting to add up.

'Well,' she said, grim-faced. 'You've put me in a very difficult position.'

'I'm sorry,' I said weakly, exhausted from the party and all the crying. 'I'm so sorry for involving you.'

'Unless...' she left a meaningful pause.

'Don't tell the school,' I begged. 'Please, let me talk to her first.'

'Mary needs to speak to a grown-up, Gus. Someone impartial.'

At the sink opposite, a tap was dripping. Jean got up and tightened it forcefully, then sat back down. My body tensed over. I knew exactly what she was asking, and I was frightened by the starkness of her ultimatum: *bring her to me, or I'll tell.*

'You've enjoyed our sessions together, haven't you, Gus?' Jean smiled tetchily towards me, through the steamy bathroom air. 'Haven't I made you feel so much better?'

My tongue darted across the tiny mouth ulcers which were developing along my lower lip from the pills. '*So* much better.'

'Why wouldn't we want that for our other friends, too?'

There was something off, I knew, in the stern little nod Jean gave me; the triumphant way she reached into the water and jerked out the bath plug. But I didn't pursue the thought further. There were far more painful things to dwell on. My mind kept going over the grisly details of what I had witnessed: Lawrence's blunt fingernails pawing over Mary's body. His pronounced chin nuzzling the soft pit of her neck. The sight of her back, arched with pleasure against him. I was coming down and facing the bleak embarrassment of Mary's rejection. Why would I want to introduce her to Jean now? She didn't deserve it. I had already lost Mary to Lawrence. I couldn't face sharing Jean, too.

Halfway into the portrait session, there was a knock on the door. It was Lawrence, dressed in a camel-coloured coat, his hair slicked back. My body stiffened with anger. Mary looked at him and immediately coloured.

'Can I do you now, Mary? Before I head off to that dreary lunch.'

Mary glanced anxiously at her canvas, then rested her paintbrush down in the slot at the bottom of the easel. I shifted out of my usual position on the plinth and stretched my arms. As I watched Lawrence approach, I was bracing myself, still used to him representing trouble for her. But as he gazed at the portrait, he didn't criticise it as he usually did. He made sounds of approval.

'Almost there.' He beamed, his eyes flitting between the canvas and me. Then he clicked his fingers, as if to wake me from hypnosis. 'Gus, come take a look.'

'Sure,' I said, pulling my straps up, though I was startled. I wasn't ready to see the portrait. Not yet. Mary had been so protective of her work, and I had spent so long fantasising about how she perceived me, that I had expected this moment to be more ceremonious. Or, at the very least, private. Mary and I needed to be alone to appreciate the material expression of everything that had passed between us. More than twenty sittings. Plus, the observation outside of school, too. Across the table from each other, in bars, in pizza restaurants, our heads facing each other on the pillow. But when I rounded the canvas and looked up at the portrait, everything about it was wrong.

The shock of how wrong it was brought tears to my eyes. I bit down on my bent finger to prevent them falling. The softness of my image disarmed me. Mary had changed the black sheet I'd been posing in front of into a misty, lilac background. In fact, everything about me had been altered: the surface of my face had a blurred film on it, as if she'd seen me through gauze, or fine rain.

The rest of my face was homogenous, identical to the faces in her other canvases that hung sloped around the school. She'd rounded the angles in my face, shaping them into more classical features, smoothing out the bumps in my nose and softening my jawline. Even my hair had been tidied. There was no way that it wasn't a flattering portrait, but I was basically unrecognisable: much more womanly than I was comfortable with. My chin, in particular, was desperately off.

But what hurt me, most of all, was my anxious expression. I had the frightened look of someone who'd been interrupted, perhaps pulled back on the shoulder by someone unknown. A stranger. My mouth had been almost comically reddened and rounded open, in surprise. Through Mary's eyes, there was nothing magnetic or appealing about me. I looked dull, like a woman on the cusp of absolutely nothing.

I thought, then, of something Jean had said in a previous session. We'd been discussing love, and she'd mentioned how true love could only develop if we understood and appreciated the absolute uniqueness of the other person. If we paid full, worshipful, attention to them.

But there was no tenderness in Mary's rendering of me; it was formulaic. I knew, then, that Mary didn't love me at all. The pain of that knowledge hit me in successive waves.

'Thoughts, comments, reflections?' Mary asked, chewing her thumb. I could tell she was delighted that Lawrence was happy with it. Her leg was fidgeting with pleasure and tension, like a spaniel awaiting its next command.

'You've made me look very young,' I said, trying to smile.

They turned back towards the painting then, teacher and pupil. I had to stand there for a number of excruciating minutes while they deconstructed my painted image. I was sickened by the glowing praise she received. Lawrence kept stepping towards the canvas, suggesting improvements, using his fingernail to mimic future brush strokes. It was so obvious to me now that they had been lovers. He patted her back and shoulders as he instructed her, while she leaned loosely into him.

When there was a lull in conversation, Mary finally looked at me.

'Gussie, you look upset,' she said and sighed, her frustration at my reaction evident. 'It's not finished, you know. There's still the hands to do, and the hair.'

I shook my head and turned away from them both. 'I'm fine,' I said. 'Just a bit overwhelmed.'

Mary insisted that we go out after the sitting ended and I couldn't resist one more – and it was our final – outing with her. The bar where we met the wider group was near Piazza Navona. We pushed plastic tables together to accommodate the size of the group, and I sat at the opposite end to Mary, watching her quietly. She'd changed in the toilets at the school and was now wearing a long silver column dress and biker boots, bangles running up her arms. Bright gold earrings were hanging from her ears, the heavy kind she got from India. They swayed prettily around her face as, with every drink, she grew more and more animated, telling stories, and greeting strangers who approached our table simply to kiss her cheek, flitting in and out of Italian.

I should have left when the bar closed, but I was feeling destructive. When the group moved on to a nightclub nearby called *il Gioco*, 'the Game', I followed. It was a low-ceilinged, carpeted little room; an old *bunga bunga* dive with mirrored walls, the kind of place where politicians abused their privileges. Apart from Mary, the rest of us were dressed too scruffily to be there, in Converse trainers and jeans, but somebody knew the doorman and, since it was a weeknight, they let us through.

On our table were three or four bottles of vodka. Everyone was distracted because, sitting at the table next to us, was the national rugby team. Mary went straight up and asked for photos with one of them, posing with one foot lifted in the air and a hand placed delicately on his tank of a chest. *She'll fuck anyone*, I thought, *anyone at all, because she loves being admired*. Watching her, I was suddenly struck by how moronic that was. I wondered if, together with Jean, I'd projected an intricacy to Mary's character that was never actually there.

I helped myself to the vodka, enjoying the way it burned as I swallowed. Then someone grabbed me roughly, by the shoulder. It was Cleo, and she looked frantic.

'Have you seen my sister?' she asked. 'She was meant to meet us. But she's not answering her phone.'

I shrugged and turned away to pour myself some more vodka. My insides were twisting at the taste, but I also liked the harshness of it. I wanted to corrode all the softness inside me, the animal shame. I wanted to harden over the hurt.

To the right of the bar, I found a narrow conservatory where you were meant to smoke. Inside, I slumped into a leather chair and watched the floor tilt dangerously from side to side. Rubbing my face with my hands, I thought once more of the portrait. She hadn't seen me. Couldn't possibly claim to know me. She had been thinking of Lawrence all along.

Then there was a sound at the door. It was Mary. She couldn't open it and was getting frustrated, flapping at the handle. Deep down, she was just a yob, I realised, as I went over to let her in. A rich yob.

'Gussie!' she said hoarsely. '*Dove vai?* You know, you don't have to be out here. People are smoking at the tables. It's cool.' I took in her appearance. Her silver dress was stained with alcohol and there was red-wine scum around her lips. Crumbs of coke in her nostril. I dabbed at it, roughly, with my thumb.

'I'm going,' I said.

Mary sat clumsily on the sofa, spilling the drink she'd been carrying. With two fingers, she mopped the vodka up from the table and sucked them clean. I was also extremely drunk, but I could never behave like that because I wasn't a rich girl like her. If I openly wandered about in stained clothes and took drugs, it would mean something different. It wouldn't be charming. It would only affirm someone's idea of how a person from my background might behave. The injustice of this provoked a swell of anger.

'You're a state, Mary,' I said, quietly. 'Look at you. You should get home.'

She looked taken aback, but only momentarily. Grabbing hold of my hands, she brought me down to sit next to her, her earrings tugging her lobes as she moved. I hated that my body still shivered at the closeness of her.

'What's the matter with you tonight? What have I done wrong?' Her eyes searched mine earnestly. 'Was it the painting? You know, it's not finished, anyway.' She leaned towards me and massaged my hands. 'I've still got these to do.'

I withdrew my hands quickly.

'What does it matter?' I said. Tears were stinging the back of my eyes. 'Law will pass you whatever happens, won't he? I saw you and *Vincenzo* together at the party.'

There was silence. Mary's face darkened. She lit a cigarette and exhaled. Her mouth carried a twisted, half-mirthful expression. 'I didn't know you'd seen us,' she said.

That *us* was unbearable. I had thought that *we* were an *us*. But when we'd shared a bed, she'd carried that secret with her. Warmed herself against it. I began to feel angry.

'He's ancient, Mary. How can you sleep with someone that old?'

'Gussie, please don't.'

'Look at you. You're so beautiful. You could have anybody. Why him?'

'Please. Stop. You don't understand,' Mary said, bringing a hand to her forehead, then her neck. 'You don't know anything about it.'

'I know I don't. And I'm glad, because it disgusts me.'

'See?' She pointed her cigarette towards me. 'I actually tried to tell you before, and you know what, I'm glad I didn't bother – you're too judgemental!'

I laughed and shook my head. Nearby, a group of women stood smoking, oblivious to our conversation. I took in their thickened upper lips and ugly, sharp-heeled shoes. I hated places like this and I hated myself for following Mary here.

'Go on, then,' I sneered, wanting to hurt myself with the details. 'How did it start?'

Mary bit down on her cheeks. 'Sorry if you think I've confused you or whatever—'

'—When Mary? This term, or did it happen before?' I nudged her with my arm. 'Tell me.'

There was a pause as Mary leaned forward to stub her cigarette out in the ashtray. Then, in a quiet voice she said, 'Years ago.'

My head jerked to face her. Our eyes met and she nodded, so that I understood the full gravity of what she meant.

'Before you came to Rome?' I ventured, quietly. She looked sullen. 'Earlier than that?'

'The summer before sixth form.'

The club noise fell away. The seriousness of what she was saying made my body weak.

'But – why are you here? Why did you still come here to study?' I asked, hating as I uttered the question that it sounded as though I didn't believe her.

'I didn't have a choice.'

'What?'

Mary cast her eyes downwards and began to cry. 'It was my mother's decision.'

'Mary...' I breathed, wiping her tears and feeling my own forming. 'I'm so sorry, this is just so *unbelievably* dark.'

'I know.' She gulped. 'I'm so sorry to burden you with it. I've been so stupid. And so confused.'

'Not stupid, Mary. Never stupid, okay? Confused over what?'

'About him. Things were better with him once I started here. I don't know how to describe it, but it felt more equal. More on my own terms. I honestly think I started to like his attention.' She looked up at me. Tears filled her eyes again. 'At least, I thought I liked it. I liked it when I thought I had control.'

She collapsed into me then, folding straight into my arms. As we embraced, that picture of Lawrence in the background of Mary's holiday photo reappeared in my mind. Jean's question: *I wonder when this started?* My stomach lurched at its pertinence. But as I considered her words, there was a growing sense of relief. Mary never actually wanted to be with Lawrence. They weren't a romantic thing at all. The sick man had only groomed her, taken advantage. Guilt struck me then for my elation; my shameful condescension at the banality of the situation. *Only*. But I would not dwell on this now. No, the main thing was to get him out of her head.

I released Mary, but held her by the shoulders. 'Listen: he's the older guy. A trusted family friend. You were, what?'

'Sixteen.'

'So, you were never in control. He's been grooming you. *Completely* fucking with your mind, your self-worth. Your entire practice. You can't stay here for next term. Will you promise me that?'

Mary's face turned blank. I sensed she couldn't really conceive of leaving the school. I worried that deep down, she didn't want to.

'I can't leave. Mum will kill me.'

'Then we'll tell your mum,' I said, grasping her hands. I noticed she was gripping me back in a strange way, curling her fingertips around my fingertips like an anxious child. Then she let go.

'We're not telling my mum, Gussie.'

'Why?'

'It won't do anything.'

'Why?' I said. She hesitated. 'Tell me?'

'It just wouldn't help.'

'Meaning?'

Mary stared up at me, her gaze rigid. 'I've told her other things like this before. She never takes it seriously. In fact, it wouldn't surprise me if she already knew about us. You should hear the way she talks about rape. Like half the time it's just *rough sex*.'

A bunch of rugby players spilled out noisily into the smoking area and Mary, despite her emotional state, still straightened a little in her seat so they'd notice her. Was it her mother who had encouraged this endless pursuit of male attention? I remembered the way Anna basked in Lawrence's praise at the party; their pressed-up dancing. What if Lawrence was just using Mary to try and get to Anna? And what if that were true, that Anna turned a blind eye, that she didn't really care about her daughter at all?

Mary gradually shifted her attention away from the boys. 'You didn't tell anyone about us, did you?'

'Don't talk about you and Lawrence in that way, Mary,' I said, bringing her towards me again. 'Please don't say *us*.'

Half desperate, I kissed her. A kiss she didn't return. There was the mesh of Mary's teeth. Her hands pulling against my jacket. The sweet blast of alcohol, as her mouth reluctantly yielded to mine. A few of the rugby players cheered.

'You're sure no one else at the party saw?' she gasped, pulling quickly away.

I reassured her, just as an idea was gradually taking shape in my mind. If Mary was going to escape the school, she'd need somewhere to go. Somewhere that wasn't home. My mind seized upon Jean's place in Primrose Hill. It was perfect. The two of us could make a base there while she collected herself together; then we could plan our next moves. Maybe the American design school was actually a good idea. My chest gave a slight kick when I imagined it. Maybe we could move to New York together?

'But if you don't want to go home...' I trailed off as I opened my phone, which had a pocket for cards. I pulled out one of Jean's, which I had started carrying with me. 'There's this woman I've been talking to.'

I see us from the view of a bird, or imagine we are like those starlings who once soared high above the river, before swerving, disastrously, in the wrong direction.

Two girls, drunk and shivering, stepped out of the taxi I had hurriedly booked from the nightclub. Mary's fingertips curled around mine as we crossed the quiet courtyard and mounted the stairs to Jean's apartment. Lingering there at the threshold, we already felt relief; a homecoming calm. You always smelt the floral scent of Jean's home before you entered it. Once, twice the door was unbolted, then opened. Jean rushed us inside, dressed in an elegant paisley robe, smiling first at Mary, then at me. I had done well.

Not well enough, apparently, to be allowed to stay the night. That privilege fell to Mary, who was given a sedative. I was much better off, Jean assured, sleeping in my own bed. By the door, she hugged me, but woodenly. I reminded her about my trip to Venice the following day and she promised to see me when I was back. My stomach knotted as I counted the number of days that would be. Then she bent down and opened her wallet.

'A holiday contribution,' she said, and smiled.

'But don't I owe you?' I protested weakly, holding the spray of notes.

'Forget about that for now, Gus,' she said, her finger beneath my chin, the other on the door handle. 'Go and have a good rest. Enjoy Venice. And merry Christmas.'

The following day, I caught the train north, unsettled because I hadn't received my usual morning message from Jean. I called her twice. It went straight to voicemail. There was also no response out of Mary either, but that was less unusual. She was travelling back to London today, and I guessed she felt afraid and awkward about her confession in the nightclub, now that she was sober. Then, as my train was nearing Bologna, she texted, thanking me for the introducing her to Jean.

I love her energy! Staying in Rome a bit longer and doing a few sessions to help me manage Christmas!

I pressed my forehead against the train window, my insides squeezing with envy.

Well done! I eventually replied. *She's magic.*

Mary read the message but didn't respond. Over the next few days, I sent pictures, in the hope of engaging her: the bold red font of a restaurant sign; a traghetto gliding through the mint-green waters of the lagoon; Marino Marini's horseman and all the Man Rays in the Guggenheim. I got nothing from either of Mary or Jean. Venice was bone cold and beautiful, but it felt too remote without Jean's presence at the end of my phone. By the mid-afternoon, the city was surrounded by ribbons of disorientating fog. I kept getting lost, pursuing dead ends or walking in circles.

The days passed. My mind also started to spiral. Mary must be angry for how moralistic I'd been about Lawrence in the nightclub, or upset because I'd publicly kissed her, or both. Jean probably agreed with Mary – they were probably discussing it – and now she was disappointed in me. As I wandered the city, I tried to break the day down into three-hour chunks. If I didn't hear from Jean by the end of each period, I would allow myself to send a text message. Before bed, always, a call. My chest would grow tighter and tighter as the tenth, twentieth ring went unanswered. There were six strangers in my hostel dormitory and I was anxious not to disturb them. When I gave up the calls, I turned into my pillow, crying as quietly as I could.

Before long, my mind started to summon Jean instead. First, it was the peal of her laughter, ringing from an open window above me. Then it was a brief vision of her with Mary, walking along the Zattere: the pair of them were in beautiful green woollen coats, Mary gripping onto Jean's arm like an invalid, like she was taking her first steps outside after a fortnight of flu. Had they come here to surprise me? Did that explain the cruelty of their sudden silence?

A day later, I saw them again, a couple of rows in front as I sat in St Mark's Basilica on Christmas Day. One head with long, blonde hair; the other jaw-length and brown. My heart leapt with recognition, but when the choir processed in and they turned around, I recoiled at the unfamiliarity of their faces. Tears raced out of me as the choir sang 'O Come All Ye Faithful' in Latin. I was frightened at how frightened I was; ashamed, too, for the freakish hallucinations; for letting the city send me mad. My mind kept looping with Mary's words: *I thought I liked it, when I thought I had control.* Resenting her bitterly, I now felt the same about Jean. Yet she was also the only one in the world who could make sense of how I was feeling.

By New Year's Eve, I was on my way back to Rome. Arriving at Termini, I took a bus straight to Jean's, amazed when I buzzed and was let straight in. I took the stairs two at a time, desperate to apologise if that was necessary; for things to feel normal again. I bashed the door with my fist. It quicky swung open. My chest lifted, then fell, at the sight of the person standing in front of me: a young woman wearing a cleaning tunic.

She removed an earphone. '*Salve?*' The apartment reeked of pine cleaner.

'*Dove Signora Guest?*' I asked breathlessly.

The cleaner shrugged. '*Non lo so.*'

My heart plummeted. Behind her, I could see that the apartment had been emptied: the fridge door was wide open, and all the vases that had once held those massive bouquets of lilies were washed up and drying by the sink. Somewhere further inside, a radio was playing pop music.

In my bad Italian, I told her that she must have it wrong, that I was certain this was an apartment Signora Guest owned, not rented. The cleaner shook her head. She'd cleaned it for five years, she said. The apartment did not belong to Signora Guest, but a young man.

'*Questo è Air bnb,*' she pronounced loudly, like I was stupid.

She closed the door on me and I stood there, too stunned to move. Surely there'd been some kind of mix-up? Or did the sanctuary I'd grown to depend on belong to someone else? I tried yet another call to Jean's Italian number, but, this time, the phone didn't connect at all. The awful realisation slowly dawned: I had been deserted. Jean had left the city without telling me. They both had.

The hallway sensor clicked off and the lights went out. I remained standing there, letting the darkness envelop me as I tried to make sense of how or why Jean had vanished. Humiliated, my rage reared up. I kicked, furiously, at her front door, beating it with my elbows and fists. I screamed her name over and over. Then, seized with shame and afraid Jean could somehow see me, I fled down the stairs and out through the courtyard.

I spent that evening booking flights to London and packing up my room. When the countdown came, I was surprised to hear the blaring of horns and the parties in the streets below. The date had barely registered. The New Year had crept up on me, but my resolutions were made: find her. Find them both.

PART FOUR

PART FOUR

GUEST V FINBOW: DAY FIVE

This email might come as a shock to you. I am writing to let you know I am taking a healing separation from our relationship. I need to step back and reflect on our (voluntary) parental bond. So I ask you to respect my desire to turn my energy inward. I am in good physical health and have plenty of resources at my disposal. This message is not intended to undermine any of the happier times we have enjoyed together, for which I am grateful, but please don't try and find me. I am working towards forgiveness.

'Oriel's email arrived in the summer of the year she first began seeing Ms Guest, is that correct?' Ms Carr asks.

'Correct,' Lucy Ayres replies, calmly.

It is the fifth day of the trial and Anna has summoned Lucy – another tortured mother – to speak in her defence.

'Do you believe your daughter was the real author of this message?' enquires Ms Carr.

Lucy's stare is rigid. 'There is no doubt in my mind: it was written by Jean Guest.'

'Why?'

'At that point, she was controlling every aspect of my daughter's life. No correspondence went unchecked. She wanted her all to herself.'

Ms Carr pauses, then brings to the judge's attention a second email, which is projected onto the screen. This one is signed by Mary. As Ms Carr flips between them, my skin prickles. They are eerily alike. Lucy Ayres confirms her belief that Mary's message was also authored by Jean Guest.

'Everything is the same. Oriel cut us off shortly after she began therapy with Ms Guest, too,' Lucy explains.

Ms Carr nods sympathetically. 'Did Oriel have any other reason to enforce an estrangement from you?'

'None whatsoever,' says Lucy, her chin trembling. 'She loved me.'

Ms Carr lowers her folder of notes and leaves a reverent pause. There is a shift in her manner, a softening. 'Mrs Ayres, perhaps we should have acknowledged this at the beginning. We are profoundly sorry for your recent loss.' I look up. My awareness sharpens. 'We understand your bereavement is very recent, so it must take great strength to stand here today. We are grateful for your courage.'

A cold feeling seeps into my stomach: a slow, sickening dread. Did she mean the loss of her husband? Or could it be Oriel? I look towards Anna, but her face bears no surprise. She shakes her head grimly. There was often talk of Oriel's hospitalisation. Had she never recovered?

'My daughter was the brave one,' Lucy says, bowing her head. I hear myself make a small cry. 'The reason I am standing here is because of what happened to her. I cannot let the same thing happen to anyone else. It's the same pattern: meeting in Rome, pressuring young girls into therapy...' She trails off, suddenly overcome.

As she pauses to compose herself, I look over at Jean, who is writing, obstinately, in her notebook.

Look her in the eye, Jean, I think, with boiling outrage. *At least have the guts to look Oriel's mother in the eye*. But her head remains lowered, and I don't know why I am surprised; facing Lucy would be to acknowledge her role in her suffering. For months, I was just as spineless, witnessing Anna suffer the loss of Mary without facing my own part in what had happened.

There was, at first, a rush of relief when, two Januarys ago, I received my own version of Mary's hateful email. Sheer dopamine, just to see the letters of her name in my inbox. It came about a month after I'd found Jean's apartment in Rome empty. I was back in London by then, renting a sublet room in Archway, and staggering about beneath a cloud of confusion and shame at the way I'd been ghosted. In the first week of the new year, Jean had texted, briefly, to say she was busy working. But Mary wasn't even reading my texts. For a couple of weeks, I blocked her. Then I unblocked her, expecting a flood of messages. Nothing. Why was I being erased? What had I done to make them both shut me out? And had Jean openly lied to me about owning that apartment, or had I just assumed it was all hers, like I assumed she was all mine?

When I remember how I responded to Mary's email, I'm ashamed at how swiftly I went on the attack. HEALING JOURNEY? I replied mockingly, trying to suppress my queasy acquaintance with the phrase. I asked her what the fuck this self-important insanity was all about. In my next message, I grew defensive. I'd tried to be helpful when she dropped that bombshell in the club, and I'd done her a *huge fucking favour* in introducing her to Jean, so it wasn't fair to *just vanish* like this.

All the wrong things to say, but I was so hurt, I don't think I really read Mary's email properly at all. As always, I turned to Jean to decipher things: *I know you're busy, but did you receive this too?* I forwarded Mary's message onto her. *Can we at least talk on the phone?*

The following day, Jean finally messaged from a British number. Her profile picture no longer showed the black-and-white image of her smiling at a party, that I used to admire, but two white curtains blowing beside an open window. She apologised that work had been very absorbing. There was no acknowledgement of Mary's bizarre message.

How's my Gus getting along? she asked. *I've missed you!*

Can I come over? I begged. *Please.*

Jean's flat wasn't 1970s at all. It was on the lower level of a 1930s low-rise building on the outer fringes of Primrose Hill. When I arrived, it was early evening. Jean answered the door, dressed more casually than I'd ever seen her before, in loose-fitting trousers and an ugly cardigan. The only expensive-looking item was on her face: a pair of new rectangular glasses. They made everything about her seem altered.

'Hello, Gus,' she said, taking a slight backward step.

For the first time ever, I came inside and there was no hug. No watchful, interested gaze. She surveyed me with sympathy, but only fleetingly; then she looked away. My body felt stung.

We went down a dark hallway into the kitchen, a damp, sloping room at the back of the flat lit by dusty lamps. It was confusing to me, as I looked about. In Rome, Jean had boasted about a gloriously minimal and airy flat which she rattled around in, but this place was cramped and depressing. Gone were the art books and records, the fresh cream upholstery. The whole kitchen was pine: the cupboards on the walls, the chairs, the table. Bright orange and oppressive.

Sitting at the table, I read Mary's email aloud while Jean got me a drink.

'"Turn my energy inward?" What does that mean? She sounds unhinged. What's she said about me? Is she cutting me out?'

'Not permanently, Gus,' she said sharply. 'She's asking for a temporary separation.' Jean brought over two glasses of wine and pulled out a chair alongside me. 'Just a short break. You should respect it.'

'How do you know it's only temporary?'

'How do I know?' Jean asked. A flicker of something new crossed over her face. 'I helped her write it.'

My stomach turned. 'But,' I stammered. 'I don't get why she has to isolate herself. Doesn't she need her friends?'

Jean sipped her wine primly. 'You know I can't comment on another client's treatment,' she said.

A slow sense of betrayal began to dawn on me. I registered, with fear, the fancy gauzy teabags that Mary liked to have before bed, propped on the side next to Jean's kettle.

'Is she coming here a lot?' I asked quietly. I couldn't imagine Mary's golden energy occupying such a claustrophobic space.

'Don't press this, Gus,' Jean warned harshly.

Jean had always let me into little secrets from other sessions before. Why not now? Hit by a fresh wave of uneasiness, I got up from my chair and began pacing the narrow kitchen. 'But is she okay?' I asked. 'Did she break it off with Law?' Four small steps on the slick linoleum floor and then back again. 'Is she returning to Rome?'

'For now, no.'

'Why can't I talk to her?'

Jean shook her head. 'She needs space, Gus. That means, stop texting. And no more phone calls.' She gave a chuckle, though her expression was serious. 'You're frightening her.'

Humiliated by the thought of them both discussing – even complaining – about me, I collapsed back into the kitchen chair.

'Oh, my God,' I whispered.

Jean placed a warm hand on my back. 'Poor girl,' she murmured, stroking my scalp and then down again. I leaned into her, feeling a rush of wellbeing, not only from Jean's touch but also that soft voice she used. 'My funny girl.'

I tried to cling to the thought that Mary would know Jean's comfort, too. But my sadness wouldn't lift.

'Will you tell her that I miss her?' I sniffed, once I had gathered myself together. I reached into my bag and pulled out a letter I'd written. 'I'll give her space, if that's what she really wants. But will you give her this?'

Inside the envelope were photos of us. Silly drawings we'd made together on the stationery in Beaker's hotel suite. A list of the films we'd watched, with pompous reviews I'd made up when we were drunk one evening at her flat. There was an apology for how term had ended. A post-script promise that she could tell me anything and I'd always be there for her. I signed it off using a jokey nickname she'd used for me once: *your scowling muse*.

Jean took it from me quickly. 'Of course. I do know she misses you, Gus. She mentions you a lot. I'm sure she'll be back in touch soon. She just needs a break. We all do from time to time.'

'But I'm worried about her. I'm sad about her feeling so sad.'

Jean sipped her wine. 'I am, too.' For a moment, she fell quiet. 'None of this has been easy on me, either, Gus. It's taking such a lot out of me.' She adjusted her glasses to dab at the tears that had formed. 'Some of the early memories that Mary's retrieving are very disturbing.'

'You mean about Lawrence?' I said. Jean looked pointedly at her hands. I felt my rage flare. 'Shouldn't she be speaking to her parents?'

A bitter expression crossed Jean's face. 'Telling them won't help, Gus. They're the biggest part of the problem. We both know what those kinds of families are like. It's all about outward appearances. From what she's telling me, they completely ignored the situation. They just pretended it wasn't happening. They neglected her when she needed them most.'

The kitchen grew smaller; no longer warm but uncomfortably overheated. I brought a hand to my neck, remembering the Finbow funding of Lawrence's school; her mother's acceptance of Lawrence's kiss. Then Mary's words in the nightclub: *it wouldn't surprise me if she already knew*. How evil of Anna Finbow, I thought, to look the other way and ignore what was inconvenient. Just as my own mother had flatly ignored what she perceived as a problem in me. My whole being ached for Mary then. I wanted so much to console her. To tell her I had known that rejection, too.

Jean rose from the table and went over to the sink. 'I shouldn't have told you that, Gus, I'm sorry—'

'—No,' I said, still stunned. 'Thank you, for telling me.'

She turned to the sink. 'I hope it explains why Mary needs the silence...'

'Yes,' I said uncertainly. 'It does help. The context. Thank you.'

'It's you I should thank, for recommending me. Now I can help her.'

That word jarred on me: *recommended*. I felt a growing shame for engineering a situation that was causing me pain – a pattern Jean had told me I must break.

I tried to ask more questions, but Jean insisted it wasn't right to discuss Mary any longer. Instead, she poured me another glass of wine and tried to engage me on different matters, but the conversation often felt forced and one-sided. She was acting so politely that I began to feel a creeping sickness, as if I was being dumped. We talked about the room I had rented in Archway and what I might try to do now I was back. Her own offer of a home with her glided by, unmentioned.

'That reminds me!' Jean took out her phone and sent me a link to a news story about a programme for ceramicists in the north of the country. I stared at her in disbelief.

'Stoke-on-Trent?'

'They're selling studios in the old pottery factories really cheaply.'

'But it's so far away?'

'Live-in studios. With other artists. When I read about it, you sprang immediately to mind. You're never far from my mind. I said to myself: now that would be absolutely perfect for Gus!'

I paused to read a few lines of the article. 'Stoke,' I repeated. 'Isn't that where Mary's mum's business is based?'

A lopsided smile passed across Jean's face. 'Oddly enough, yes. Not that you'd ever see her, I expect.' She paused. 'Not unless you wanted to.'

I turned the screen of my phone over. 'I can't move there,' I stammered. 'I'd be hundreds of miles from you.'

'You did the same thing when you went to Rome and look how well you did! When I saw the piece, I thought it was fate. I said to myself: just think what that could mean for her work!'

'What about *our* work?'

There was another awkward pause. Jean removed her glasses and blinked at me with her naked, mouse-like eyes. In an instant, I was back in Mr Greening's office, facing my teacher, my parents; all their grave and angry faces. A pain rose up into my chest.

'I think we might need a break from each other,' Jean said, curtly. 'Just for a little while.'

Her words burned my ears. Here was the moment I knew, instinctively, was coming. Jean was ending things.

'My work has to take priority, Gus. *Mary* has to take priority. You understand that, don't you? You know she's in trouble. We have to make sacrifices.' There was a pause. The walls around me began to slide slowly backwards. 'And I have to be a little bit selfish here, Gus,' she said, then chuckled. 'I have to make a proper living.'

I couldn't speak. It shamed me how little I had paid her.

'I can pay more,' I whispered, eventually. 'Get a job again. I can match the others—'

'See what happens in Stoke, perhaps. When you get an income going…' As she trailed off, she opened her arms for a hug. 'You do know how much I'll miss you, don't you?' she said, bringing me close. 'And I promise it won't be forever.'

'How long?' I whispered through tears, wanting to remain there, safe in her smell.

'You're such a strong girl, Gus,' she said, releasing me, but ignoring my question. 'I'm so proud of how you've grown.' Briefly, she held my chin as tears poured down my face. 'But sometimes the hardest part of loving someone is also letting them go.' She nodded as she said this, to make it clear she was also referring to Mary. 'Do you understand me?'

When Jean offered a bed for the night, I grasped the invitation with a sense of bleak, defeated nostalgia, combined with foreboding: she was like a lover proposing one last intimacy before we separated. She showed me to a single bedroom with textured walls, just off the kitchen. I felt a queasy contentedness because, as she prepared me for sleep, things were almost feeling normal again. Almost.

The bed was dressed in fussy peach linen, all tucked in around the edges. She switched on the heated blanket and gave me a pill to help me go to sleep. When she turned off the light, leaving without kissing me, I remembered Mary and Jean, both complaining about my phone calls. Mortified, I turned to the wall and covered my face with my hands. Then I shrieked with pain.

Not long after dawn, there was the sound of the doorbell, a violent rapping of her letter box, and what I thought was a woman's voice shouting through it. I rolled over and covered my ears from the sound.

'Who was at the door this morning?' I said later, as I tucked into the elaborate breakfast Jean had cooked. I remember eating it slowly, wanting to delay our separation. I had no idea, then, where I would go next. The stark truth was that I had blown the last of my savings on that miserable trip to Venice. London was unaffordable for me now. Jean's suggestion of Stoke was starting to seem like a valid alternative.

'No one was at the door,' snapped Jean. She was standing at the stove, writing a message on her phone. 'Now, eat up. I've got a client in ten minutes.'

My throat hardened as I cut down into my bacon. I was unable to say what I was thinking: that now I was awake, I was fairly certain, even beneath the haze of my sleeping pill, that I had heard something very specific. A girl's name, over and over.

A woman – a mother – calling for Oriel.

The voice belonged to Lucy Ayres. As she stands here in court, I realise that, of course, it was her outside Jean's door in that early dawn, banging and shouting through the letter box. Several months later, Oriel tried to sever herself from Jean, just as I have tried and failed to do.

'We wanted to reintegrate Oriel back into normal life,' Lucy explains. 'But how do you recover from such complex manipulation? Jean turned Oriel's childhood into a horror movie. She was tortured by what she had been made to believe. At the same time, she also felt completely foolish for absorbing all the lies.'

Ms Carr draws parallels between Oriel's experiences and those of other individuals who have left cult organisations. 'In your bundle, Your Lordship, we have summarised a number of cult-exit studies. It is very common for recovering cult members to fall into deep despair whilst trying to recommence life outside of their restrictive regime. Many individuals suffer from feelings of worthlessness and shame about what they have endured. They experience drug addiction, depression and even suicide.' The lawyer pauses to take a sip of water. There is a hollowness in my chest as I consider the starkness of the road ahead. My future, without Jean playing any role in it. 'Do you recognise these behaviours in your late daughter's experience?'

Lucy swallows. 'Back at home, Oriel became severely depressed and withdrawn. She still craved Ms Guest's company like a drug. She never got over the absence.'

My stomach churns with recognition: *neither will I.*

Ms Carr proceeds gently. 'Is it your evidence that these experiences contributed to your daughter's death by suicide?'

A painful hush falls over the gallery. Justice Larkin leans forward. 'Take whatever time you need Mrs Ayres. . . we know how difficult this must be.'

Lucy presses her lips with her hand. 'I'm still coming to terms with the *why*. It was barely a month ago. She said she was going to Notting Hill Carnival with a friend. We were happy for her. It was the first time in years.'

'Where did she go instead?'

'She took a train to Brighton. Walked a long way up the beach. Waited until it was dark. Placed stones into the pockets of her coat and waded into the sea.'

Tears streak my face. I picture Oriel clutching at the fistfuls of rocks. Her defiant gasp as she is dragged under. Behind her lawyer's desk, Jean emits a quiet sob. The judge frowns.

'To clarify,' Ms Carr ventures softly. 'Is it your evidence that your daughter's tragic suicide this August, and Ms Guest's influence, are connected?'

'Of course they are. It takes time – a dreadfully long time – to come to terms with the fact that you have not been loved, but exploited. A month before she died, my daughter even tried to make amends with Ms Guest.'

'Why was that?'

'She had made a statement for Mrs Finbow, but was terrified about being questioned over it. The prospect of standing up in front of her abuser was just too much. You see, my daughter's dependency on Ms Guest was never really severed. Not until—'

Suddenly, I have heard enough. I rise from my seat and grasp my way to the exit, hearing a horrifying echo in everything Lucy Ayres has said. On Monday, I am due to speak against Jean, but how will I manage it? Stumbling through the grand atrium, my mind conjures images of Oriel's floating, lifeless body. Her corpse morphs into my own, then Mary's. Frail Mary, gripping on to her baby girl. Mary is so dependent on Jean, I have no idea how she will cope without her. Isn't it reckless to break them apart?

Striding away from the courthouse, I take out my phone and begin reading the statement I have submitted against Jean. I imagine her listening to it, those watchful eyes moving rapidly, as they always did when I recounted my memories. I can even hear her voice, telling me that this isn't really the truth, just another false narrative I'm telling myself. She's tutting and calling me out for self-sabotage. For that weak way I always cave to external voices;

endlessly seeking the approval of others. She offers her own threatening insight: *You know I dreamt about this happening, Gus. I had a very vivid dream that one day you'd betray me.*

Like any self-appointed messiah, Jean often spoke of my betrayal, wielding it as both prophecy and threat. As I consider defying her, those words pierce through me again. I always laughed away Jeans' paranoia. I always promised it would never happen.

I exit the statement, and instead, open an email to the Finbow's legal team. *Not yet*, I think. *Not Monday. I can't do it.* Jean asked for my dedication and I gave it.

With shaking hands, I type out a long email to Anna's lawyers. It starts with an apology.

GUEST V FINBOW: DAY FIVE

Perhaps the greatest falsehood in my statement against Jean was that I found it difficult to lie. I've written that concealing my history with Mary whilst keeping in contact with Jean over the Finbows' legal strategies caused me deep personal anguish. But that is a fiction.

There were moments of shame, of course, but it was frightening how easily I withheld things; the fluid ease with which I slipped into the roles Anna cast for me. Her carer, but also someone to care for. Sometimes, I think back to the word-association game I played with Jean those years ago, and the quietness that fell over her as she sketched a profile from my impulsive answers. We both knew she had divined a darkness in me: a dishonesty that eventually became useful to her. At the time, I loved her for perceiving it. For seeing the mess of who I was, and loving me anyway.

But Jean's love was never steady. The bright beam of her attention brutally shifted and dimmed. When I got the job with Anna, I rushed to tell Jean, who began to answer my calls again. In turn, I helped her wherever I could, with whatever I overheard at Anna's, or could find. But, as always, it wasn't enough. My findings were never as sensational as Jean hoped they would be. Anna and Bonamy were just two people clawing their way through an ambiguous loss they could neither grieve nor understand. Jean wanted more. She wanted dirt.

I began to feel that pressure again, the same feeling I'd had when we began our therapy, of not being able to come up with anything rich enough for her to exploit. The mediocre findings, and then my growing affection towards Anna – of course, Jean sensed it – began to frustrate her. She withdrew. My calls went unanswered, while at the same time, my sympathy towards Anna deepened. When I heard about Mary handing out the flyers in the Tube station, and knew that Jean was lying when she said she'd be giving any gains from the lawsuit to charity, I felt a revulsion towards her that I could no longer contain.

So, it was a conscious decision to drop the perfume at Anna's apartment. Listening to the Finbows row, and watching their misery so close at hand, was unbearable. I wanted the nightmare over. A wave of fear filled my mouth as Anna studied the tin, and I waited for her to make the connection. It was Mary's, of course. She used to dab it on her wrists and neck, then, maddeningly, into the tips of her hair. I stole it because I missed her, carrying it with me like some tragic totem. I dropped it to make her parents understand we had a history.

How on earth did I get hold of it? This was Anna's question as she turned suddenly, her eyes still red from her tearful row. Adrenalin surged through me, then a steady pulse of relief. I could help this family now. I wanted to do whatever I could to support them.

'I stole it, Anna,' I replied calmly. 'I opened the drawer of your kitchen dresser and I stole it.'

But they hadn't taken me seriously. They both just laughed.

'Very good!' Bonamy roared, slapping the table. I could have shrunk to the ground with smallness. 'Too funny,' he chuckled.

Anna joined in, shaking her head, saying, 'Mad girl,' and pinching my arm. There was a heat between the pair of them that lingered from their argument and which now re-emerged as violent and carnivalesque. Bonamy passed me my rucksack, then waved me off, chuckling still, as he turned his attention back to his phone.

It hurt me that my connection to Mary was so far-fetched to them, it was laughable. But I also felt embarrassed for resenting the fact I had been robbed of some moment of great revelation. If we were still talking, Jean would have explained that I just wanted to be observed; another sign of the attention my parents had deprived me of. When I imagined her words, and the forgiveness Jean would have shown me, I missed her, bitterly.

In Her Defence

After that evening, I vowed to distance myself from the toxic triangle I had created. June turned into July and Anna returned to London. Still, Jean and I were no longer in contact. With Anna gone, for the first half of July, I stayed inside, avoiding the good weather and making very bad art that I put up for sale for cynical sums of money. I searched online, desperately, for traces of Mary, in the background of other people's photographs or even on music-streaming sites. I emailed Jean until I was blocked. Then wallowed in the shame of it. I was always getting in my own way. Jean blocking me was just another sign of how I'd blocked myself.

Then, an email arrived. Following that, a driver with a soft shoulder bag containing Quill. Anna and Bonamy would be in Corfu until the end of August and wanted me to take care of him. An envelope of money was tucked inside the bag, along with a gift basket of tatty crockery: seconds from her factory floor, which would have been hastily compiled by her team. The Finbows never asked, they simply assumed I was available to help, but in a small way, it tempered my guilt towards them. I was glad to serve the family from a distance.

I composed many different emails over the rest of that summer, outlining the truth about my involvement with Jean, and what I had done. When I didn't send them, Quill was my excuse. With no contact from Jean, he lightened my days and I depended on his company. Knowing that at the end of the summer I would be returning him, allowed me to put things off. Soon it would be August. I would explain myself then. Perhaps not all the story, but part of it. Enough to offer my help for the Finbows' case.

I didn't yet feel able to admit everything Jean had made me do.

Anna messaged me as soon as their flight landed, asking me to bring Quill down from Stoke to London.

Stay for our party if you want!

It took me a moment to work out that Anna was referring to their annual Carnival party. The Notting Hill Carnival commemorated the neighbourhood's healing from brutal race riots in the 1970s. But, for the Finbows, it was just an excuse for an event which was notoriously fun and, for a certain social set, a summer fixture, in the way that Glastonbury and opera festivals and tennis tournaments are. The show went on, even without Mary.

As I travelled down to London with Quill, I was ashamed by my curiosity; how quickly and compulsively I had accepted Anna's invitation. My excitement only grew as I made my way through the crowded neighbourhoods and sound systems. The roads were already littered with crumpled cans of beer, leaflets for local churches and after-parties, cobs of corn that had been bitten bald. Rain earlier in the day had produced that wet-pavement smell mixed into other, richer Carnival odours that were driving Quill wild: cooked meat and sticky hash.

He was strapped to my chest, as we shuffled slowly forward through the dense crowds and approached Pembridge Villas. Then, I began to notice the grander houses and the blonde-haired Mary lookalikes standing in window frames, gazing down on the carnival like princesses in royal boxes. When they danced past me on the street, they linked arms and threw their blonde heads back in laughter, all confidence, plimsolls and creaking leather jackets. All Mary. We had to get her home, I pictured telling the Finbows that evening, after the party had wound down. They would be shocked, of course, to learn about my past with Mary but I would persuade them that I could help. I harboured indulgent fantasies of the three of us sitting at the kitchen table together and concocting a rescue strategy. Fantasies even I couldn't quite bring myself to believe.

Eventually, I found the Finbows' pink detached villa. An ornate metal balcony ran along the width of the house at first-floor level, and its porch was covered in heaving wisteria. Of course, it wasn't my first visit to the Finbows' London house. In the month after I returned from Rome, I had, on occasion, waited nearby for Mary; a sad hangdog in her pursuit. Now, there was a weightless thrill to be making my way up the pink front steps and pressing the bell.

'Gussie! And my hound!' Bonamy opened the door. From downstairs, I heard laughter and music, but the look on his face made me realise the invite had come from Anna. 'So good of you to come!' He had bottles of wine in each hand, which he passed to Clover as he brought Quill and me inside and strode down the wooden-floored hallway. 'We're just out in the garden playing a game. Come and join us. Clover, take her jacket, will you?'

I followed him down into a beautiful, dark-green kitchen, with a domed glass roof overhead. Clover busied herself in the fridge, showing something to the caterers, while I lingered awkwardly near the entrance to the garden. It was just like the Finbows, I thought, not to sense the bad optics of throwing a party like this, so close to the trial. Venturing out into the garden, I encountered at least a hundred people. *They just partied on*, as Mary used to say.

'Let's find you something to drink.' Bonamy beamed, placing a warm hand on my shoulder and guiding me through the crowd.

Towards the back of the garden, there was a large grill spitting meat juices, and, to the right of it, a long table, which a number of the guests were sitting around. They were a mixture of young and old, all dressed in colourful clothes, big smiles pasted across their faces. Anna stood at the far end, a drink and cigarette in hand. Like Bonamy, who was wearing an orange waistcoat with a Nehru collar, Anna was also wearing vaguely ethnic items of clothing: a long skirt made of a red-and-black wax material; a matching bra top which showed off her ageless waist. Her dark hair was plaited into two long braids and there were big gold hoops in her ears. On her forehead, was a piece of paper which read, *Anna Finbow*.

'Do you know the name game?' a man next to me whispered as I slipped into the nearest seat. He wore mirrored aviators, but his face was familiar, and, moments later, I realised I knew him from a famous television show about life on a Cornish farm. Before long, a tumbler of milky punch was placed in front of me, clinking with ice. Next, a plate of grilled meat, served with a heap of grains and a minty dressing. I drank fast, wanting to catch up with the party around me. It was exhilarating to be there among all those famous faces; to sit back in the Finbows' magical garden and just bask in the belonging. I had to remind myself my stay here was only temporary. Once I told them the truth about what I had concealed, my role on the inside of this family would be over.

'You're all laughing,' Anna said, smiling coyly around the table at her guests. The piece of paper was fixed in the middle of her eyebrows like a bindi. 'Am I very bloody difficult?'

That provoked more laughter. She took a final drag from her cigarette and stubbed it out on the empty dinner plate of a young boy who was sitting on his mother's lap, sucking his thumb. 'Okay!' she shouted. 'Who's on the clock?'

'Me,' shouted a man over in the corner. My heart froze at his voice. Scottish. Frighteningly familiar. I looked over. There were his ridiculous round glasses, his thick painter's hands, a blue paisley shirt which strained at his chest.

Lawrence.

Fury coursed through me. The sheer guile of that bastard turning up here. Then my anger shifted to fear. He wouldn't remember me now, or would he? I turned my head to face away.

'Go!' Lawrence shouted.

'Am I male?' asked Anna.

'No!' everyone called.

'Am I on the television?'

'Yes,' they chorused.

'Am I an actress?'

There was a pause. 'A drama queen,' piped Bonamy, who was now standing to the side. Anna laughed along and stroked her chin.

'On the television,' she mused, 'but not an actress... Am I in reality TV?'

'Sort of,' said a gamine girl about my age, wearing a thin white vest and a Jamaican hair scrunchie. And, when half the table disagreed, she protested. 'Well, she sort of is!'

'Okay, then,' said Anna. 'Half reality.' She hesitated. 'Is my family famous?'

That question quietened all of us, many of the guests looking away. Anna sensed the change in mood and narrowed her eyes, letting the question linger and studying the expressions of those around the table. She hadn't greeted or acknowledged me, and that was thrilling; how readily I'd been absorbed into the retinue.

'Yup,' my neighbour's voice boomed. 'You are well known.'

'Sounds scurrilous,' Anna said. 'I must be a politician. Do I belong to a political species?'

'Only when it suits you,' someone said. 'Otherwise, you act as if you hate us.'

Everyone laughed heartily to dissipate the tension. Anna's lips moved as if she was remembering her previous questions. 'On the television...' she began again. 'Oh! Do I present things?'

'Yes!' everyone roared, relieved that the family question had been forgotten.

'Am I popular?'

A burst of hilarity at that. A blonde woman with taut, beautiful skin lifted her wine glass and said, 'You're adored, darling.'

'By kids or adults or both?'

'Too many words!' someone protested.

But Anna fixed me in her gaze, and tilted her head in exaggerated supplication.

'Help me out here, Gussie, will you?'

Her sudden address startled me. The guests turned and stared, including – I was sure of it – Lawrence. I clutched my glass tightly, feeling my cheeks burn with terror at the thought of him calling me out in front of everyone. Not now, I thought, my heart thudding as I pictured the scene that would follow. Not here. He cannot expose me here.

Anna clapped her hands and turned her attention away. I had dithered for too long. 'I don't trust these drunk goons,' she said, pouting. 'Am I for grown-ups, or do children love me?'

'They all love you,' my neighbour piped up. 'All ages. Even if the kids don't know you, they still somehow love you, if you get what I mean. You're sort of everywhere.'

'Okay and, um, am I very beautiful?'

'The most heavenly creature to have walked this earth,' called Bonamy, leaning against a tree.

'Hang on a minute,' Anna said, in a voice like a detective. She drummed her fingers against her cheek. 'Am I at this table?'

'Five seconds!' shouted Lawrence over the laughter as he counted down.

'Oh, bloody hell I *am*!' Anna laughed. 'I'm not Anna Finbow, am I?'

'Yes!' we all shouted as an alarm began to ring loudly and Lawrence called for time, slapping his huge hand down onto the table.

Anna wiggled her hips with triumph as Bonamy kissed her on the mouth. When they pulled away, her face shone with affection, her eyes twinkling and thickly outlined in mascara. She laughed heartily at something someone said behind her, then sucked on her cigarette. Bonamy was right, she did look beautiful. Beneath that beauty was Mary.

I thought back to the time Mary had told me about Anna's affair with the MP. Despite the horror of their circumstances, Bonamy and Anna had found the depths of reserve to love each other again. Their resilience shamed me as I turned away to fill my glass. I had hidden so much from them and in search of what? These flashes of Mary's expressions in their faces? Or was it the affection she had withheld? These were all excuses, I knew. I had been guided by a darker, sadistic comfort: the pleasure of witnessing Mary's parents suffer her absence; to observe them in deeper sadness than my own.

I turned towards the television presenter and pretended to listen to a long story he was telling, all the while keeping track of Lawrence's movements and interactions. After ten minutes or so, I rose quietly from the table, ready with the excuse of wanting to help tidy up. But no one saw me leave.

Gradually, the guests departed while I cleaned dishes at the sink. Still, there were a hardened few, perhaps a dozen, who stayed on drinking. An art dealer tried to engage me in conversation while I rinsed glasses. I asked polite questions about his business, but then he slumped sideways onto a window seat, his drink slopping out of his glass and onto the cushion. All the time, Bonamy and Anna were clattering in and out of the garden, retrieving old records from the living room upstairs, dancing together and getting in the way. I kept sight of Lawrence through the kitchen window as he sat on a striped garden swing smoking Silk Cuts, talking to the television presenter. I tracked him as he meandered past me and into the house.

I'd got away with it, I realised then. Lawrence hadn't noticed me. Quill was lying in his bed in the corner, happily settled. The party was winding down. For some moments, I considered it. If I left now, there would be no rupture and no great scene. I should tell them on a different day, because the Finbows were too drunk, too occupied to hear my confession. What compelled me to stay, where it was dangerous? There was somewhere I had to see. Just once. Only briefly, then I would go. Wiping my hands on a tea towel and checking over my shoulder, I crept quietly upstairs.

The ceramic letters on her bedroom door were wonky. I paused to straighten the *M* as I pushed it open and took in the dim stillness of Mary's bedroom. The space was a museum to Finbow textiles as much as it was a temple to Mary's girlhood. The drawn curtains were upholstered in the same Finbow fabric as the little armchair, the headboard, the lampshade. It was a familiar print: rows of pale pink ballerinas, entwined with roses.

On a pinboard was a collection of Mary's old riding rosettes, and tacked on the walls were faded posters of rabbits and watercolours of her houses in Scotland or Greece. Next to me, on the wall by the bed, I noticed the grubby smudge marks that her fingers had once made. The sight of them made my stomach curl with guilt; how had I just sat there at the table, avoiding Lawrence's gaze? I found myself going over to Mary's desk, where I knew I could hurt myself. I opened drawers, searching for evidence of us: a photograph, a little sketch; anything that would prove I'd meant something to her.

And then a sudden sound close by. A toilet flushing. In the corner of the room, a disguised door, which had been wallpapered over, opened abruptly. Anna appeared.

I froze. Desk drawer open. Chest fallen into the pit of my stomach. Pulse hammering my neck, my fingertips. She jumped when she saw me, then recovered herself.

'Gussie!' she scolded, playfully, wagging a finger. I noticed that in her other hand, she was gripping something. 'You know, guests aren't supposed to be up here!'

'I'm just—' I stammered as she walked over and tried to bustle me from the room. 'Leaving. Someone took my coat. I wondered if—'

We were at the threshold when the bathroom door-handle rattled again. I swivelled around in surprise, Anna turning more reluctantly. Someone else had been inside it with her. Another flushing sound, a familiar cough, then the door sprang open. Lawrence walked out of the same bathroom, pinching his nose.

'Hullo,' he burred, glancing mischievously towards Anna. 'The other one was busy.'

Mary's childhood bed was between us, the eiderdown rumpled from where I'd been sitting, a wide gulf of cream carpet surrounding it. Anna stood by the open door, coaxing us both downstairs.

In Her Defence

'Guests aren't supposed to be up here!' she repeated, matron-like, as if they hadn't emerged from the same place.

But it was too late, for as Lawrence approached, he also caught my eye. One second passed. Then another. He held my gaze. I wanted to turn and place my forehead against the bedroom wall forever, but there was no chance of it. He lifted his glasses.

'Aha, it's you!' He squinted at me and I cursed him inside: his thick neck, the hair on the back of his hands, the threatening alignment of his neat, sharp teeth. 'Now, I know you from somewhere.'

We were by the door now, all three of us. The room felt unbearably crowded, but there was no escape. Anna folded her arms and looked at me with impatience. She was high, I could tell. Agitated with it. 'Do you two know each other?'

I smiled thinly. 'Not really—'

There was a pause. Law squinted at me again, then his face shifted in recognition. I wanted to collapse. Fall to my knees or fight him.

'Rome. We met in Rome,' Lawrence said, his eyelids flickering. 'Don't tell me. One of my students. What year were you? Don't tell me – was it Grace?'

'Gus,' I said quietly.

He beamed, and I knew I was discovered. 'That's it! I'd never forget a face like yours. You were one of our models, weren't you?'

'I don't think so.'

'A couple of years ago, wasn't it? That's it! You kept emailing us about your portrait!'

'Don't be absurd, Laurie,' said Anna. 'You're pissed.' She looked apologetically at me. 'He thinks everything is always about that bloody school!'

Anna strode out onto the landing. We followed. My limbs felt light as I estimated how many stairs existed between me and the front door. I wondered if this was now the moment. If I could run now.

'You were Mary's model.'

Anna turned, laughing, on the top stair. With her hand resting on the banister, and the great staircase beneath her, she was beautiful, like she'd stepped from a portrait herself. Then a shadow crossed her face. Her jaw tightened.

'Gussie doesn't know Mary. She's our help. She lives in the north.' There was a pause. Her gaze searched me, seeking reassurance. I couldn't meet it. 'Please tell me he's confused,' she whispered. 'Please?'

'He's not confused,' I said, my voice shaking with self-disgust.

'No?' said Anna, softly. 'No?'

'But I can explain—'

'—No!'

Lawrence and I stared at each other. The skin on his neck was flushed, and I wondered if he regretted what he'd just blurted out. Whether he knew that it might implicate him. In the horror of my uncovering, this was a shred of consolation: I would share Mary's confession. Anna and Bonamy had to know. I would not go down alone.

'He's not confused,' I said, rushing my words. 'I knew Mary. But it's important you understand: she wouldn't be gone if it wasn't for Lawrence.'

Anna was too furious to listen. She fled down the stairs and when she reached the bottom step, she looked up in outrage. Her face was full of motion, like the hard edges of a rock loosening and giving way to reveal more hard rock beneath it. 'Not you, Gussie,' she cried. 'Not you as well.' A sob escaped from her as she turned and fled. '*Please*, not you as well!'

I raced after her into the kitchen. The room was empty now, wine bottles littering the kitchen counter like fallen skittles. Anna crouched over the sink, breathing deeply. When I approached her, she flinched.

'I knew there was something strange about you. You were always just *there*. Always hanging around, hanging on. Normally, I can spot them. Fantasists. But you! Wow!' She gave a cruel laugh and pointed. 'You were really fucking good.'

'Please,' I stammered.

'You *leech*. We told you everything!' She spat out the words. 'We *trusted* you!'

'Anna, stop. Please, calm down.'

'I think she should go,' Lawrence muttered, sidling up to her. I hadn't seen him enter the kitchen. Fury coursed through my veins as he started talking about how much I'd had to drink.

'Please, Anna. Just let me explain! It's that man, that *bully*, who should terrify you.' I walked over to where Lawrence stood by the kitchen table. 'Do you get a kick out of being here?' I snarled. 'In her home? Doing *coke* with her mum in her bathroom?'

Lawrence laughed scornfully and shook his head, though the skin on his face was growing red too.

'Is this your coat?' He picked up the nearest garment to hand, which he pressed hard into my stomach. 'I think it's time to head off now, isn't it? You've had a lot of punch—'

'—Not enough to forget the truth, Lawrence.'

'—Are you still in touch?' Anna interrupted, seizing a glass of wine and walking towards me, her eyes travelling angrily over my face as she spooled backwards through the last few months. I could feel her replaying all our little trusting chats; the details she had relayed about the trial. The questions I had asked about Mary. The breadth of my betrayal. 'Please tell me you're not communicating with her?' I hesitated, remembering Anna only knew about my relationship with Mary; nothing of Jean. I bit my lip as Anna gestured at me, clumsily, with her glass. 'I let you hear everything. Everything!'

'I don't know any more than you do,' I snapped, bitterly.

'Oh, so you weren't actually friends,' she jeered. 'Of course not.' She laughed to herself. 'You're a complete *nobody*.'

'We were close enough for her to tell me the fucked-up things he did to her,' I cried, pointing across at Lawrence.

'What?' said Anna, aghast.

'When she was sixteen!'

'She was like this in Rome too, Anna.' Lawrence boomed in a bored tone. '*Completely* obsessed with your daughter. Deluded about her. The other students talked about it. Wasn't healthy. Now, now.' There was frightening force in his chuckle as he reached for my arm, gripped it. 'I think it's time to leave, don't you? Come on, let's go.'

'Get off me!' I shrieked, shaking him clear. In an instant, I was Mary at the party, stumbling away from him, toga unravelled, her hair all matted. I blinked, feeling light-headed as I tried to suppress the memory.

'Oh, I get it,' said Anna sarcastically, going over to the kitchen table and sitting down. 'She's swallowed all those rumours about you, Lawrence.' She winced. 'That's what happened.'

'In Mary's case, it's true.'

A look of dread passed over Anna's face. 'What do you mean?'

I knew then that Mary had it wrong, that Anna had no idea about what had happened to her as a teenager. Jean had twisted things, consciously misinterpreting Mary's misgivings to weave the far darker story that Anna and Bonamy had known about, or even condoned, Law's behaviour.

'Listen to me, please.' I rushed on. 'You can't have him speak at the trial. You categorically *cannot* call him as a fucking character witness—'

'—This is *outrageous*,' said Lawrence, stepping towards me again.

'It'll destroy Mary. She'll never come back, not to any of us—'

'—You've said your piece,' said Lawrence. 'Now, out!'

'—Just, let her finish, will you?' Bonamy stepped into the kitchen from the garden, pulling the door behind him. I felt a wave of relief at his presence. Weakly, I smiled at him. He looked away.

'Do you remember the costume party in Rome, Anna?' I asked, speaking quickly. 'The one on the island? You won't remember it, but we actually talked. I remember your outfit, so clearly.'

Lawrence called from behind me. 'Enough with this madness—'

'—You had all these paper butterflies stuck to your eyelashes.'

'You shouldn't have let her anywhere near your family,' Lawrence said, now addressing Bonamy. But Anna looked rattled. A flicker of familiarity crossed her face.

'I saw them together at that party,' I said flatly. 'Lawrence and Mary.'

Lawrence interrupted angrily. 'Anna, don't listen to this *parasite*.'

I turned on him then. 'Mary told me everything. How much you fucked her up. On family holidays. At parties. She thinks you knew, Anna!' I said, a sob escaping from me. 'She told me you've always known!'

Anna gazed, glassy-eyed. There was a moment's pause, and I wondered if my words, although difficult to hear, might actually have reached her. Then her manner shifted. Her jaw reset in utter distaste.

She turned, slowly, to face me. 'How *dare* you come into my home and spread this utter bile about my closest friend? Lawrence has been a part of our family for years. Whereas *you* are a liar. A liar who we trusted with everything!'

'A *fucking* fantasist!' said Lawrence.

'You didn't really trust me, Anna!' I snapped. 'You just argued in front of me. No wonder Mary wanted out of your family. She said it was toxic.'

Anna made a cry of outrage, then steadied herself. 'Bonamy,' she said, breathing deeply. 'Get her out. She's dangerous. Where's the dog? Does she still have the dog?' Then she looked me up and down. I was wearing the dungarees she'd once admired. 'Are those my fucking *clothes*? Did you steal them from Mary? This is too much! You actually *terrify* me!' Bonamy approached me slowly, and Anna kicked at the table leg. 'Get her out, now!'

'I'm telling the truth, Anna,' I sobbed as Bonamy guided me upstairs and towards the front door. 'I promise you, it's the truth.'

'Liar!' she shouted. 'Get out!'

After a moment, Anna stomped up the stairs and prowled after us. By the front door, she grabbed my arm.

'Hang on, I think I do remember something actually,' she said, leering viciously into my face. 'Mary did mention you once. She came home one weekend and talked about her *model*. She said that you had rather a crush on her, I think.' The door opened, but she held me there on the step and leaned even closer towards me. 'You embarrassed her.'

She slammed the door, but, to my surprise, Bonamy led me right out of the front gate, pausing under the lamplight. I started to feel faint. I looked around helplessly for somewhere to slump down.

Grip the earth, I said to myself. *Name the smells.*

'We gave you a chance,' Bonamy said. 'We made you quite comfortable. All we asked for was a bit of loyalty in return—'

'—I'm sorry,' I gasped. 'I never meant—'

'What is it you want from us? Is it money? Is that what this is about?'

'That's the last thing I want.' My voice trembled. 'I don't want money. I just want Mary to be...' I paused as I searched for the words. I knew I couldn't say *mine*. 'Free.'

'But this stuff about Lawrence?' His face was pale, the muscles of his mouth puckered with emotion.

'Bonamy, please believe me,' I begged. 'Mary thinks you and Anna knew. And ignored what was happening, or even supported it.'

Bonamy's lip quivered. 'I'm just realising that I mentioned him. I *bloody* said his name when I saw her at the Tube. No wonder—' Then he turned, interrupting his own thoughts, surveying me with seriousness. 'You said you knew her in Rome?'

I nodded. 'That's when I first saw them together.'

'But, hold on. If you knew Mary as you claim to do, then why didn't you say?' His voice cracked. 'You might have helped us.'

'Because,' I stammered. 'Because it was Mary I wanted to help, not you. I thought she needed help, from someone outside her family. An adult she could trust.'

There was a long pause. I could hear Bonamy's mind piecing together the facts. 'So was it you that took her to—' Bonamy brought a fist to his mouth. He turned from me, unable to utter her name.

'To Jean?' I nodded, my chest tight as I confirmed it.

Bonamy swore. I stood there numbly for a moment, then I tried to explain. 'This thing with Lawrence, it really fucked her up. At the time, Jean was treating me. I thought it might help. She means well, I promise. At the beginning, she does actually mean well. I definitely believe that.'

'—I'll kill him!' Bonamy roared suddenly into darkness. He turned back, wild in his eyes and breathing loudly through his nose, 'You're still in touch with her?' he stammered.

'With Mary?'

'No,' he hissed. 'Jean.'

I held my breath. 'Sometimes.'

'And you've, you've *told her things?*'

'She asked me to,' I said, hating myself as I sobbed and lied. 'It was her idea to—'

'Hang on,' Bonamy cut me off, looking at me with an expression of utter loathing. Then a thought seemed to pass through him. A jolt of realisation. 'And you *claim* you wanted to help my daughter?' I glanced up, hopefully. 'Then you will find yourself a solicitor and make a statement. Against Jean. You can join our defence.'

The thought of betraying Jean in public made me want to be sick. Still, I nodded.

'And then?'

'And *then?*'

'What about Lawrence?' I ventured.

Bonamy's gaze travelled all over my face. First, there was sadness in his pale blue eyes, then anger. Finally, a ghost in his glance, fading away as I was outcast: Mary.

'And then, Gussie, you will leave my family *the fuck* alone.'

GUEST V FINBOW: DAY FIVE

Evening

In the recording, we are back in Jean's living room in Rome. I recognise it from the long cream sofa, and the carpet that was so thick, you left footprints in it. On the ottoman between us, there is Jean's infinite supply of tissues and a warm teapot. The heavy curtains are drawn, something she used to insist on during our later sessions. At the time I didn't notice it, but they acted like blinders on a racehorse, keeping my focus in the room and concealing the passing of time.

At first, there is a giggling sound; the camera's on but I'm not yet in shot. Instead, you hear me calling to Jean from the kitchen, asking what there is to eat.

'Anything.' Jean's voice comes from behind the camera. 'Help yourself.' Then the frame fills. I walk into view.

'Woah,' I say, raising my hand like a film star. 'Paparazzo! Is that an actual camera? I thought we just did audio?' There is food in my mouth which I chew playfully.

'You don't mind?' says Jean. 'It'll be helpful.'

I sit down heavily on her sofa with my plate of focaccia, and look directly into the lens. 'Just not me eating.' I grin broadly. 'I'm a pig.'

There's something in that grin – in its silliness, its joyful trusting – that makes me want to cry. It's not my vulnerability that upsets me, but how confident I seem. At the time, I felt so insecure, but I see now that I came across differently. I marvel at how I just walked into Jean's living room – a sure-footed, big-booted, lanky lope, dressed in some old purple suit that Mary had probably complimented at some point, one hand plunged deep in my trouser pocket. How trusting I was then, just throwing myself onto the sofa, right into the centre of the camera frame; how brave I was, to tilt my head backwards and talk.

Abruptly, the video cuts, and there I am again, coyly shuffling some sheets of paper and passing them over to Jean.

'These drawings are so embarrassing,' I say, glancing at the camera. 'I'm supposed to be an artist.'

'You're coming up with homes again and again. Interesting.'

There is a silence. Noisily, I swallow tea. Then we both laugh, acknowledging the awkwardness. It is a terrible sound.

'Was home a lonely place, Gus?' Jean asks in a soothing tone. She supplies that detail so swiftly that I feel my hackles rise.

'I suppose so. It's hard to remember how I used to feel—'

'—You're very protective of your parents, Gus, considering what they put you through. To my mind, they were *toxic*. They make me want to do this.'

Although she is behind the camera, I know that Jean is cradling her arms. She'd often demonstrate these soothing gestures when I spoke of my home life. I liked how she'd flinch and shiver. Soothing herself was more proof that I'd suffered.

'I wonder why you protect them? Do you still feel ashamed of how they let you down? You do realise how seriously they let you down, don't you?'

My face darkens at Jean's suggestion, but then I start nodding.

'What did you think about the reading I sent you?' she continues.

The book was called *Begin Again* and had been written by two American psychotherapists in the late 1970s. It contained lists of physical and mental symptoms that were supposed to indicate buried trauma in the mind and body: Jean's little bible.

'Quite eerie, actually. It made a lot of sense.' I nod. 'Thanks.'

'The pages I folded over for you, the checklists. Did you see much of yourself in those?'

'It was, like, every single one.' I laugh in a rasping way. 'Except the bed-wetting.'

'Why don't you read out some of the statements you identify with?'

'Um, sure.' I pick up the book and begin reading: '"I have a great deal of unused capacity which I have not turned to my advantage. I feel unable to protect myself in dangerous situations."' My voice wobbles at the last: '"I feel that there is something wrong with me deep down inside; that if people really knew me, they would leave."'

Jean's arm leans across the ottoman towards me. Though only her wrist is visible, I notice the brand of her watch: far more expensive than I'd ever realised. My stomach begins to hurt.

I shut the book theatrically. 'And that's the end of the story!' I try to laugh again.

'Is it?' she asks, with calm authority. 'Not unless we first forgive ourselves for these thoughts. Shall we go back to when they might have started? You see, our memory functions a bit like this video I'm taking of you. Or a roll of film. It's all in there, we just have to spool backwards and locate it.'

There is a pause. Jean stands up then and helps me into the position she always had us lie in. Eagerly, I let her arrange me. The slow head massage begins.

'Let's rewind the tape, Gus,' she whispers softly.

Imogen Carr leans over for the remote control and presses pause. I cover my eyes, unable to bear the sight of Jean's fingertips greedily stroking and pressing upon my hair, as though she were polishing a rare piece of jewellery.

'Augusta,' Ms Carr says gently. 'Augusta, are you alright?'

The video is too excruciating to watch in full. It is like seeing myself without skin. I lower my forehead on the table so that it rests on the barristers' chambers' stationery: a pad of paper and two sharpened pencils that were set out for every chair around the glass table of the conference room. I had sent Anna's legal team the email only a couple of hours ago, requesting the withdrawal of my evidence, but my vacillation only brought on their charm offensive.

I can't pretend I didn't enjoy how quickly Bernard's car pulled up next to me by the Tube station, with all the suaveness of a spy in some television drama. As a key witness, I knew they couldn't afford to let me panic and flee London. There was an offer of a more luxurious hotel room to spend the weekend in, too, so that I would be well-rested before my evidence. They fussed around and got me a pizza for dinner. Then I was brought into Ms Carr's brightly lit conference room for a serious talk.

'I know this recording is confronting,' she says soothingly, as I eventually lift my head. 'But it's fantastic evidence, Gus, and we're so glad you located it for us. It's just a reminder of the importance of what you're about to do. It's *exactly* why you must be brave now and speak up for the truth. Look at the way she touches you. The way she puts ideas into your head—'

'They weren't all her ideas. We were discussing my life!'

'She must be stopped.'

I glance at the screen, then away. However crooked Jean's analysis was, a large part of me still wished I was back there, basking in her attention and the comfort of that apartment. My mind wrestles with the yearning. *It wasn't hers.* I tell myself. *It was rented. Her whole life was rented.*

'What about Lawrence?' I say, folding my arms. 'What about the way *he* touches people?'

'Gus,' Bernard warns. 'You know what we said about bringing him up.'

Beneath the table, my foot stamps. 'I don't see how he gets to carry on living his charmed life in his *atelier*, while we're all forced to go through this.'

Ms Carr glances at Bernard. 'I take it you have warned her about courtroom libel?'

Bernard clears his throat. 'You can't just go in there making accusations about random men, Gus. You need to be really careful.'

'He's not random.'

'No,' Ms Carr agrees. 'He isn't random.'

'I told you, other students are speaking against him!'

'So let the story come out! They aren't your accusations to make. The truth is, whatever happened with him and Mary, this is still a vulnerability that Ms Guest has exploited. If it wasn't Lawrence, there would be some other wound she'd be prising open for her own benefit.' I shiver and she proceeds more carefully. 'Which is why your account of how she coerced you is so important.'

It irritates me how glibly Ms Carr describes my experiences as an *account*.

'But it's not that easy,' I snap. 'Look at Oriel. Look at what happened to her.'

'Exactly, Gus,' Ms Carr snaps back. 'Think of Oriel and all the other lives this woman will destroy.'

There is a heated pause. Bernard tops up my glass of water. For a while, I gaze forward, unwilling to face the full significance of what Ms Carr has just said.

'But there's other things I want to make clear,' I venture quietly. 'Jean's not all bad. She also made me feel better.' I turn slightly, to appeal to Bernard, but he won't meet my eye. 'You don't understand how caring she could be.'

Ms Carr removes her glasses. 'She encouraged delusions in you for her own gain.'

'Yes, but she also gave me hope.'

'That hope bred a dependency which she exploited.'

'It was still hope.'

Frustrated, Ms Carr and Bernard eye each other warily, then she nods at him. Bernard removes his phone from his pocket and places it on the table. 'You've got the weekend to think it over now, Gus.

No one can force you to do anything.' He hesitates. 'But perhaps this might help you to see straight.'

He turns the handset over. On the screen, there is a map with a pin the middle of it. My mouth turns dry. 'This is Mary's last known location.'

A tense quiet falls over the room.

'You're saying I can visit?' I ask, breathless. It has been so long since I've known of Mary's whereabouts.

Ms Carr releases a sigh of disapproval, gets up from the table and looks out of the window. 'If it helps you understand how critical your evidence on Monday will be, then, yes.'

'Are you sure she's there?'

'Not certain, no,' Ms Carr says. 'This is our best estimate.'

'Go there,' Bernard says simply. 'See if she'll talk to you. If not, just take a look at how she's living. A pregnant woman. The state Jean's got her in.'

I hurry to copy the location down. 'Thank you,' I stammer. 'You don't know how much this means.'

Ms Carr faces me with folded arms. 'Giving evidence is a civic privilege, Gus. Everything you say under oath is a serious matter. We are trusting you with this information. But can we trust *you* on Monday?'

I murmur some acknowledgement, but, in my mind, I am already back with Mary. I begin to pack my coat and bag, now guided by a strange purpose: she might listen to me. If we spend real time together, like we have before, I can try and get through to her. The two of us can discuss what we've been through. We can give Jean up together.

Ms Carr repeats her question more urgently, bringing my attention back to the room. 'We are trusting you to keep this address to yourself. But Monday morning, Augusta. Your evidence. There is nothing more you're keeping from us, is there?'

I shake my head, but my mind is running away with itself. Anna had looked at me with such loathing at the Carnival party, but what if I got her everything she wanted? What if I was the one who could break the spell and bring Mary home? Would I finally be forgiven?

'We're depending on you, Gus,' Ms Carr repeats. 'Your evidence must be rock solid. Can we trust that you'll be there?'

By now, I am standing by the open door. I give them both a quick nod, but I cannot deliver any real assurance. Why should I be asked to make promises, when no one bothered to keep theirs to me?

SUNNYMEDE, SATURDAY

The entrance to Mary's squat is marked by a hand-painted sign and two wheelbarrows filled with old flowerpots and bits of driftwood.

Welcome to Sunnymede.

Online, Sunnymede styles itself as an artists' collective, but in person, it's much bleaker: a woodland gathering of a few makeshift cabins. Every dwelling looks filthy, and the wind chimes hanging from the trees tinkle eerily over the drone of traffic from the M1 nearby. In the middle of the clearing, an old, mossy greenhouse stands; once a studio perhaps, but now filled with collapsed easels and old sleeping bags. I am peering through the window, looking for signs of Mary's work, when a young woman with bleached white dreadlocks approaches.

'Everything alright?' She smiles, dreamily.

'I'm here to visit someone,' I stammer, feeling conspicuous in my clean clothes. 'Mary Finbow?'

The girl's expression falls. She eyes me with suspicion. 'You're not the health visitor, are you?'

'No,' I say, shaking my head. 'A friend.' She hesitates and twists her fingers in her hands. 'Of Jean's.'

Her name is a crude password. The girl points in the distance, towards a second clearing.

'Right at the top there. Head through the trees – there's a few more cabins. Can't remember which one's hers. If I were you, I'd just shout.'

'Does she live alone?' I ask, suddenly nervous of what I might encounter.

The woman raises her palms to the sky as if feeling for drops of rain and shrugs. 'None of us do.'

Her directions lead to a line of four cabins with sloping corrugated-iron roofs and flattened plastic bottles peeking from gaps. *The state of this place*, I think, remembering the frescoed walls of Mary's apartment in Rome; its silky, wide bed; her daily housekeeper. In court, Mary described this place as "simpler," but how did she fit in here? How could she tolerate it? My evidence in court on Monday takes on a frightening significance: if Jean wins her case, she'll retain Mary's other properties, consigning her and the baby to this dump forever.

'Mary?' My voice echoes, hopelessly, in the clearing.

No response. Only the twitter of birdsong between the grind of plane engines flying low overhead. A brief image returns: how excitedly I would stand outside her apartment on the Lungotevere for the sight of Mary's long brown legs in her pyjama shorts when she opened the door. The fruit smell of her when she brought me inside. *We were something*, I remind myself as I search the desolate surroundings. *The two of us had something. A future. When she sees me, she'll remember.*

Then, from behind me, the sound of twigs, snapping underfoot.

'Hello?' she calls in a voice that, although thinner and airier, is still recognisably hers. I spin around. There is Mary, emerging from the trees. I raise my hand, so struck by the sight of her that I can't speak. She looks like a park ranger, in a pair of worn chinos and a murky green jumper. The brown boots on her feet are carelessly laced, and in one hand, she leads a thin, trembling dog – perhaps a whippet – on a length of neon rope. In the other, she holds a packet of tissues. She stumbles as she sees me.

'It's you,' she says.

'It's me,' I say and smile, but something inside me has splintered. Mary checks around nervously. 'Who told you I was here?'

'Can we go and talk somewhere?'

'How did you find me?'

'Five minutes, Mary. That's all.'

We stand facing each other. Mary stays rooted a couple of metres away in the tall grass like a shy animal. 'I promise you, it's just me. No one else.'

She begins to walk towards me. 'You've actually caught me on a really busy day.'

'Mary,' I say, 'please.'

'I'm really sorry,' she says, briskly folding her arms against her stomach. With a shoot of pain, I register its swollen curve. 'Now isn't a good time.'

I take another step towards her. 'Please.'

At that moment, the whippet starts barking: a high-pitched bowing sound. 'She doesn't like strangers,' Mary says, squatting down and cradling the animal's juddering jaw. 'You're making her really anxious.' She hushes the dog for a moment longer, then sighs. 'You better come in.'

Mary's hut is warm and dry but in a dense, organic way, like the inside of a vegetable drawer. Towards the back of the room is a wood-burning stove, and a cardboard box, which the dog picks her way into. Mary busies herself making tea and the dog watches us with seal-like eyes, a whine caught in its throat.

'Comfy bed,' I comment as the kettle hisses and chimes to a boil. Once again, I am back in Rome, propped against the headboard, watching Mary get ready for a party or dinner I wasn't invited to. The tantalising sight of her body as she wriggled into her clothes, admiring herself in the mirror, before snake-hipping out of them and opting for something else. Today, Mary bears no resemblance to that girl. There is an intense nervousness about her. A guarded, simmering paranoia. She washed her hands for a long time after we first came in, drying each finger individually. Her gaze falls anywhere but on me.

'Biscuit?'

I accept, as she lowers her pregnant form onto a lambswool blanket to sit cross-legged on the floor, about a metre from the bed and within arm's reach of the dog. I check around for any photographs or paintings of her own, but there are none. Nor can I see any objects that might signal she is shortly due to give birth: no cot prepared, or maternity vitamins, or guides to surviving labour. The only books around are self-help tomes – many of which Jean had also encouraged me to read – arranged on the rotten windowsill. Other than that, the set-up is hopelessly monastic. The walls are bare, except for a sign near the entrance which reads: *The first step to a better world is the belief that it is possible.*

'Does anyone else live here?' I ask, aching to know about the baby's father.

'In the other cabins? Mainly creatives. Some travellers. It's nice.'

The biscuit forms stale clumps in my mouth as I think of Jean. How powerful she was, and how completely sick to set her prized client up somewhere like this and convince her she was happy.

'You're up north now?' She smirks. 'Working for *my family*?'

'Did Jean tell you that?'

Mary throws me another withering look. 'We both found it pretty disturbing that you'd actively seek them out. But it's your life. Your journey.'

Jean's treachery makes me want to scream. After everything I'd tried to do to help her case, Jean has portrayed me to Mary as some fame-hungry hanger-on. I open my mouth to defend myself, then decide against it. Later, I will explain.

'I wanted to find you after court the other day. To say, congratulations.' I gesture to the bump.

She tosses her head. 'That's what you came all the way here to tell me?'

'I've tried text,' I say coolly. 'You never respond.'

Mary laughs bitterly. A fresh wave of anger builds. I point carelessly at her pelvis. 'So Jean lets you have boyfriends now?' Mary ignores the question, concentrating on fishing something out of her cup of tea. I press her again. 'Doesn't he live with you?'

'There's no dad, Gussie,' Mary explains quietly. 'No boyfriend. This was an accident. One night. I went out on my own and drank. It was a lapse. I regressed. I'm lucky to have Jean's support.'

'—A total stranger? And you never considered letting it go?' Mary shakes her head as if the idea revolts her. 'Why not?' I say, exasperated. 'You're letting your own life go to waste, aren't you?' Mary says nothing. 'You know, when I first heard you were pregnant, I wondered if it was Lawrence's.'

Mary surveys me with disbelief. Her eyes grow an instant film of tears that fall down her face. From the right eye first, then the left. She swipes at them with a knuckle.

'Fuck you, Gussie,' she whispers. 'Fuck you, for even mentioning his name.'

I shift from the bed to the floor so that we are facing each other. 'Sorry,' I say gently. 'I don't know why I had to bring him up.'

Although I did know. In the recording yesterday, I had watched as Jean guided me towards conclusions that were falsely overblown. There was no doubting Lawrence and Mary's relationship: I had seen them together with my own eyes. But when Jean insinuated that her parents knew about the affair, hadn't this also suited her aims? In fabricating a far darker tale of their complicity, Mary became bound to her.

'I'm working to forgive Lawrence,' Mary says. 'With Jean.'

I reach for her hands. 'Mary, you know what they're saying Jean does, right? That she makes people believe things happened that never occurred at all?'

My question hangs limply in the air. Mary stares at me, livid.

'Here we go,' Mary says. 'Someone else who doesn't want to believe me. How can you question this?' She shudders. 'You even *saw us*.'

'I know you were together,' I say, soothingly. 'But I don't think other people did—'

'I think it's time you left, Gus.'

'I'm just scared Jean has convinced you of something far worse than...' I say, then leave a pause, aware of how tenuous it sounds. '... than the reality. Does she tell you about bad stuff in your past? Stuff that you've apparently forgotten?'

'We don't forget anything, Gus. We just can't—'

'—*Bear to remember?* She used that line on me, too.'

Chastened, Mary brings her knees to her chest. I inch closer.

'I need you to listen to me now. Jean is *dangerous*. Just look at what happened to Oriel; how Jean broke her down with all her lies about her family. And now she's dead. I'm not trying to doubt you, but as your friend, I owe you the truth—'

'—*Friends?* We're not friends, Gus.' Mary's eyes glint with angry tears. 'When I told you about him, you called me disgusting!'

'I could never be disgusted with you,' I say quietly, my head hanging low. 'Not ever.'

'Then where were you?' she storms. 'You let me down, just like my parents did!'

My temper flares. '*You're* the one who disappeared. You stopped picking up my messages. You left Rome without even telling me!'

Mary frowns and sits up a little straighter. 'No, I didn't. I sent you a letter, along with your portrait.' She begins to stammer as she recalls the sequence of events. 'At the end of term, Jean brought the painting and letter with her to London.' She frowns again. 'She said you picked it up during a session. That you laughed at it. It was fucking brutal to hear, actually. You were always so down on my work.'

My stomach lurches. I talk quickly, gulping for air. 'That's not true! The only contact I had from you was the email, cutting me off. A round fucking robin. No painting. No letter. Your profiles deleted, your number changed. You *vanished* Mary. For months, I tried to contact you. I *begged* Jean for news. She said you wanted me to leave you alone.'

'Right,' she says doubtfully. There is an uneasy pause, as she picks up a shiny beetle from the floor, cupping it in her hands and placing it carefully outside. The door wobbles shut. Leaning against it, she continues spitefully. 'You know, when you gave up on therapy and fucked off, you hurt us a lot. Jean and me.'

Revulsion floods my body. I spring up from the floor to face her. 'Why did Jean say I left London?'

She shrugs. 'You lost interest. You drifted. That's what you do, isn't it? And now,' she says, shuddering, 'you're Anna's little *puppet*. How much is she paying you for the appearance on Monday, out of interest?'

A shiver passes through me. Jean always kept me hanging on, promising that Mary would find her way back to me soon. This was a *necessary separation*, she claimed. First, there was the parental influence that she had to shake off, and the whole trauma of Lawrence. Then: Mary will be in touch *when the trial's over*. I turn towards the window, repulsed by how naïve I've been. But beneath that fear, a darker acknowledgement: for a long time, I believed Jean would prevent Mary from being with anyone else. Hadn't that suited how I felt about her? Annexed in her treatment, Mary could never reject me.

'We need to get you out of here, Mary,' I say flatly, turning back to her. 'This isn't an artists' collective; you're living in a forest squat. A ruined *fucking* jungle. And Jean is lying to you. You need to come with me now. For your own safety. For your *child's* safety.'

Mary goes over to the sink and concentrates on pouring food into a dog bowl. But she is agitated, and in a different way from before. Rattled, as if some element of our interaction has broken through and disturbed her.

Then she sighs and spins around. Her expression changes. My heart lifts.

'I didn't ask you to come, Gus. I didn't ask you to cosy up with Anna, or involve yourself in any of this. I don't know how you found me. Or what you want here. But I'm not asking you to support my choices. I just want to be left alone.'

'They're not your choices, Mary,' I explode. 'Can't you see that? They're *Jean's* choices. She's got you living here like a tramp. She's turned you against your parents. And, whatever you think of them, they are – you have *no idea* – falling apart without you. Your mother always carries a birthday card with her, wherever she goes. Just in case she bumps into you. She even sleeps in your childhood *bed*.'

'My mother is taking me to court,' Mary says blankly. 'And she's calling Lawrence as a witness. That tells me everything I need to know.'

'I told them about you and Lawrence, Mary.' I blurt it out suddenly. 'I'm so sorry, but I had to.'

'They've always known.'

'Trust me, they didn't. They were shocked. Your dad—' I say, and my voice chokes at the memory of Bonamy's anguish. 'Your poor dad was horrified.'

Mary watches my mouth for a moment, as if trying to focus her attention on what I've said. But then the blankness falls back over her eyes. 'Wrong, Gussie. You don't actually know my family. They've always known. It was just too ugly to address. They failed in their duty to protect me, so I had to say goodbye to them. It was the only way I could greet myself.'

I recognise that as a line of Jean's. I take her chin in my hand, but more firmly than I'd intended. Instantly, Mary pulls away, her lip curling in disgust.

'Jean warned me about this side of you,' she spits defensively. 'She said she did her best, but you were just like Oriel: *bitter*. And she told me about the things you used to say about me. When I think of the way you used to touch me in the night, Gus, when I was off my head, I feel *sick*.'

I hear myself utter a cry. She carries on.

'You wanted to have me, just like *he* wanted to have me. Like everyone's always wanted to have me.'

'Mary – I'm sorry – I didn't mean to make you uncomfortable—' I stammer tearfully, thinking back to how Jean encouraged it. 'I thought that you liked being with me. Wanted it. I thought it was nice. I thought we were having fun.'

'I didn't want it, Gussie.' Mary gasps, now wiping tears of her own. 'I needed a friend.' She grips desperately at her abdomen, and her voice falters. 'I want – need – a friend.'

I slump back on the bed, humiliated. The sting of Anna's words: *she said you were embarrassing*. Warm tears run down my cheeks as I imagine, with horror, that I pushed Mary into something she wasn't comfortable with. But did I really cross a line, or was this one of Jean's inventions? Another way she'd got Mary to believe she'd been exploited?

We stare at each other, bewildered. I desperately want to explain myself, to get her to understand just how far Jean has betrayed us both, but then Mary's phone starts to ring, a dull vibrating sound that shakes against the plastic worktop. My chest freezes. I recognise the sudden panic in Mary's eyes as my own.

'Don't answer it, Mary, please.' I beg. For a moment, Mary wavers. She looks down at the screen, then back at me. 'Don't answer. Don't tell her I'm here.'

Seconds pass; the old-fashioned handset hums insistently. Then, shaking her head as if waking from a dream, Mary turns.

'Hello, Jean,' she says.

GUEST V FINBOW: DAY SIX

'Augusta? Ready? It's time.'

The usher guides me into Courtroom Six. One foot in front of the other as I bow my head, unable to meet the eyes of dozens of people, all of whom, it feels, have read my private diary. I am only called into court when the recording of my session with Jean has concluded. The judge has been kind, at least, to spare me that torture. Approaching the witness box, I think of the words the lawyers, members of the gallery, and press, have just heard me speak: *I feel that deep down inside there is something wrong with me ... that if people really knew me, they would leave.* Today, standing on the raised platform, there is no hiding from it.

For most of today, proceedings have been halted as the judge considered the admissibility of some evidence. There were agonising hours of waiting in corridors and side rooms and cafés. There were last-minute pep talks from Bernard. The sickening, unsettling sense of waiting to go into theatre, laid flat and put under. Now, in the final thirty minutes of the day, I am sworn in, only to confirm the pieces of evidence which concern me. Neither Jean nor Anna are present. Only their barristers stand together, checklists tucked into their open folders. The most frightening part is still to come tomorrow: my cross-examination.

Ms Carr guides me first to the transcription of the recorded session with Jean. My vision blurs as I scan the rambling and stuttered sentences, rendered ridiculous now in typed text, framed by legal jargon.

'Do you confirm your identity in this video?' she prompts impatiently.

'Yes,' I say, my voice thin and regrettably girlish as I keep close to the microphone. 'Witness H is me.'

After the transcript, Ms Carr moves on to a series of images, which were sent as email attachments.

'Do you confirm that you composed and sent these emails?'

'I do.'

'And that the email inbox you sent them to was accessible by Ms Guest?'

'I believe it was.'

'We'll go through them chronologically. Please provide the context of each image, just briefly if you can. First, Image A, do you have it there? Sent on the third of April of this year?'

'It is a photograph,' I murmur, my fingers lightly tracing the page. 'Of Anna Finbow's front door.'

'Did you take this image?'

I pause, remembering those journalists who Jean must have coordinated. That pair of weasels who ransacked Anna's bins. I remind myself: *you were no better*.

'I took it, yes.'

We turn the page. Two other images follow. I confirm that I captured them both: correspondence between the Finbows and their private investigator; a letter from Anna to Oriel's mother Lucy. Then, finally:

'It's the pages of a notebook,' I explain.

'Who did the notebook belong to?'

'Someone in Mrs Finbow's legal team.'

A stirring sound, a frown from the judge. Anxiety crawling like ants across my chest. Ms Carr gestures over her shoulder.

'The people sitting over there?'

'The people sitting there.'

Ms Carr nods, blank and business-like with the stark facts of my deviancy. 'Thank you. That's all I have for today.'

In Her Defence

There is hardly time to take water before Ms Ibrahim speaks. She points me towards a page in the evidence bundle with the title: CALL LOG BETWEEN WITNESS H AND JEAN GUEST.

Lowering her file, Ms Ibrahim asks calmly, 'Ms Bird, is this your mobile phone number?'

'Yes,'

'Are you the caller making these unanswered phone calls?'

'I am.'

She asks me to keep turning the page. Then again, and again. Hundreds of missed calls, night after night, spanning at least a year. Longer.

'Who were you trying to reach?' Ms Ibrahim asks, her voice full of derisive pity.

My throat narrows. Of course, this is not the full picture. Jean would call me, about once a week, always careful to use a private number. 'Ms Guest.'

The lawyer then moves to screenshots of my text messages. 'Did you write and send these text messages to my client, Ms Guest?'

I hesitate as I scan the pages. It's not the first time I am viewing this evidence, but I still struggle to recognise myself. The frantic desperation, the repeated requests for news of her that went unanswered.

Did you send Mary my number?
What's this I heard about a painting exhibition that Mary held?
Why didn't you tell me?
Will you tell Mary I say hello?

Despite my hounding, Jean was careful not to reply. But here, for the sake of balance, an exchange is provided to the court.

No news from Mary, Gussie. If there was, I'd let you know x

'Do you confirm that this message from Ms Guest is genuine?'

I turn the word over in my mind. 'Her words were not in the least bit genuine, but she sent the message, yes.'

Ms Ibrahim snaps her file shut.

'Thank you, Ms Bird,' she says, avoiding my eye. 'That's all I have. We'll see you tomorrow.'

Just as she goes to sit down, an anguished sound comes from the gallery. Coughing or crying, I can't tell which. I turn towards the balcony. The door upstairs swings open, then slams. The footsteps fade. Whether I'm guided by instinct or blind hope is unclear, but the knowledge is there, lodged in my chest. Those sounds were her. She must know it now, she must have seen it in those messages. I didn't just disappear on her. Those footsteps belonged to Mary.

Outside, in the atrium, I go and look for her, but it is too late, Mary has already gone. Instead, it is Anna's team that now approaches. They move like a many-headed animal, their biscuit-tan tights sparkling officiously in the streaming sunlight. As Anna draws nearer, I look away at my phone, wondering if it would be better to avoid her, but when I glance up again, I have mistimed it entirely. Anna's group is parallel to where I am standing.

Our eyes meet. Just briefly, her gaze widens. I realise that this might be my only chance to address Anna directly and apologise in person. Her footsteps falter. My armpits prickle with fear. I attempt a smile, but Anna grips the strap of her handbag, as though I might snatch it.

'Anna,' I hear myself stutter. 'Please ... please can we talk?'

I want to tell her about Sunnymede. The state of Mary's home and her mind, but also the moments when I thought I might have broken through to her. I want to tell her how sorry I am.

Anna stands there, rooted. Her eyes narrow and she opens her mouth as if to say something, but then she supresses it. Her face goes blank and she looks beyond me. Of course, she knows that treating me like a stranger will hurt more than any confrontation. It was a weapon Anna used time and again, reducing others to worthlessness, dismissing them as irrelevant. It was the bitter understanding of an ostracised woman. A lesson learnt from estrangement.

I stand there, justly discarded, as Anna climbs into the waiting car and speeds away. From behind me, Ms Carr approaches. She assures me that despite the hostilities, the Finbows are actually very grateful for what I'm about to do. She tells me they think I'm brave. Pathetically, my heart lifts.

'You'll be fine tomorrow, Gus. Ibrahim's pretty formidable, but just keep in mind everything we've discussed and we'll be okay.'

I nod, but my mind lingers miserably on Mary's filthy cabin. Bonamy was right about the trial: neither outcome guarantees his daughter back. My appearance in court tomorrow will make no difference to Mary's welfare. Even if it goes well and the judge rules in Anna's favour, it only plays into Jean's hands, fuelling her claims of family conspiracy, pushing Mary and her baby further away. I feel the hopeless weight of everything then. There is no way to win.

Ms Carr notices my expression and smiles gently. 'It's a mild evening. If I were you, I'd take a walk. Escape the zoo for a bit. Clear your head. Then do your best to get some rest. Bernard will be at your hotel first thing in the morning. One more day and you're free of all this.' She lays her delicate hand on my shoulder and a surge of warmth spreads through me. 'You know, you were incredibly lucky to get out of this mess when you did, Gus.'

When we part, I take her advice and follow a longer route back to my hotel, through a narrow park alongside the river. Victoria Embankment Gardens is small, at least by London's standards. A curved pathway, lined with benches overlooking two wide strips of lawn and some ornamental flower beds. As I pass through it, I reflect on Ms Carr's words. In her view, tomorrow I'll be free, but I haven't *got out* of anything at all. Not when Mary is still festering alone in that hut.

I pause on a bench, staring towards the river, then in envy at the office workers sprawled leisurely on the grass, scrolling their phones and drinking canned cocktails. I imagine them reading the highlights of the trial to each other, laughing at its salacious details. It's hard to remember a time when I felt such lightness. For years now, my life has been shaped by Jean's presence or absence. This was why Ms Carr was wrong when she said, *just one more day*. Despite everything Jean has done to me, there is no chance that my evidence tomorrow will simply spell our ending. Jean always found a way to claw back.

For a long while, I sit there. The evening slowly creeps in. The Thames shimmers between the traffic on the Embankment like silver tape. Now and then, someone approaches me on the bench and asks me for money or a cigarette. I give the first woman my last change, the next man a water bottle from my bag. They leave me in peace. Then, after five minutes or so, another figure sits down.

'It's funny you're here,' says the voice. 'This was Oriel's favourite park.'

I freeze. There is the scent of her tuberose perfume, the familiar gasping in-breath before she speaks. Jean.

I jump up from the bench. 'What are you doing here?' I cry, terrified. 'Did you *follow* me?'

Jean fixes her gaze upon the evening sky. 'I knew you'd be out on an evening like this. To think, we're in September! And just look at that moon rising! Almost but *not quite* full.' She squints. 'Like a nibbled biscuit, isn't it?'

'You shouldn't be here, Jean,' I warn her breathlessly. 'It's forbidden. I'm a witness – I have protections—'

Jean interrupts, pointing at the river. 'And the way it shines on the water.' She sighs. 'It might not be Rome, but London's not all bad, is it?'

'Leave me the *fuck* alone!'

'Sit down, Gus,' Jean says, calmly. 'Don't make a fuss.'

'What you are doing now is illegal.' I check the park, fearful to be alone with Jean. But there are no onlookers I could rely on later; our interaction passes unobserved. 'What do you want from me?'

Jean smirks, as if amused by my need to follow the rules. She gestures to the bench and I catch sight of her hands. Her fingernails are no longer opal and glossy, but cracked and yellowed. There are liver spots by her knuckles; those coloured rings that once enchanted me were just ugly plastic props. Disgusted, I turn and walk away. But Jean calls me back, always summoning.

'I want you to know, Gus. I've managed to forgive you.'

I pause and press my palms against my eyes, but my anger can't be forced down. I thunder back and stand over her, raising my phone like a weapon. Jean doesn't flinch. She blinks up at me with kindness.

'That's what I came here to tell you. I don't want anything from you, Gus. I just wanted to let you know, you mustn't feel guilty about what you said in your statement.'

'Guilty?' I say, incredulous. I make a low sound of disgust. Of course, Jean has named my feelings exactly. She always could.

'We're disappointed by what you did, but you mustn't feel any guilt towards us.'

Not us, I think. *Do not use the word us.*

'It's not productive,' Jean continues. 'So, I don't want you to harbour it. And I wanted to let you know I share it too, Gus. The feelings of shame. The guilt.'

Gradually, I lower my arm. My phone goes back into the top of my bag. Standing here, with Jean, in the growing darkness, feels terrifying, but I can't help wanting to listen. The saddest part of me craves an apology.

'When I read your statement, of course, I was very hurt. You see, when someone you love lets you down, you feel angry. Will you just sit, please, for a moment?'

Again, Jean gestures to the space next to her, but it feels important – vital, even – to stay standing.

'You didn't love me,' I say, buoyant now, with rage. 'You used me.'

Jean sighs and shakes her head sadly. 'I'd hoped you might be strong enough to deal with Anna and Bonamy. But I knew they'd get to you, eventually.'

'They didn't get to me.' I shake my head at my stupidity. '*You* got to me!'

'They really are a tricky pair,' she murmurs. 'To think of the damage they've inflicted on Mary. Her mother's torturing her. Even in Mary's condition, she just will not stop!'

My heart races. 'You're deluded, Jean. It's you who inflicts pain. Anna and Bonamy aren't perfect, but they had no idea about Mary and Lawrence. Yet you've convinced Mary the opposite.' I pause, stricken. 'Just like you managed to convince me that Mary might one day want to be with me.'

Jean purses her lips. 'I only go with what my clients tell me, Gus. Anna and Bonamy may deny any knowledge, now that you've confronted them with the truth about that awful man. But do they actually care? What have they done about it?' Jean fixes me in her gaze. 'Don't tell me you're not appalled by that.'

Jean's perception was a pincer; a great gift she abused. There was a grain of truth in what she was saying. Lawrence was still due to give evidence at some point this week, and, as far as I knew, Anna still funded Lawrence's programme.

I slide down next to her on the bench. The corners of her mouth turn upwards. 'Why are you smiling?' I ask quietly.

'I just…' Jean says, then falters. 'I give so much to my girls.' She turns to me. Again, a smile. 'They occupy such a large part of me. And now I'm seeing you, I realise that everything you said in your statement hasn't even touched me. All I know is how hard I found it to let you go.' She reaches towards my face. I duck away from her, but she just chuckles. I tell myself, *she isn't sincere,* and yet her words puncture me. 'I've missed you, Gus, so much. You're such a special girl. So much heart. Such *talent*. If only your parents could have nurtured it.'

Tears spring to my eyes. Humiliated, I wipe them with the back of my hands.

'Gus,' Jean coos, suddenly busy with her handbag. 'Oh! My poor girl.'

I take a tissue from her and blow my nose, hating the comfort I still take from her presence. She pats my arm, then rests her hand there. Electricity travels along my skin. I can't shrug her off.

'You know, I so wanted to meet you today. I'd asked the universe for a chance. And I'm so glad to see you. I've been worrying about you, going up there on the stand.' She winces. 'Such a breach of trust. But we've both had to do it. Tomorrow won't be any better for you, I'm afraid.'

'What do you mean?'

She chuckles. 'I've had to fight fire with fire. You told untruths in your statement, you mentioned my ordeals. I've had to mention yours.' She pauses. 'It's your parents I worry about. They're not coming, are they?'

'No,' I say, feeling a stab of fear.

'Are you sure about that?'

There is a pressing feeling in my chest. As far as I know, my parents have no idea about any of this. Has Jean told them to come?

'It's fine,' I lie. 'We're actually talking again. I've told them all about it!'

'Well, phew,' she says, with a satisfied sound. 'Because some of the things that you said in our sessions. And then afterwards, what you wrote to me. Some of it was *really* quite vicious. And I'm afraid you – or they – don't come out of it very well. What was it you called them? *Small-minded. Obstructive. Cruel.*' Jean leaves a purposeful pause, just to make it known what she means. 'It would be awful if they heard those words, or read them, wouldn't it?'

A pebble of fear lodges in my throat. I imagine my parents sitting in the gallery, watching down on me as, once again, I bring shame upon our small family. Defeated by Jean's last betrayal, tears fall freely over my cheeks. She looks down and taps my hand.

'Don't pick your fingers,' she says sternly.

'Sorry,' I whisper. Suddenly, I'm so tired. Despite myself, I let my head droop on her shoulder.

'I'm scared, Jean.' I cry, softly. 'So scared about tomorrow. Today was so terrifying.'

I feel her whole body relax as I lean against her.

'Poor girl,' she says, stroking my hand. 'You know that I always wanted my girls to be independent, in the end. To stand on their own two feet. That's why I was always so proud of you and everything you achieved. If you decide to go ahead tomorrow, just make sure it's from a position of strength, of independence. Not just because *the Finbows* asked you to.' I pull away then and we stare at each other. She reaches for my chin, tilts it. 'The case is already wrapped up, Gus, everyone knows it. Your evidence won't make a difference. So, forget everybody else. What do you need in this moment? Is it that awful courtroom? Or is it back home in your studio, away from all this madness?'

That's when I notice her hair: the greys now collecting in wiry strands around her ears. The elegant, cosmopolitan woman I once knew has been replaced by someone grasping and dowdy. Her breathing is quick; the cold-cream plump skin that used to glow with goodness looks greasy and congested.

This time, I start laughing.

'Bullshit, Jean.' With trembling hands, I reach into my bag and carefully, so as not to press any buttons, remove my phone from the top of it. As I check the screen, I feel a wave of joy. The red button remains on. Eight minutes have been carefully recorded; our whole conversation. The milliseconds are streaming gloriously by. I have captured Jean Guest, the claimant, the healer and the hopeless fraud, intimidating a witness: a criminal offence. Jean knows it, too, as she glances down at the handset, she gives a little gasp. When she looks up me, her eyes are pleading.

'Is this how you dreamt it, Jean?' I ask, smiling brightly with exhilaration. I rise from the bench. My heart is beating wildly in my chest; a bird breaking out of its cage. 'Is this the way you thought I'd betray you?'

Jean jumps up and tries to grab the handset from me.

'You're very confused, Gus,' she warns. 'You're frightened. I can tell.'

'You're right, I am frightened of *you*.' My voice chokes as I swerve her grasp. 'But I'm terrified for Mary. She needs her friends. Her family and friends. People she can trust.'

'What do you want?' Jean interrupts, in a low, rough tone. Her eyes flit back again to my phone. 'If it's money you need—' Jean reaches for her wallet, and I almost start laughing.

'All that therapy and you can't actually listen. This.' I wave my phone. 'This could ruin you.'

'Name it, Gus. I'll do it.'

I hesitate, thinking first of Oriel, and then of my own devastation when Jean stopped working with me. How would Mary cope? But then I remember the baby. A little girl. That sign on Mary's wall: the first step to a better life is the belief it is possible.

'Drop her,' I say, quietly. 'Leave Mary and the baby alone.' Jean's eyes dart nervously. 'No more sessions, no more phone calls to check in, no more bubble baths or dinners—'

'—I see what you're asking,' she interrupts. 'You jealous girl.'

I tell myself: *don't rise to it*. For the first time in years, I feel bigger than Jean.

'But what about tomorrow? What about your evidence?'

There is a long pause. We study each other and I shrug. 'I'll tell the truth.'

Jean's eyes fill with tears. 'But I've read your statement. I know all know about your relationship with the truth. You sculpt it in whatever way suits you best.'

'Must be why we once got along.'

Jean looks at me pleadingly. 'But Mary needs me, Gus. She's almost better. Don't make me abandon her. Not at this point.'

The woman's capacity for manipulation still astounds me. I open the maps browser on my phone and type into the navigation bar. With a shaking hand, I wave it at her.

'It's a twelve-minute walk. Wow. Quicker than I expected! Scenic, too. Like you said, it's a lovely evening. I'm feeling quite up for a stroll to the police station, aren't you?'

Jean's face darkens. 'You've always had this vicious side to you. A pathetic hanger-on—'

'—To you, Jean! I clung on to you. And now, I'm walking away. I'll let tomorrow go the way you want. But only if you promise, if you swear you'll walk away from Mary, too.'

Jean nods, her mouth trembling. There is a powerful feeling surging in my chest. Nobody could prove that she was doing anything criminal before. The proof is now in my possession. It will remain always in my possession.

Suddenly, Jean's phone starts ringing. I watch her, half fascinated, as she sits back down and scrabbles for the handset in her bag. It is a strange sight, this hateful woman who once was everything to me, now frantic and snivelling, sat alone on a bench in London.

'Is that Mary?'

Jean winces, as if she is already missing her. 'No, not Mary.'

'Show me.'

Guiltily, Jean flashes the screen. Someone called Tabitha is ringing again.

'Don't let me keep you, then,' I say, collecting myself and beckoning her upwards. 'Answer it! I'll see you tomorrow.'

Jean rushes to answer. 'Darling,' she coos as sweetly as she can manage, rising from the bench. For a moment, my heart almost strains towards the sound. Jean glances over her shoulder and we gaze at each other. Then she turns back around and I hear her sickly tone.

'Nothing's the matter. I was just a bit concerned. I had a dream about you and I got worried. I thought I should check in. Tell me, how was class today? Is everything alright?'

GUEST V FINBOW: DAY SEVEN

The following morning, I stand hardly ten paces from the woman I was once devoted to and study the oath. All the while, Jean surveys me, her expression fixed in a muted scowl. Does she understand, I wonder, how far our power dynamic has shifted? I think of the way I towered over her last night in the park, phone recording in hand. The evidence I now possess that could collapse her case instantly, even incriminate her. For the first time in my life, I have collateral over Jean; she owes *me*. We made a deal over it, a deal for Mary's freedom. I am to tell the truth: that is all that is demanded of me. Why, then, do my legs threaten to buckle from underneath me? Why now, do I doubt if I am capable?

'The whole truth,' I say, one hand trembling on the red book, the seismic pressure of what I am about to do building inside me. I can feel, from the left, Anna's wounded glare moving across my body. I gaze at her with a deeper remorse than she could ever understand, taking in the soft-pink cardigan she has draped on her shoulders, her slim wrists and forearms triangulated on the desk. 'Nothing but the truth.'

'Tell me about the sessions,' Ms Carr asks, standing tall at her desk, treating me with exaggerated kindness to emphasise that I am Jean's victim. 'How did they start?'

I speak about my residency in Rome, the model casting, our encounters at her apartment, my studio. For several minutes, I am questioned over how Jean cultivated my dependence. I stammer over my words. It is painful to articulate all the sweet things I let Jean do for me – the meals cooked, the scented baths she drew, all the tips on Rome she provided – in order for Ms Carr to argue that she had an ulterior motive: control.

'She didn't seem controlling, at first. I thought she was glamorous and charismatic.'

Ms Carr nods. 'How did you feel when she wanted you to commence formal sessions of coaching with her?'

'Excited. Lucky. It was appealing, the idea that she might fix me, or turn me into a better person.'

'Did this happen, during the course of your relationship with Ms Guest?'

I hesitate. Her phrase catches on me: *the course* of my relationship. In a second, hot tears form and blur my surroundings, but, quickly, I blink them away, training my mind instead on the portrait, the letter, the freakish predator Jean made me out to be.

'The opposite,' I say. 'Jean Guest shaped me into the very worst person.'

Jean's head jerks upwards, and I am seized with the pleasure of hurting her, of speaking the truth. Briefly, Anna and I lock eyes. The slight nod of encouragement she gives is unbearable, knowing what else lies ahead.

'In your witness statement,' Ms Carr continues, 'you allege that Ms Guest exploited your discomfort around acknowledging or accepting certain aspects of yourself.' She points a pen. 'Specifically, pertaining to your sexuality. Do I have that right?'

'You do,' I say, feeling my cheeks flame to acknowledge this so openly. 'Jean – Ms Guest – can detect the shame on you very easily. It is like a magic power. She extracts it from you and then holds it, out here.' I extend my arms and make a cupping gesture with my hands. 'Making it external. Making it safe.'

'But it wasn't safe, was it?' Ms Carr asks, her eyebrows raised theatrically.

'No,' I say, softly, watching Jean at her desk. 'It wasn't safe at all.'

Ms Carr refers then to the transcript of my session, quizzing me over the reading I was set; the websites I was asked to study; the regularity and length of our meetings. 'You've said in your statement that you would interact with Ms Guest for astoundingly long periods of time,' she notes. 'And that Ms Guest exploited your fatigue, bringing you to conclusions that, out of sheer exhaustion, you could only agree with. Is this still the case?'

'Yes.'

'What, specifically, did these conclusions relate to?'

'Every aspect of my life. Mostly around my upbringing.'

'To remind you,' Ms Carr explains carefully. 'We are here to ascertain the truth of my client's statement, that Ms Guest creates false memories in the minds of those she coaches. Can you expand on how Ms Guest might have reframed episodes from your past to contaminate or change them, for instance?'

'The truth is,' I say, 'I don't really know *how*. We talked about my childhood all the time. Jean was always adamant that I'd suppressed certain episodes as a coping mechanism. She called my parents a toxic influence. You saw,' I stammer, 'the recording. At the time I found it helpful. Liberating, even.'

'—How is your relationship with your family now, Ms Bird?' Anna's lawyer cuts in.

'Distant.'

'In your statement, you use the word *estranged*. Which is it?'

My hand clutches my chest. It's still painful to admit this publicly. In the moment's pause, my gaze travels upwards to the upper gallery, checking once again for my parents. Despite what Jean said last night in the park, there is no sign of them. I feel, at first, a tragic flutter of relief, then rage at Jean for making me fear that she'd encouraged them to come. Her threats were empty, just another desperate attempt to keep me from court. *Fuck you*, I think as I glare over at her. *Fuck every single one of your cowardly threats. Fuck you for what you made me say about them. Fuck you for recording our sessions.*

'Estranged, yes,' I say, bringing my attention back to the lawyer. Ms Carr watches me carefully, anxious that I might misstep.

She has no idea how much worse is to come. 'Yes. Sorry. That's more accurate. In subtle ways, Ms Guest made me fixate on my parents' flaws. If I wanted to develop, if I wanted to grow, it was critical to cut them off.'

'In order to isolate you? And to depend on her?'

I nod miserably. For the purposes of the court recording, I am asked to confirm aloud: *yes*. The lump in my throat swells and rises. Satisfied, Ms Carr turns the page.

'Let's go now to another part of your witness statement: how Ms Guest purposely exploited your feelings for Mary Finbow, the defendant's daughter, in order to proliferate her network. What, precisely, did she convince you of?'

A tense silence falls over the courtroom.

'She made me believe there was much more to our relationship than there really was.'

'Such as?'

I lower my head, remembering Mary's words, how she had accused me of touching her against her will: *I needed a friend*. Surely, this was another of Jean's lies? I had to believe that. The alternative – that I had misread things, that Mary hadn't ever wanted me, not even fleetingly – was too unbearable.

'Jean made me think there could be a future. But only if Mary forgot her old life and her family.' My legs shake as I admit my pathetic gullibility. 'Yes, Jean implied that Mary's parents wouldn't have it – her being with a girl. That if it wasn't for her family – specifically Anna – I'd be able to be with Mary, romantically. And I was naïve enough, in love enough, to believe it.'

Ms Carr pauses, training the judge's attention on my words. 'How did that make you feel towards Anna Finbow?' she asks carefully.

My tone lowers. 'Resentful.'

'Is this the reason that you introduced Mary Finbow to Ms Guest? I believe the phrase you used in your statement was "cure her?"'

'There were multiple things I wanted to help Mary with,' I say. My mind crowds, suddenly, with Lawrence. That holiday photo; the reflected flash in his eyes. 'But I also felt a financial pressure.'

'Go on?' A tremor of pleasure passes across Ms Carr's face as I raise this. She makes a little swipe of her pen against her notes. 'Throughout this trial, we've heard reports that Ms Guest's sessions were very expensive. Was this also your experience?'

'I could never have afforded our sessions. And Jean knew that. I paid her almost nothing, which she never let me forget. It made me feel very bad, like I owed her more.'

'Like you owed her Mary?'

'Yes,' I whisper, too disgusted with myself to say it any louder.

'And what else?' Ms Carr booms. 'How else did you pay her back, once Ms Guest launched her legal battle?'

The judge turns to me with interest. I take sip of water, then stare straight ahead, steeling myself for what I am about to admit. *Mary. The baby. The squat. We have to get her out. The first step to a better life is the belief that it is possible.*

'I paid her back by helping her in this case.'

Ms Carr glances around the courtroom, to ensure that everyone is following her line of argument. This is her volta, the crucial shift in her approach, and I hate that I am about to disappoint her. 'In your statement, you allege that Ms Guest pressured you into obtaining information about Mrs Finbow – her legal opponent – on her behalf. Will you tell us, as carefully as you can, what exactly happened?'

My heartbeat quickens. If I keep to the script, I'll now be talking about Stoke. How Jean encouraged me to move, then to apply for roles within Anna's team at Bellinter. My statement describes how, under Jean's duress, I manipulated my way into Anna's confidence and trust, gathering all I could find about her legal strategy, the witnesses she was summoning. I'll explain how I was coerced; that I complied with Jean's insane demands for one simple reason: I was afraid of her.

Instead, I hear myself stuttering an apology. Closing my eyes, I bring my fists to my cheeks. The next words come shakily. 'There is something in my statement that I want to correct.'

Silence falls over the courtroom. As if I have fallen into a well, I am left with the lonely echo of my words. I look over at Jean, and for a moment we are back in that living room, my head cradled in her warm lap. The chandelier above us, gently moving, refracting rainbows. *Who is showing you love, Gus? I am.*

No, Jean, I think to myself. *This here is love. An act of sacrifice. For Mary, not for you.*

'My witness statement contains a lie,' I begin to say quietly. 'Several lies. And I need to correct them.'

Anna watches my performance in horror. Ms Carr, too, who had begged *no surprises*.

'What lies?' she snaps back furiously.

'It was my idea to help her. Jean never asked me to do anything. It was my idea first. I passed information to Jean to try and make myself useful. To win back her favour.'

'Because she threatened you?' Ms Carr urges now, through clenched teeth. 'Because you were frightened of her?'

'Frightened of my life without her.'

A ripple of excitement passes along Jean's legal team. I gaze, half-pleadingly, at Anna and Ms Carr, for what I am now admitting to. The idea had always been mine; a desperate attempt to win back Jean's attention. I couldn't stomach admitting it to Bonamy that night of the Carnival party. I persuaded myself it was immaterial, how and why I'd first intruded into Anna's life. Until now, I had barely acknowledged my original part in what happened; could barely admit it to myself.

'But you assert in your statement that you were obliged to act because she had recordings of your private sessions,' Ms Carr insists, growing frustrated. 'You've stated that she threatened you!'

'Then my statement is false.' I try to speak as calmly as I can. 'She never threatened me. It was the other way around. It was my fault. It was me who put Jean in that situation.'

I glance briefly at Anna, desperate to communicate how sorry I am, but her gaze, full of tears, is fixed to the table. She doesn't understand yet that undermining my own performance on the witness stand might actually help get her daughter back. Anna has never fully grasped the true risk of her legal undertaking: that if Jean loses in court, Mary's debt to her beloved healer will deepen. Jean's public disgrace galvanises Mary's social isolation because she will blame herself.

Last night, when Jean saw that I had recorded her, and that she was compromised, she vowed to abandon her relationship with Mary. In that moment, I understood it: Jean wants money more than Mary. She craves power over phoney parenthood. In the deal we struck, I am to discredit my own pivotal evidence and acknowledge in court that I offered Jean clues into the Finbows' defence of my own accord. Admitting that I lied may mean Jean wins the trial, but it is a risk I have calculated: by losing the Finbows' case, I will set Mary free. And, however flawed they might be, in her freedom, Mary might find her way to her family again. But that is another gamble: an outcome no one can be sure of.

Ms Carr makes a shaken appeal to the judge, her case crumbling along with my credibility. 'I wonder whether we ought to take a break,' she stammers. 'I believe my witness has become confused—'

'I don't need a break,' I interrupt, eyes trained forward, fingernails dug deep into my palms. 'I need to be honest.'

The judge turns to me with harsh reproach. 'May I remind you that you verified your witness statement with a statement of truth? Any false statement made there, or, indeed, inside this courtroom, risks the serious charge of perjury, and with it, very grave consequences.'

Jean scribbles fast in her notepad. I hate how she crouches over it; the childish and possessive way she takes space on the desk. I hate how I am letting her win. I glare at her, so she is left under no doubt why I am admitting this. An image guides me: Mary back in her flat, raising her daughter safely at home. Will she allow me to visit, eventually?

'I was ashamed to admit it before,' I say, staring at Jean so she understands the full meaning and weight of my words. 'Or I just couldn't *bear to remember*.'

'You little *liar!*' cries Anna. 'You *bitch*!'

The judge issues a furious warning against all contemptuous conduct in his courtroom.

'Ms Bird,' he continues, 'this witness box is not a therapy couch. We are, frankly, not interested in hearing about your feelings of shame or embarrassment, only the veracity of your statements. Can you assure us that you are speaking the honest truth?'

'I am.'

Ms Carr shakes her head, mystified at my collapse. 'Then that brings us to the end of our engagement, Ms Bird,' she says, in quiet, clipped voice. I hang my head low. 'No further questions.'

'Do you understand the difference between truth and a lie, Ms Bird?' Ms Ibrahim asks, standing well apart from the witness box. Moments before, she watched me placing my hand on the oath with open disgust, her lip curling with contempt.

My body pulses with shame, and the voice that answers is choked and small. 'I do.'

'Because my client's case is that you do not always tell the truth. So, despite our lengthy preparations, we will try not to waste too much court time on your testimony.'

I nod, merciful that Ms Ibrahim's dismantling will at least be swift. I had waited out the short adjournment in the bathroom, first backing up the voice memo of Jean I'd recorded, then silencing the calls that came in from Bernard or other members of Anna's PR team. Now, as I stand in front of Jean's lawyer, I realise Anna has not returned to Courtroom Six. I wonder if she's waiting for me outside, preparing to pounce. For a second, I imagine the brawl, even crave it; the sharp square of her fingernails, the ball of spit summoned upwards, then hurled in my face.

'Were you angry?' Ms Ibrahim continues curtly. 'When my client could no longer afford to treat you for free?'

Ms Ibrahim's question turns me to ice. 'No,' I stammer. Then I cast my mind to the stranger at the open door to Jean's apartment. The door I kicked. I hesitate. *The truth. Nothing but the truth.* 'At first, yes. Then I was sad. Sad and confused.'

'Would you say that you still feel confused?'

I look across at Jean. Her expression is lowered. 'Not anymore.'

'Then perhaps it is just we who feel confused!' Ms Ibrahim counts on her fingers. 'First, you claim Ms Guest bullied you into stealing evidence for her. Then, you say you proposed it of your own accord. Are there any other falsehoods in your witness statement that we should be aware of?'

'Nothing else. Honestly, just that part.'

'Did Mrs Finbow pressure you into the very serious allegations you originally made?'

'No.'

Ms Ibrahim pushes back. 'Is it not the case that you submitted your witness statement simply to please Mrs Finbow?'

'No. It is not the case.'

'It would be understandable, though, wouldn't it? The wealth and influence of a family like the Finbows must have been *dazzling*, Ms Bird. And unrequited love?' Ms Ibrahim winces. 'No pain like it, is there? Ms Guest states that you put her under immense pressure to, for want of a better term, *match-make* you with Mary Finbow. Do you agree?'

My cheeks flush with anger. Indignant, I shake my head.

'Were you resentful when she failed to bring the two of you together?'

'I was sad at the situation,' I stammer. 'And I admit, I am still sad at the situation.'

'So, did you try to alleviate that sadness by working with Mrs Finbow? From daughter to mother: swiftly replacing one obsession with another?'

'Obsession?' My temper flares. 'No! I liked Anna. And, once I started to understand her situation, I felt sorry for her.'

'And yet you *stole* evidence from her home?'

'Jean had made me so dependent,' I say, my voice trembling now, 'that without our sessions, I felt like I was drowning. For a while – yes – I did everything I could to please her. I desperately wanted our sessions to resume again. I missed her—'

'Yet you claimed she ruined your life?' Ms Ibrahim frowns, cynically.

'In hindsight I realise—'

'—But which is it?'

I pause then, unable to articulate the messy truth of it: *both, it was both. Your client shaped me, just as she broke me down. Made me, just as she undid me.*

'Do you agree that you harassed Ms Guest over calls and text messages, Ms Bird?'

'I wouldn't say so.'

'My client says she felt harassed. And we saw the evidence yesterday. The text messages. The call log.' She sighs, pityingly. 'You press her, Ms Bird. You are *quite* insistent!'

'Jean reciprocated the contact. Once I offered help with her legal case, she wanted more and more from me.'

'But we see no evidence of this in your exchange—'

'—Of course you don't!' I explode. 'Jean phoned me from a private number!'

Ms Ibrahim leaves a dubious pause. Ms Carr sits back in her chair, arms folded.

'Ms Ibrahim,' the judge interjects. 'We took you at your word that this would be quick.'

The lawyer raises a deferential hand. 'Only a few further questions, My Lord.' She turns back to me. 'Let's go briefly to Rome, where you first met my client. You strike up a special connection. You commence formal coaching sessions together. At the end of term, you introduce Mary Finbow – your crush – to Ms Guest, because of the improvements you are seeing in your life.'

My vision swims. 'One of the reasons—'

'So, may I ask, when did you last *recommend* something to someone?' Ms Ibrahim leaves a little hesitant pause, pretending her next question is a merely an afterthought. 'A film? A book? A holiday destination?'

My breath catches in my throat as I reflect on the emptiness of my recent days. 'I'm not sure I can remember.'

'But *typically* when we recommend something, it is because we have enjoyed it very much, is that not the case?'

'Of course it is,' I say, tight-lipped. 'Or *believe* we've enjoyed it.'

'So, how do we make sense of the fact you earnestly recommended my client's services, only later to state that she, in your own words, 'eroded your power, freedom and wellbeing' from the moment you met her?'

'At the beginning, things were different,' I snap curtly. 'I had no idea what was happening.'

Ms Ibrahim raises a hand to her forehead. 'This is really starting to stretch logic here. Because, according to my client, you were so positive about your sessions that you didn't just make one recommendation, but several. Is that not the case?'

My palms begin to sweat. Across the courtroom, my gaze falls on Jean, who smiles to herself, and in that moment, I make an inward vow: once Mary is free, I will use it. I will take that recording to the police. I will ruin Jean, just as she ruined me.

'Who else did you bring in for life coaching, Ms Bird? Could you provide their names to me?'

I pause. A moment too long. 'I might have mentioned Jean to one or two people.'

'Truth and lies, Ms Bird!' Ms Ibrahim's voice thunders suddenly. 'I thought you said you knew the difference? Please name the two young women for whom you *enthusiastically* made introductions to my client, Ms Bird, or I will.'

There is an awful carousel of emotions: shame first, but also relief, at finally admitting my role out loud. Remorse for the relief. On it spins. I glance over at Anna's vacant chair, grateful she is no longer present to witness another hideous confession.

'One girl was called Decca,' I say, bile rising to my throat. 'And there was another girl that I also met in Rome: Bea. I regret it now.' I gasp, unable to look up as the judge calls for quiet. 'I regret it so much.'

I am remembering how freely those girls, Bea and Decca, danced in their white togas at the party. My shock to see Jean there, out by the banks of the Tiber, talking to some student. The trespass of it. That wasn't how it was meant to go. She'd asked *me* to bring her new clients, and I wanted the recognition for it. In a hurry the following day, I had given Jean the girls' email addresses and written a quick introduction. I told them I'd met Jean through my own residency. I called her my art doula. Bea replied gratefully, joking that she felt she needed professional help to deal with her Christmas-party comedown. There was no response from Decca. But I never saw or heard from her again.

Ms Ibrahim raises a hand. 'My Lord, to be transparent, my client often welcomes personal recommendations from clients. If time permits, she likes her details being passed on. Both individuals have waived their right to anonymity, and have provided written statements attesting to their contentment with my client's methods.'

What happened to those girls who had such gilded futures ahead of them? At the time, I resented the contented way they obliviously stepped through life; their boisterous self-assurance. Did a part of me want to see them humbled and reduced? Wrenched open, in the same way Jean pulled me apart?

The lawyer turns back to me. 'My point here, Ms Bird, is that you felt you *deserved* something for your perceived role in growing Ms Guest's client base. Just as you felt you deserved something from my client for spying on her legal opponent. When you didn't get what you wanted, you launched a vendetta against Ms Guest, making all sorts of statements that you now undermine at your own choosing.'

Ms Ibrahim turns to the judge, lamenting his wasted time. 'My Lord, Ms Bird's statement must be struck through. Not only has this witness harboured a personal vendetta against my client, but her version of events, as we have seen, is wholly unreliable.'

She turns back to me. 'Speaking truthfully under oath is the backbone of this country's legal system. Your meddling in this courtroom's events may have grave consequences, and so I bring my questioning to a conclusion now, to avoid any further interference or confusion. Thank you, My Lord. We have nothing more.'

As I am brought down from the stand, I become aware of someone staring intently: not Ms Carr's furious gaze, but the court illustrator. The last time anyone observed me in this way was years ago, when I was sitting opposite Mary or Jean. There is a strange flicker of pleasure at being looked at again, objectified in the way those women once studied me. So far, the court drawings published at the end of each day have been grossly exaggerated: Jean's bearing is hunched and mousy. Anna, by contrast, is a Disneyesque icon of womanhood, her cleavage like a deep gorge, her lips plump and her hair dark and flowing.

I step away from the witness box and wonder: how will this artist portray me? Jean's ruthless handmaiden, or a pitiful weak link?

Anna's aide or Jean's victim? Not a hanger-on. Not a leech. No, I was once at the centre of things.

A somebody. Whatever may be said of me, however I will be sketched, not a nobody.

PART FIVE

STOKE-ON-TRENT, DECEMBER

Three months later
Not long after the trial ended, I read an article about those migrating starlings. It was in an old copy of *National Geographic* that I found in the waiting room of my doctor's surgery. This summer, for some reason, large numbers of them had started falling out of the sky. Residents were sweeping up great heaps of dead birds in the Porta Pia neighbourhood of Rome, an ancient gateway to the city. At first, they thought the heat was to blame. But when the experts tested their bodies, they found the starlings to be in good health. What they had suffered were broken bones, the physical trauma you would associate with collisions.

'We don't understand what would cause the creatures to suddenly collide with each other, when before they flew in such perfectly choreographed harmony,' a scientist was quoted saying. 'Something has caused panic in the murmuration. It could be an electromagnetic force, it could be another creature, a predator.'

The journalist called it a 'complete riddle'.

A resident of Porta Pia described it as a 'bloodbath, like something from an Alfred Hitchcock movie'.

When I read the piece, I thought first of Jean and Lawrence, then myself too. Predators, the three of us, disturbing the harmony of things.

After my evidence, I returned to Stoke and tried to re-establish some semblance of normal life. The judgement is to be announced in a matter of weeks, so all I can do is wait. In the day, work helps to quell the anxiety, but, at night, my mind plays endless reruns of that moment with Jean in the park. I wonder if I will be forever living through that decision, wavering between the reasons why I withheld that criminalising recorded evidence, and in whose interests.

It was all for Mary, that's what I try to remind myself. I agreed to tell the truth in court, admitting to my part in everything, on the condition Jean left her and the baby in peace. But I have no idea if Jean has aborted their sessions yet, and it terrifies me that she is still working with Decca and Bea, as well as others. Ruining more lives, as she did mine. Then, as I acknowledge this, another creeping thought lingers: was I reluctant to see Jean legally condemned? Despite everything that has happened, was I still too attached to let her lose?

The *idea* of Jean, I correct myself. Not the reality. My projection.

Earlier this week, I was working late when an email arrived from Thea. Where in the world was I? How were things? She was curating an exhibition in Rome. Would I consider contributing a piece for her?

My heart soared: the first good news in a very long time. I rushed to accept, sending photographs of my current project. When she replied encouragingly, saying that she couldn't wait to have me back in Rome, I felt like bursting into tears. Thea never called me *blocked*, as Jean had. Accepting me on my own terms, she was the first person who had given me permission – and you do always need permission – to think of myself as an artist. I had ignored her emails at the end of my residency and failed to make anything new for my end-of-term show, so fixated was I with Mary and Jean. Now here was Thea, giving me a second chance. That evening, I began searching for places to stay when I visited.

2br apartment in elegant, art-filled palazzo: Centro Storico

Halfway down the listings, there it was: Jean's old apartment. My mouth turned dry as I followed the link, navigating straight to images, hypnotised by the most anonymous, inconsequential features of a holiday let that had once meant everything to me. The posters on the wall were all reprints, the pink bathroom a little mouldy now, and the spare bed was tightly made up as if I'd never slept in it. Back then, it seemed a sanctuary, but now it was just an eery blank canvas; a rented stage for Jean to strut about on. Her life, like all her ideas, and the girls who followed, were borrowed from someone else.

Months after I ceased contact, I take comfort in the fact that my ideas are my own now; that I am free to use the ugly things that have happened to me as inspiration. The project I'll submit to Thea's show is a departure from my other stuff, and reflects the coercion I lived under. The idea came from an old photograph Jean took of me in Rome. In the image, I am standing at the Porta Portese flea market, carefully holding an old vase. Something about the tender way I carried that ceramic piece moved me to recreate it in my work.

Experimenting at first, I began to take plaster casts of my hands, blending them carefully onto vases and pots, or other pieces I had thrown. The results were thrilling. I loved how affectionately my sculpted hands held on to my ceramics. It felt vital, too, that Jean had taken the original photograph; as if I was somehow shedding her influence. Winding these casts of my hands around my own work, made me feel I was giving myself a layer of protection that Jean had never provided. The certainty that what I loved would be held safely, and not broken.

These pieces are nearing completion when, one freezing afternoon, my studio swings open. Instead of a person, there is a big parcel; rectangular, wrapped in brown paper. A large canvas.

A postcard falls out onto the floor. As I pick it up, my legs weaken. Printed on the front is an image of an adult woman and a tiny baby: Mary and her new daughter, standing next to a grubby canal boat in a patch of weak sunlight. She still wears her knitted hairband, but she is grinning with joy. I almost choke at the hopelessly small size of the infant. A knot of envy rises as I wonder who took the photograph.

The card reads:

Gussie in the North light.
You should have had this years ago, I'm sorry.
Merry Christmas, from the two of us!

Tears spring to my eyes. I am seized by excitement at the message, but also fear. That apology; the sense of hope and freedom conveyed by the exclamation mark. I read the card again and again until the words blur and float away because my eyes, and then my whole face, are wet.

I slowly make a cup of tea, as if the canvas is a living entity that I must exert power over. Finally, I take a breath, and unwrap it from the protective sheathing, laying the canvas flat on the surface of my workbench. Immediately, my vision swims. My only impression is of the background; that dense, lilac grey: the colour of a summer thundercloud.

I prop it on the shelf opposite my windows to see it better. There is a lamp nearby, which I turn on and position towards the canvas. Then I pause. I take a step backwards. Then another. I hear myself gasp. My hand moves instinctively to my throat, as if she is still painting me.

There is a half-gothic intensity to the portrait now. Either Mary has worked it up, or I hadn't seen clearly at the time. Before, I had despised that dubious figure seated in the middle of the canvas; all its milky, pastel tones. Today, there is something different: an aliveness. The shy expression that I had found embarrassingly passive when I first saw it at the school, actually has an ageless presence. The dark space between my upper and lower lip is wider than I remember it, as though I am half way through a word, or even laughing. My eyes are flecked-green gems, almost photographic in likeness. They follow me as I move to view the painting at different angles, giving the portrait, for all its superficial shyness, an uncanny, unassailable reality.

I sit down at my workbench and rest there with my chin in my hands as I continue to take it in. What had set me so firmly against Mary's canvas when I'd first seen it at the school? Was it all because of Lawrence? Had Mary improved the painting, or was I only just learning to see it? I'd been furious at the portrayal but it would always have been wrong; nothing could have reflected the chaos on the other side of my appearance.

When I think of everything that happened, I realise that none of us were seeing each other properly. All we perceived were outlines from which we derived stories; competing narratives: contradictory, overlapping, very few of them objectively true. Anna had argued for a perfectly happy daughter in Mary, while Jean summoned a vulnerable victim of her mother's fame. I saw my soulmate in Mary, my sexual other, my socialite saviour. She only saw me as a friend.

I wonder if Mary's card means we can go back to that. After the judgement is released – sometime after Christmas, they think – I can approach her, gently, and see if she wants to talk. Perhaps I can meet the baby, even help her out with her. I imagine this with a smile as I go over to my studio window. Outside, you can see the moorlands, which span northeast from here; bright-green ground that stretches up towards the fringes of the Pennines. I rest my head against the glass; press my nose against my reflection. Then I reach up to the window, pull it open and let the cool air enter. I turn my face towards the grey, flat light – north light – and try to breathe it all in.

NEW YEAR'S EVE

Anna's email arrived during my first Christmas at home in three years. The email address was anonymous, but the plain energy and spite of the writing was unmistakable.

> *Congratulations on your pathetic court performance! You let us down again and again. Just as you lied OVER and OVER. Forget therapy, you need actual MEDICAL ATTENTION. If you ever come near my family again, I will ruin you. You are UTTERLY DELUDED to think you ever had a chance with our beautiful daughter.*

My heart plummeted. Anna wouldn't have written this if she'd won the case. I immediately searched online for the judgement, but nothing had been published. Then I checked Anna's profiles. She'd posted multiple childhood photographs of Mary, with captions which were hardly cryptic: *we'll never be separated,* she wrote, under an old picture of herself and Mary at a film premier.

The news outlets caught on and ran wild with speculation over what was due to be announced. Then, for two days, Anna fell silent. It was illegal to make any reference to the outcome of the trial until the judgement was formally handed down. Perhaps Anna had learnt from her ordeal and finally worked out when to shut up. Just as I did, with the long responses I typed out in my notes but never sent back to her.

Christmas at home was subdued but, in its own way, significant. After the trial ended, I gently prised open channels of communication again with my parents. I kept waiting for their questions about what had happened, why I had been so quiet for so long, but they seemed unwilling to mention it. Instead, we talked by text on safely neutral subjects. In our sessions, Jean had reinforced their failures, forcing me to dwell on the different ways my parents let me down. But, as we began speaking again, I started to value their consistency. Our exchanges were curt and often quite dull, but no message I sent was left unanswered.

I sent unoffensive photos of winter skies, or the cat that lived in our studio building. My mother replied with pictures of one that had been visiting her back garden. One day, I noticed that she was leaving a saucer of milk out for the animal. When I noticed it in the right-hand corner of the image, and saw that it had been present in the others she'd sent, I found myself in tears. She had carefully warmed that milk – probably nervous of wasting it – and placed it on the step, hoping and coaxing the creature inside. Through my tears, I remembered Anna's words from months before: *at the moment you work it out, bam. Your children are gone.*

I knew then that it was time to go home and try again.

The judgement is finally released on New Year's Eve. I am back in Stoke, returning from the shop with food and drink for a party that is taking place in my studio building. The news alert illuminates my screen, and my body starts to shiver uncontrollably: *Judge rules against Anna Finbow in blockbuster libel trial.*

Justice Larkin's judgement runs over eighty pages. I scroll through the headline findings. His first points explore the meaning of the burden of proof; how the civil court differs from a criminal trial in that the truth of something can be ascertained if it is *probable,* but not wholly proven. At this, my hopes almost lift, but then he goes on:

There can be no doubt that these costly and lengthy proceedings point to the need for a closer regulation of the therapy sector, but that dispute was not at the heart of this case. Ms Guest's methods may be unconventional, even maverick, but I cannot find evidence that the central sting of the libel asserted in The Peony, that

Ms Guest is a modern-day cult leader, can be substantially proven to the civil standard that is required.

He describes Mary's evidence in favour of Ms Guest as "compelling." He comments on her age, the claustrophobia of her family milieu, and her freedom to spend her income on whatever she chooses. *It may be evident that Ms Guest is transgressing the conventional boundaries between coach/ therapist and client. Yet, as we heard from many of the claimant's current clients, they consider it a privilege they are willing to pay for, and they are perfectly within their rights to do so.*

One piece of evidence which shocks me is a statement from Robert Bute. It was Beaker who was cross-examined in a closed court during the second day of the trial. He was granted anonymity on account of his recent rehab stint for his own substance issues, which had attracted unwanted press attention. Mary easily developed infatuations, Beaker said. She was also a determined young woman, deeply committed to whatever path she chose to follow. His character reference is used by the judge as an illustration of Mary's right to autonomy and self-improvement, not her susceptibility. I wonder, as I read, whether Beaker was simply on his own healing path and ready to salute anyone taking drastic steps of their own. But it is a reckless statement that only underpins the script Mary sold of herself.

Eventually, I find the judge's response to my evidence. Scarcely three sentences. More than I deserve. I have shown contempt of court by failing to admit that I initiated the intrusion into Mrs Finbow's most private exchanges. I am described as a "wholly unreliable" and "meddlesome individual" who complicated proceedings and wasted court time, risking "the gravest of consequences".

There is some relief to see my reproval in print. Here it is, finally made known. The unreliable parts of me that have always existed. The parts that I hadn't wanted to hear, but Jean did. Those tendencies she exploited for her own gain. I'm furious to think of the justice she has evaded, but she has won. For now, at least, she has won.

I skip the party. Instead, I go online to see if she is there, as she often is in the late evening. There is a community I belong to, a closed group, all about Lawrence Melrose. I'm hopeful that the judgement might have triggered a post from her.

He was never called as a witness by the Finbows, in the end. Apparently, an urgent health issue kept him in Rome. I read about that earlier on the forum, and felt some slanted encouragement that the Finbows were finally taking my allegations seriously.

I discovered the group a few months ago. It had begun years before with a few ex-students posting anonymously but it soon spread wider. I read the stories – some of them going back decades – with grim indulgence. There was an uneasy comfort in the banality of his acts; how similar they were to Mary's experience. He had also bullied these girls into an infatuation with him. They, too, had believed they were in control. He was helping ignite their craft, they reported, until suddenly, he extinguished it.

The girl I sometimes talk to there goes under the name of a Joni Mitchell song she used to paint to: *shadows+light*. I assume a different name entirely, never revealing that it is me she's engaging with, but proceed on the assumption that it is her. Mary.

She's candid with everyone on the group about her experiences with Lawrence.

It started when he came on a family holiday. I had just turned sixteen.

Did you tell your family? Someone asks.

I thought they knew about it before, but turns out not... Now they are aware.

Mary sometimes shares updates on everyday life: she posts on the group that she has recently had a baby and that motherhood has reawakened her. She says that hearing the news of Lawrence's dismissal from his position at the school has liberated her, too. In between all the feeding and the naps, she's making the best paintings of her life.

I desperately want to ask if Jean's retreat has freed her as well; anything that might absolve me from the guilt of withholding the evidence I recorded, but I'm too afraid to tell her who she's really corresponding with. Instead, beneath her comment, I tell her I'll be exhibiting soon in Rome.

I feel like going over to his apartment and confronting Lawrence in person! I type, feeling an uneasy twinge as I post this. These are not my accusations to make, but she likes the post. A few others do, too.

Emboldened, I write a reply, suggesting we meet for a coffee one day and talk about our work. I lie and tell her I'm a painter, too, that I live in London. Mary likes the suggestion and for a moment I feel hopeful.

But that is our last interaction. Shortly after that, she disappears.

FIVE MONTHS LATER

A light evening in May, with the smell of wisteria in the air and the promise of summer beyond it. I am walking towards a small neighbourhood gallery just off the Portobello Road. In the window, there is a wide piece of hanging silk, and painted on it are letters in green ink: *Melrose Academy Fundraiser Sale.*

Cleo is smoking outside as I approach, talking to a dark-haired man in a long grey mackintosh and pearl earrings. I steal a glance but only very briefly, so she will not notice: her looks have aged considerably.

Your fault for what you did to her sister, I taunt myself, until another, kinder voice overrules it. *Not your fault. Jean's fault.*

The sale has been organised to raise support for the school, which lost most of its funding around the time Lawrence was permanently dismissed from his position in early January. Without the support of key donors, like the Finbows, the school was struggling to stay in its building on Via Renella. When I heard about the sale online, I knew I shouldn't attend. That it would be foolish to allow myself anywhere near that crowd again. However curious I was, I resolved to do the sensible thing and stay away.

But then, by chance, I was in London that day anyway, participating in a group sale with some other ceramic artists. My own show was only a couple of stops further west. Would anyone recognise me if I briefly stopped by?

It was the wrong thing to do, which compelled me towards it.

The Finbows had not only withdrawn their funding for the Melrose, they also ended up closing Bellinter. The damages Anna had to pay Jean were so significant, they were forced to move manufacturing to Asia, where it was cheaper. But, however much she lost, Anna continued to profit from the trial in her own way.

A defensive PR campaign was quickly mounted after the judgement, announcing her intentions to appeal the High Court outcome. I always scoured each article for news of Mary. For months, there was nothing, then, at the turn of spring, a pixelated image of Anna jumped out at me in the supermarket queue.

Anna had penned a column all about how she fought valiantly for her marriage during the trial. Halfway down the page, Mary's name was mentioned. There had been some shaky attempts at reconciliation. She was living on a canal boat near their home in London.

Close enough for us both to feel comfortable, Anna wrote. *I am told that her status on Regent's canal waterways is a 'continuous cruiser'. Perhaps I must get used to her permanently living this way.*

Back in the spotlit gallery, there is no sign of Mary in the crowds. None of her pieces are on the walls either, from what I can tell. Weaving my way through the tightly packed bodies towards the back, I encounter a huge canvas that is staggeringly different from the other portraits. It is a self-portrait, depicting a beautiful blonde girl in front of a mirror. She is propped on one elbow and surveying herself, her legs folded prettily beneath herself, like a deer. Around the mirror, there are books and other canvases, but the most arresting detail is in the centre of her forehead. Under the artist's skin, there appears to be a drop of black ink, paler at the edges, but racing outwards in straining black branches. It looks to be a terrible blot, an imposition on the girl's mind.

A woman draws next to me. I glance at her. My heart lifts.

'What a talent she had,' I say.

Lucy Ayres nods and adjusts the strap of her handbag. 'Hello again,' she says, in her kind, breathy voice. Together, we study the painting.

'Truly remarkable,' I add.

Lucy thanks me modestly and asks a female attendant to reserve it with an orange sticker.

'This is my fifth,' she says, turning more squarely to face me. 'I come to buy all of Oriel's works. Apparently, she made a bunch of canvases in between her portraits, then just left them at the school. People keep thanking me for my support. But I couldn't give a toss about the school. I just can't bear the thought of anyone else having them.'

I ask Lucy if she'd like to get some air. She tells me she's heading home.

'I'll come out with you then,' I say.

She hesitates. 'I've driven here.'

'Then I'll walk you to your car.'

Together, we stroll past the pub on the corner, then uphill along the brightly coloured facades of the antiques shops. Our elbows lightly touch as we walk.

'All that.' She gestures backwards towards the gallery, where the swell of boisterous laughter still chases behind us. 'All that was very confronting for me. You know, I used to walk up and down this road at night. We had a flat right around the corner, and just after Oriel went missing, I kept searching for her. It drove my poor husband to despair, but it became an obsession for me. I'd try every pub.' Her eyes lower. 'Every doorway.'

'And now?'

Lucy shrugs. 'I'm still looking for her, but now,' she says, pointing to her temple, 'it's up here.'

She mentions that since the judgement, more victims have come forward. The police have reopened a file about Jean Guest. 'It's a bit like that business with Lawrence. The news spreads and people start to reassess their experiences. They realise, perhaps, what they experienced was wrong. Or they start to feel guilty about what they didn't stand up for.'

I feel my pulse quicken. 'But what charges can the police bring?'

'There are new laws in place now, criminal laws, against coercive manipulation. And there are other pieces of evidence at our disposal. For the first time, the police think we might eventually have a case for a criminal prosecution.'

'What kind of evidence?' I ask. I picture Jean being arrested. Despite everything, the thought still scares me.

'Oriel's note, for instance. We couldn't use it before.'

Her walking slows and she gestures to a muddy Volvo. 'This is my battered old thing.' We pause and face each other. 'Well,' she says briskly, 'nice to see you again.'

'Have you eaten?' I ask, suddenly desperate for Lucy to stay with me. 'We could get a pizza? I think there's somewhere just on the corner. I've heard it's really nice.'

'Thanks, but I have to get back. The dogs...' She trails off.

'It's just up there,' I persist. 'We could talk a bit, about the trial? You know, I'm sorry I wasn't completely honest with you about who I was when we first met. I was told not to talk to anyone.'

'Don't worry, Gus.' Lucy shakes her head, sympathetically. 'I always knew exactly who you were.'

As she says this, I feel an unexpected warmth, and with that, the certainty that I can't let Lucy go. When she turns to put her key in the door, I panic.

'I had a dream about her the other day,' I blurt out suddenly. 'About Oriel.' I feel my face colour at the lie I have told; the lineage of this phrase I can trace back to Jean. I walk over towards the passenger door. 'She was just visiting me, she said. Just asking me if I was okay.'

Lucy and I survey each other over the car roof. A sad shadow crosses her face. 'Is there something you need, Gus? Perhaps a lift somewhere?'

I accept a ride to the Tube station, feeling a thrill as I settle next to her on the worn leather seat. But accompanying that thrill is another voice that tells me to leave the case alone. It reminds me that Mary is safe now. It's time to start over.

Let's rewind the tape, Gus.

But then I notice Lucy's keyring dangling by the steering wheel. The faded image of a young girl and a horse, held between plastic. It rocks to and fro as Lucy makes one, then two, attempts at the ignition. Oriel.

'There isn't anything I need, Lucy,' I say as she lifts the handbrake and the car rolls forward. 'But I do have something to tell you.' I remove my phone from my pocket and leave it to rest, warmly on my knee. It is the handset with Jean's recording. I take a deep breath.

'Not something I need, necessarily. But something you might want.'

ACKNOWLEDGEMENTS

To my agent, cheerleader and dear friend Juliet Mushens – I can never thank you adequately nor apologise enough for the length of voice notes I send you. The guidance from you and the Mushens Entertainment team has been the greatest asset as we worked on this book together.

To Lily Cooper, my very first art doula. Thank you for acquiring the novel and drawing out such vitality in it. Thanks also to Jo Dickinson, Kit Nevile and the rest of the team at Hodder and Stoughton for bringing it to UK publication with sensitivity and enthusiasm.

Across the water but nearest my heart, thanks to my star US agent Jenny Bent and the formidable team at Scribner; Marysue Rucci and Anne Speyer – this novel was shaped by your forensic insight. All I ever want is to impress you (both).

The seed of this book first germinated on the Prose Fiction MA course at UEA and I am deeply indebted to those teachers who first gave me permission to think of myself as a writer: Giles Foden, Trezza Azzopardi, the late Ian Jack, Amit Chaudhuri, Ian Rankin and Tommy Karshan. Then to the brilliant students who read early drafts of these chapters, sharing their feedback amid a cloud of syrupy vape smoke: Tim McGabhann, Sophie Kirkwood, Alan Murrin, Campasbe Lloyd-Jacob, Sara Byatt and so many others – thank you for all the encouragement and ideas you shared.

There are many people who have supported the writing of this book by providing a peaceful place for me to retreat and work. Thanks chiefly to Roy and Roz Simpson for the Irish woodshed, Bertie Troughton for the central heating, Emilie Pugh for the ergonomic Hackney desk chair, Rosanna Cundall for the spare room without internet, Jessie and Sam Jackson for the garden office and

Giles and Alexandra Fitzherbert for the loan of their Venetian apartment. Thanks too to the librarians and caretakers of the Tate Library in Brixton, the BL and Edinburgh Central Library for giving me a beautiful place to tinker and edit when it seemed a sensible idea to get dressed.

And in between the libraries and stints of solitude, thanks to all of those who read drafts and corresponded with me over matters of plot, clay or courtroom dynamics: Michaela Rhode, Gemma Reeves, Molly Pierce, John-Patrick McHugh, Pravin Fernando, Monique Charlesworth, Philippa Donovan, Naomi Ishiguro, Megan Davis, Emily Ford, George Gordon, Guy Brain, Joseph Rizzo-Naudi and Trisha Brora. I am so grateful for your generosity and wisdom.

Lastly and most tenderly, my beloved friends, hype-men and family for keeping me going. To Jenny, Mikey, Wilfy and Rupert Palmer for providing such irreverent and otherworldly joy when the road ahead seemed stony and long. To Axel Grapengiesser for the steadfast love as I cheerily concluded then rewrote each draft; life with you is always vodka and lobsters. And finally, to my parents, Hilary and Nick Malicka for all the gifts you gave and still give. This book is dedicated to you.